W9-CHX-245

✳ HEARTLAND ✳

HEARTLAND

The Best of
the Old
and the New
from Midwest
Kitchens

✳ ✳ ✳

MARCIA ADAMS

PHOTOGRAPHS BY DOROTHY HANDELMAN

MUD PUDDLE BOOKS, INC.
New York, New York

In memory of my father, Merle Grabill,
who taught me to love the land

✳   ✳   ✳

Mud Puddle Books, Inc.
54 W. 21st Street
Suite 601
New York, New York 10010
info@mudpuddlebooks.com

Manufactured in China

Design by Jane Treuhaft

LIBRARY OF CONGRESS CATALOGING-IN-PUBLICATION DATA
Adams, Marcia. Heartland: the best of the old and the new
from Midwest kitchens/by Marcia Adams.
Includes index.
1. Cookery, American- Midwestern style.   1. Title.
TX715.2.M53A33 1991
641.5977—dc2O   90-27260
1-59412-018-8

10   9   8   7   6   5   4   3   2

✳ ACKNOWLEDGMENTS ✳

This book has involved so many friends and individuals who shared time, information, and recipes that I feel very humble about calling it "my book." Essentially, it was created by the farmers who till this luxurious Midwestern land to feed the rest of us, and all of the cooks and restaurant chefs across the country who shared their favorite dishes, as well as insights about their communities and food styles. Gathering the material has been a stimulating and rewarding experience.

My editor, Pam Krauss, was constantly and cheerfully helpful, and I so appreciated her dedication to quality and the long hours she spent on *Heartland.* The entire staff at Clarkson Potter was graciously tolerant of my phone calls and my obsession for detail—their patience never wavered. Martha Schueneman, Katie Workman, Tina Zabriskie, Hilary Bass, Gail Shanks, Robin Strashun, Phyliss Fleiss, Mark McCauslin, Jane Treuhaft, Teresa Nicholas, and all the others who I never see but make books happen—thank you, thank you. As always, Chris Tomasino provided practical solutions to knotty problems; as an agent, she leavened our work with objective good humor.

Photographer Dorothy Handelman, and my husband, Dick Adams, and I traveled about the Midwest, lugging cameras, guide books, and a laptop computer. From soaring balloons to the backs of bouncing pickup trucks, the images of the Midwest came to life through Dorothy's camera lenses and her special vision. The Heartland never looked better and I am so grateful for her talent. Special thanks go to Mel Quinn, Carole Berglie, Gail Bryan, and Laura McCaffrey for the help they gave me on researching the material, which frequently sprawled, just like the land of the Midwest!

WBGU-TV 27 in Bowling Green, Ohio, where the television series is produced, has become my second home, and the entire staff welcomed me as a member of the family. Denise Kisabeth, my gifted director, Ron Gargasz, Patrick Fitzgerald, Dave Drury, Mark Henning, Jan Bell, Deborah Beweley, Lois Hamilton, Doris Kisabeth, and Betty Weaver were a close-knit team that turned a book into a television series. Their efforts were mind-boggling, and I cannot thank them enough. And to *Heartland*'s sponsors, Maple Leaf Farms, Sauder Woodworking Company, and Merillat Industries, Inc., I especially wish to acknowledge my deep gratitude for their ongoing support.

I freely admit that living with a writer is not easy. And I do not exaggerate when I say this book could not have been written without my husband's help and his good nature; I am so grateful to him. *Heartland* is really "our book," not mine, and I hope there will be many more.

✳ C O N T E N T S ✳

✳ NOTES ON RECIPES, ✳
INGREDIENTS, AND EQUIPMENT

Writing this cookbook has been a joy as well as an intellectual exercise, for I have learned so much more about a part of the country that I thought I already knew. Deciding which recipes to use was the most difficult part of the job; we began with six hundred —all tested, all worthy of inclusion. I do believe I could have easily picked a hundred marvelous recipes from each state, but that would have created too weighty and too intimidating a tome for anyone to even consider using!

The recipes on the pages that follow are a mix of the old and the new. The older ones were generally chosen because they are so delicious, but a secondary reason was to get them recorded before they are forgotten. Some were included because I have frequent requests for them—lost recipes or, as I call them, "attic receipts."

The newer recipes come from Midwestern cooks and restaurant chefs who are committed to using local regional foodstuffs and combining them in updated ways, always allowing the freshness and integrity of the food to shine through the sauces and seasonings. There are some I doubtless and regrettably missed, and exciting new restaurants are opening every day.

As I traveled about this region, it was heartening to discover a new generation of cooks who want to know how to cook "from scratch." They cherish the seasons and their bounty—the rhubarb of May and the mushrooms, the June lettuces and berries, and the last of the autumn garden that appears as relishes and chutneys in rows of gleaming glass jars. They are making bread, preserves, and pie crusts, and enjoying it all. As our daily lives have become more complex, the satisfaction derived from the tangible hands-on experience of food preparation is coming full circle, and to see it touches my heart.

INGREDIENTS

- *Eggs:* All recipes use jumbo eggs. This goes back to my days as a girl in the country— the biggest eggs made the highest cakes.

- *Flour:* The type of flour is specified in each recipe. Each kind is available at your supermarket.

- *Shortenings:* In some recipes (but not many) I suggest using lard—it gives a certain richness and flavor you don't get with other fat. I prefer to cook with salted butter, as do most cooks in the Midwest. You can substitute margarine or unsalted butter if you prefer, unless I have rather sternly indicated no substitutions.

- *Brown sugar:* This always means light brown sugar, unless otherwise specified. Pack it so firmly into the measuring cup that it will keep its shape when you shake it out.

- *Herbs, wines, and brandies:* Midwestern cooks have used these ingredients since they first climbed out of their Conestoga wagons and looked around for a place to start the fire to cook dinner.

EQUIPMENT

My own kitchen is rather spartan for a food writer, and that's by design. I don't want to be dependent on a lot of accessories and space-eating appliances when I cook, because most of my readers don't have those things and I am writing for them. But I do encourage you to have the following:

- A heavy-duty electric mixer with dough hook, grinder, and extra bowls. Buy the top of the line; you will have this machine most of your life.

- A heavy-duty food processor or blender. Again, buy the top of the line.

- A deep electric frying pan, which can also double as a french-fryer.

- Deep metal pie tins, available at hardware stores.

- A pastry cloth and rolling pin with stocking.

- An assortment of whisks, and I am old-fashioned enough to suggest a rotary egg beater.

- A timer. I have one that hangs from a cord around my neck, and I couldn't cook without it.

- A meat thermometer and a candy thermometer.

- A good set of knives, and keep them sharpened please!

- Heavy pots and pans. Don't buy cookware with wooden or plastic handles, or you won't be able to use them in the oven. Buy pans that can serve a number of purposes; I am especially fond of deep sauté pans that can be used for sautéing, frying, and roasting. A deep stockpot is essential.

- Good kitchen scissors. These speed up messy little jobs like herb snipping and bacon chopping like nobody's business.

- Parchment paper for lining cookie sheets and cake pans. This makes baking a breeze. Once you've used parchment, you'll never want to grease pans again.

✳ INTRODUCTION ✳

The peace of the great prairies be for you.
Listen among windplayers in cornfields
The wind learning over its oldest music.

CARL SANDBURG
"Harvest Poems," 1910–1960

■ ■ ■

Recently I attended a food media conference in Kansas City. As everyone does at such functions, I was wearing a name tag. Mine read "Marcia Adams, Food Writer, Indiana." ✳ On the way down to breakfast the first morning, a fellow conference attendee, probably intending to be witty, looked at my badge and observed, "I didn't know there *were* any food writers in Indiana. Is there anything out there to write about?"

I was polite. I assured her gently there was. The next day, another writer from a West Coast food magazine asked me curiously, "Do you really find enough good material in the Midwest to write about?" I assured him, smiling, that I did manage to keep busy.

Out of those two encounters, plus my lifelong appreciation of the incomparable bounty of the Midwestern land and how it has influenced America's cookery, this cookbook was born.

Defining Heartland cuisine is difficult, for though there are many recurring themes and flavors, it is not as readily characterized as other regional cuisines, like Southern or Southwestern fare. Certainly our food is as much a part of Midwestern culture as our long hazy summers, rippling green fields of corn, our church suppers and family reunions, Little League baseball games at sunset, and the haunting sound of trains keening through the night. But here in the sprawling Midwest the food styles of many cultures have come together in a unique way.

Sampling my way around this Midwestern smorgasbord I found each of the eight states—Illinois, Indiana, Iowa, Michigan, Minnesota, Missouri, Ohio, and Wisconsin—has developed its own unique characteristics. To call it a melting pot is not quite correct; rather, Midwestern food is an amalgam of indigenous foods and country dishes that have interconnected with many ethnic traditions—a melting down, if you will. For instance, Minnesota's cooking bears the indelible stamp of the diverse ethnic groups that moved there to work the land and mine the earth, while much of Missouri's fare has a distinctive Southern cast. Iowa's cuisine is stolid, straightforward farm cooking, and the food in Illinois is influenced by the exciting innovations coming out of Chicago.

Yet the backbone is the wondrous bounty of the land. We have an embarrassment of riches at our doorsteps: grains, vegetables, tree fruits, game, fish, and range-fed cattle. It is in understanding how the divergent groups in this vast region have integrated indigenous foods while retaining and nurturing their individual ethnic heritages that the true essence of Heartland cooking can be found.

Ripening tomatoes line the fence outside a door yard gate in Wisconsin.

The early pioneers who migrated from New England in the late 1700s laid the cornerstone of contemporary Midwestern cooking. Their recipes reflected a blend of traditional English cookery and the influence of Native Americans, who contributed sweet potatoes, squash, maple syrup, pumpkins, beans, and, most important, corn to the pot. Who could have ever guessed that the kernels of corn the friendly Indians pressed on the reluctant pilgrims in the face of starvation would develop into the Heartland's corn belt?

Ethnic settlers followed those first restless colonists almost immediately, and just as quickly the groups began coupling their recipes. In the mid-1800s came a tremendous influx of immigrants fleeing political and religious difficulties in Europe. Germans settled in Milwaukee and established their breweries and bakeries, sausage shops, and a wallopingly successful cheese industry. And the migrations west and north continued. Lured by the rich lands of the Mississippi Valley, Southerners came up the Mississippi to Missouri to plant corn, cotton, and tobacco. Perhaps most significant was the arrival of the Rhineland Germans who had settled in eastern Pennsylvania at the end of the seventeenth century. With an almost religious devotion to food raising and preparation, these Mennonites, Amish, Old German River Brethren (Dunkards), and Moravians have retained to this day many of the European food styles. And from that particular group millions of descendants scattered all over the Midwest and other parts of America.

The immigrants and pioneers were not inhibited by Puritan Yankee attitudes of plain food and niggardly portions. The soil was fertile and black, and the farms reached beyond what the men's eyes could see. The women planted large gardens and the dairy and beef cattle herds multiplied. Chickens provided Sunday dinners as well as eggs, and of course there was always the ubiquitous porker, which provided America's meat for 300 years. The woods were filled with game and wild fruits and the streams with an abundance of fish. One explorer marveled that the salmon were so thick in the rivers at spawning time that "You could walk across on their backs."

Everywhere, tables were laden with produce: tomatoes, corn, peas, beans, onions, potatoes, cabbages, and carrots. Smokehouses bulged with curing hams and bacons and sausages. Well-fed cows produced milk year-round.

This is our tradition, and a lasting cooking style from those early farm wives endures, even in the face of two-career families, boxed mixes, and convenience foods from the supermarket. These cooks, and there are many, remain fundamentally close to the foods of their land and climate. They understand taste and texture and authenticity.

With innate skill and sensitivity, they prepare and present home-grown ingredients as if they were a blessing from providence.

Today these good home cooks are being joined by a burgeoning rank of professional chefs who are rediscovering and embracing the bounty of the Heartland. In elegant urban eateries and modest country inns they are combining the best of the old and the new, applying sophisticated techniques and presentations to the indigenous ingredients and cherished recipes they discover all around them. Exciting new food industries are springing up across the Midwest, providing native caviar, wines, cheeses, and produce to an increasingly appreciative nation.

The Heartland, always a treasury of good cookery, is now emerging with pride into its own. In this book I have collected a representative group of recipes that truly reflect the way Midwesterners cook, both yesterday and today. I especially treasure the older recipes, those from a period before the industrial age, with its mixed blessings, brought us fast food and mass marketing. We now have a generation of people who have never cooked with their mothers in the kitchen; they do recall with pleasure, though, eating and enjoying pot roast, corn fritters, tomato butter, and buttermilk pie. Those family recipes, many from an oral tradition, generally passed from mother to daughter and were not written down; now we know they tell us where we came from and link us all to our past and our unique Midwestern experience.

There are myriad innovations occurring daily in Midwestern kitchens, as immigrants continue to arrive in our cities, bringing with them the unique flavorings and food styles of their homelands. Our supermarkets and ethnic groceries provide us with everything from balsamic vinegar to lemon grass, so we cook as our neighbors do—dishes ranging from Italian to Huang. Home cooks and professional chefs continue the tradition of incorporating new ethnic cuisines with the old with great cheerfulness and an innocent sort of enjoyment.

Still, the basis of Midwestern cookery at its best is simple and unpretentious. Underscoring it all are the basic fresh, high-quality ingredients, often presented simply. Tomatoes still warm from the patch, fish only minutes out of a sparkling lake or stream, corn stripped from its stalk and cooked before its freshness has faded are glories that need few adornments. The food is real. There is no reason for contrived sauces and garnishes.

At heart, our native cookery is rooted in the tradition of cooking seasonally from the land, with a nod to frugality and to memories of fellowship. Food has been a lifeline, holding people and traditions together. The old recipes tell us about our past, and these roots spiral back three centuries, a ribbon of memory and bonding that unfurls into the furthest reaches of American history. ✳

I am the prairie, mother of men, waiting.
They are mine, the threshing crews eating beefsteak, the farmboys driving
    steers to the railroad cattle pens.
They are mine, the crowds of people at a Fourth of July basket picnic,
    listening to a lawyer read the Declaration of Independence, watching the
    pinwheels and Roman candles at night, the young men and women two
    by two hunting the bypaths and kissing-bridges.
They are mine, the horses, looking over a fence in the frost of late October
    saying good morning to the horses hauling wagons of rutabaga to market.
They are mine, the old zigzag rail fences, the new barbwire.

CARL SANDBURG
"Prairie," 1918

■ ■ ■

Rich topsoil, "10 feet deep and black as gunpowder," was the lure for the hordes of Illinois settlers who arrived overland and by waterways. Down the Ohio, up the Mississippi, over the Cumberland Trail, through the Erie Canal, they came to settle this state noted for diversity and mobility. A hub for transportation since the beginning, the railroads fanned out from Chicago to provide foodstuffs to the rest of America and to bring in grains for world export. ✳ Illinois boomed as

America boomed. As the century turned, people from all over the world—Italians, Poles, Germans, Slovaks, Irish, Chinese, and more—poured into Chicago and the other cities of Illinois, looking for work and a place to make a new life.

Yet Illinois is hardly an industrial urban entity. In the breadbasket flatlands that stretch across the middle of the state, undulating fields of corn create swaying green vistas. The hot humid summers, with the occasional tumultuous dark thunderstorms, create the perfect medium for lush harvests. Small white-painted corn storage barns dot the roadsides, their cupolas giving them the look of small country chapels.

Still, the electric presence of Chicago dominates the state. "I have struck a city—a real city—and they call it Chicago," wrote Rudyard Kipling. It is the city made famous by Cyrus McCormick, John Deere, Swift, Armour, Kraft, Quaker Oats, and Sears. The metropolis is a city of immigrants with distinct neighborhoods: Swedish, Greek, Lithuanian, Jewish, Mexican, and Southern blacks, many of whom still retain their old food ways.

The city has always influenced the rest of America. Chicago-based Carl Sandburg, Ernest Hemingway, Archibald MacLeish, Saul Bellow, and Theodore Dreiser left their mark on America's literary landscape just as surely as did architects Louis Sullivan, Frank Lloyd Wrig t, and Mies van der Rohe.

The metropolis is also a crucible for jazz, gospel, and blues. Chicago was a lure to rural Southern blacks, and we see names like the Alabama Bar and the Mississippi Bar, where regional foods and gossip are enjoyed.

Out on the street, ethnic groups are the common denominator of the city as well as its cuisine, and they give it an exhilarating and exuberant personality. One ethnic group that significantly influenced Chicago's cookery, as well as many other facets of Chicago society, were the Jews, who first began arriving from Germany in the 1860s. In the 1880s, Jews from Eastern Europe came, and in the early 1900s, there was an influx of Polish and Russian Jews. Many of them had trained for the needle trade in the old country, enabling them to find work in America immediately, even if they could not speak English. All brought recipes and food customs from their homelands. Hearty traditional dishes like brisket, farfel, matzoh balls, and cholent have become familiar to Chicago diners and the rest of the Midwest.

On South Halsted, Greek reigns supreme, with restaurants and shops selling an abundance of rich, flavorful food in warm, informal surroundings. Lamb comes in many guises and honey-drenched desserts weaken the sternest resolve. The North Side neighborhood of Andersonville has long been known as the city's Swedish district, where many such immigrants settled when they started arriving here in the 1840s. (At one

time there were more Swedes in Anderson-ville than in Stockholm!) This is the place to come for delicate Swedish pancakes, meatballs, herring, brown beans, and ling-onberries.

Eating in Chicago is like eating with the rest of the world—everybody comes for din-ner. This vibrant, consonant complexity is reflected in Illinois cuisine and makes it a mirror of cooking in the Heartland. *

CAVIAR AND HOT BISCUITS * CURRIED CARROT AND PARSNIP SOUP * SWEET SPARERIBS WITH GARLIC * EENIE FROST'S CHOLENT * PORK POT ROAST WITH COUSCOUS * ROAST LEG OF LAMB WITH ORZO * STUFFED BEEF TENDERLOIN * COOKOUT HAMBURGERS * CHICKEN WITH PEANUT AND CHIPOTLE SAUCE * FARFEL CASSEROLE * JANSSON'S TEMPTATION * BISHOP HILL CORN FRITTERS * VIOLET VINEGAR * COMMUNION BREAD * MARSHALL FIELD'S CINNAMON CRUNCH MUFFINS * SWEDISH RICE PUDDING WITH TWO FRUIT SAUCES * BREAD AND BUTTER PUDDING CAKE WITH CARAMEL SAUCE * NAUVOO RHUBARB PIE * NAUVOO COUNTRY PIE PASTRY * GREEK HONEY CAKE * BLUEBERRY CREAM CHEESE ROLL * PEACH COBBLER * FRANGO MINT CHEESECAKE * BLACK WALNUT ANGEL FOOD CAKE * ROAST PEAR WITH PUMPKIN SAUCE * STRAWBERRY ICE * SOUR CREAM SUGAR COOKIES * SORGHUM CARAMEL CORN * CARL SANDBURG'S FUDGE * OMA'S DANDELION WINE

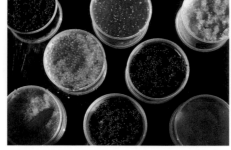

"Caviar is for everyone," declares Crystal Lake's energetic Carolyn Collins, who produces native caviar from several Midwestern freshwater fish. Her interest in caviar started as a hobby when she spent summers sport fishing. Today she sells 15,000 pounds of caviar a year to restaurants and through mail order.

"Caviar is no big secret—it is just clean salted fish eggs. The trick is how to clean and salt the eggs," she adds. But it's a secret that commercial sturgeon processors won't share. So Collins gleaned information from cookbooks and history books and devised her own process. Through experimentation she realized that the eggs of the salmon and trout that she wanted to process couldn't be screened—they were too tender. When she discovered she could cut the eggs away with one of the most common tools found in her kitchen drawer—a rubber spatula—her business was off and running. Carolyn uses a low-sodium formula and each fish yields eggs of a different texture, color, and flavor. Their taste is delicate yet assertive, and the cost compares favorably to high-priced imports. Move over, Beluga, there is a new kid on the block.

Caviar and Hot Biscuits

—— ✴ ——

MAKES 8 TO 10 SERVINGS

What better way to celebrate the best of the Midwest than by combining traditional melt-in-your mouth hot biscuits with local caviar, a burgeoning industry in this region of fish-rich waters. Guests assemble this appetizer as they eat it, so be sure to provide little plates and bread-and-butter knives for service. The biscuits can be cut in any shape—hearts, leaves, or flowers.

BISCUITS

2 cups unbleached all-purpose flour
1 teaspoon salt
1 teaspoon sugar
2½ teaspoons baking powder
6 tablespoons (¾ stick) cold butter, cut into pieces
1 cup heavy (whipping) cream

½ cup (4 ounces) salmon caviar (see Source List)
1 cup sour cream
1 tablespoon finely minced fresh dill
2 teaspoons finely minced onion
¼ teaspoon hot red pepper sauce
Pinch of salt and freshly ground pepper

Preheat the oven to 400° F. In a food processor bowl, combine the flour, salt, sugar, and baking powder. Drop in the butter and process until coarse crumbs form. Pour in the cream and process until just combined—do not overmix.

Transfer the dough to a floured board and knead 6 turns. Pat or roll the dough into a circle about ¾ inch thick. Using a 1¾-inch cutter, cut out approximately 30 biscuits. Place the biscuits on a lightly greased sheet and bake for 10 to 12 minutes, or until they are golden. Transfer to a napkin-lined basket or roll tray.

While the biscuits are baking, place the caviar in a small glass bowl. In another bowl, combine the remaining ingredients. Place the caviar, sour cream mixture, and hot biscuits on a large tray with small plates and little serving knives. Each hot biscuit should be topped first with a dollop of sour cream, then a spoonful of caviar.

Curried Carrot and Parsnip Soup

※

MAKES 8 SERVINGS

Fresh carrots and parsnips, with just a suggestion of curry and orange, create a soup that is both different and very colorful. Curry powder has been popular as a flavoring in mid-America since pioneer days, when the cooks from Massachusetts brought it with them as they came west by Conestoga wagon. The Yankee sea captains as well as English colonists had introduced the spice blend to New England, and it was immediately popular, fleshing out the cook's scanty shelf of spices, which at that time included cinnamon, nutmeg, mace, and ginger, all prized and expensive.

An old but usable tractor peeps out from its sheltering crib.

⅓ cup olive oil
4 shallots, minced
4 cups carrots, sliced ¼ inch thick
4 cups parsnips, sliced ¼ inch thick
1½ tablespoons curry powder
3 cups Chicken Stock (page 239)
½ cup orange marmalade
2 cups half-and-half
  Salt and pepper to taste
  Finely shredded carrots, for garnish

In an 11-inch sauté pan, heat the olive oil and sweat the shallots, carrots, and parsnips for 10 minutes, stirring occasionally. Do not let the mixture brown; it will cause the shallots to be bitter. Add the curry powder and stock; cover and simmer until the carrots are very tender, about 20 minutes.

Cool the mixture and transfer to a food processor bowl and process until smooth. Add the marmalade and the half-and-half, and process until just blended. Serve either hot or cold. Sprinkle finely shredded carrots on top of each serving.

Sweet Spareribs with Garlic

——— ✳ ———

SERVES 4 TO 5 AS AN ENTRÉE,
12 AS AN APPETIZER

I first ate these as an appetizer at a dinner party on Lake Vermillion in Illinois. The sweet brown-sugar glaze is a favorite sauce in the Midwest and appears everywhere—on meats, vegetables, and fruits. The lemon and garlic give this version extra oomph, and the curry is a welcome addition.

I occasionally serve these ribs as a picnic entrée with a creamy potato salad.

- 3 pounds lean pork spareribs, cut into single ribs
- ¼ cup (½ stick) butter
- 2 large onions, sliced and separated into rings
- 2 garlic cloves, minced
- Juice of 2 lemons
- 2 tablespoons soy sauce
- 4 teaspoons curry powder
- 2 teaspoons salt
- ½ teaspoon freshly ground pepper
- 2 cups brown sugar

Place the ribs in a large roaster, cover with water, and bring to a boil over high heat. Lower the heat, skim the foam, cover the pot, and simmer for 30 minutes. With tongs, transfer the ribs to paper towels to drain, discarding the water. Preheat the oven to 300° F.

In a 10-inch sauté pan, melt the butter. Add the onions and garlic and sauté over medium-low heat until the onions are transparent, about 15 to 20 minutes; don't rush this step or they will burn. Add the lemon juice, soy sauce, curry powder, salt, pepper, and brown sugar. Simmer, uncovered, until the ingredients are well blended and heated through, about 3 to 5 minutes.

Place the parboiled ribs in a shallow baking pan. Cover with the sauce and bake, covered, for 2 hours; baste occasionally. The ribs should be tender and deeply glazed.

Eenie Frost's Cholent

——— ✳ ———

MAKES 6 GENEROUS SERVINGS

Eenie Frost's career in food began as a volunteer. "My mother and grandmother were both active in Jewish charity work, so volunteer life is just part of my heritage—it is my responsibility," says Eenie. After helping to publish a cookbook for the local synagogue, she began doing TV demonstrations on how to prepare kosher food. Now she has a cable kosher-cooking show on WJUF, which is aired all over the country.

This nourishing one-dish meal is a traditional Jewish meat and vegetable stew. Since orthodox laws forbid any work on the Sabbath, the dish is typically assembled before sundown on Friday, then left to cook slowly overnight, to be eaten at the Sabbath dinner.

There are many versions of this dish, some with barley, some with rice. Eenie finds this old dish well suited to today's busy life-style because, "You can just make it and forget it."

- Generous 1 pound beef bones, cut in pieces
- 2 medium onions, sliced
- 1 cup dried lima beans
- 1 cup dried kidney beans
- 2 teaspoons salt
- 1 teaspoon freshly ground pepper
- 6 medium potatoes, peeled and quartered
- 2 tablespoons catsup
- 2 tablespoons all-purpose flour
- 1 medium carrot, sliced
- 2 pounds short ribs or chuck roast, well trimmed
- 1 pound beef shank with bone, cross-cut

Preheat the oven to 250° F. Place the beef bones in a heavy large Dutch oven, then sprinkle with the onions, lima beans, and kidney beans. Season with half the salt and pepper. Cover with the potatoes, catsup, flour, and carrot slices. Place the short ribs and beef shank on top, and season with remaining salt and pepper. Add water to cover the meat entirely, cover tightly, and place in the oven. Cook at least 12 hours or longer. Serve in large soup bowls.

Pork Pot Roast with Couscous

adapted from Printer's Row

—✳—

MAKES 4 TO 5 SERVINGS

Chicago chef Michael Foley has used indigenous Midwestern foods from the very beginning of his career. His restaurant menu at Printer's Row reflects his enthusiasm and knowledge about the region's diverse cultural influences and specialties, such as buffalo, pheasant, Great Lake fish, and the fresh fruits and vegetables he buys daily from local sources.

This succulent pork roast is braised in chicken broth and served with fresh vegetables baked along with the meat. Couscous adds style and texture to this new interpretation of an old favorite.

¼ cup all-purpose flour
    Salt and coarsely ground black pepper to taste
3–4 pound center-cut loin pork roast (it should have at least 5 chops) with the bones frenched, see Note
¼ cup olive oil
2 medium onions, peeled and quartered
4 garlic cloves
1 celery stalk, cut in large chunks
2 medium carrots, peeled and cut in large chunks
2 medium turnips, cut in large chunks
1 small head fennel, quartered (optional)
2 tomatoes, peeled, halved, and seeded
1 quart Chicken Stock (page 239)
1 teaspoon fresh thyme, minced, or ½ teaspoon dried thyme
6 black peppercorns
½ cup quick-cook couscous

Preheat the oven to 325° F. Combine the flour, salt, and ground pepper on a piece of wax paper and dredge the pork roast in the mixture. In a heavy pot just large enough to hold the meat and vegetables, heat the olive oil and brown the meat on all sides over medium-low heat, until golden brown, about 15 minutes. Do not let it get too brown, or the sauce will have a slightly burned taste.

Remove the meat, add the onion, and sauté for 2 minutes. Add the garlic, and toss and sauté for another minute. Remove the onions and garlic with a slotted spoon and set aside. Add the celery, carrots, and turnips; brown lightly for about 5 minutes, just until they begin to color. Return the roast to the pot, along with the onions and garlic, and add the fennel (if used), tomatoes, chicken stock, thyme, and peppercorns.

Cover and bring the liquid to a boil. Transfer the pot to the oven and bake for approximately 1½ hours, or until an inserted wooden skewer slips into the meat with ease.

Remove the meat and vegetables to a plate, cover, and keep warm in a low oven. Dip out 1½ to 2 cups of the stock to use as the cooking liquid for the couscous. Cook the couscous according to package directions. Reduce the remaining stock over high heat by about one half.

Transfer the cooked couscous to the center of a large service platter. Slice and arrange the meat on top of it. Add the vegetables, and spoon the reduced sauce over all.

NOTE: You can also use a boneless tied pork loin roast, which is easier to carve.

*OVERLEAF: **Country housewives hang their washing out on the line early in the morning; the dungarees come in all shapes and sizes, just like their wearers.***

Roast Leg of Lamb with Orzo

Greek cooks in Chicago (and everywhere else) have a special flair for preparing lamb. This succulent dish, seasoned with herbs, onions, and garlic and served with orzo (giouvetsi) in a tomato sauce, is a sturdy, flavorful entrée.

1 leg of lamb, about 6 pounds
4 garlic cloves, slivered
2 teaspoons dried oregano
2 teaspoons salt
½ teaspoon freshly ground pepper
¼ cup fresh lemon juice
2 medium onions, thinly sliced
1 cup boiling water
½ cup tomato puree
2 cups orzo, about 1 pound (see Note)
Freshly grated Parmesan cheese

Preheat the oven to 405° F. Cut deep slits into the lamb and insert a sliver of garlic in each. Combine the oregano, 1 teaspoon of the salt, and the pepper, and press all over the surface of the lamb. Insert a meat thermometer, making sure it doesn't touch the bone.

Place the lamb, fat side up, in a shallow pan and roast for 20 minutes. Reduce the heat to 350° F., and baste with 1 tablespoon of lemon juice. After 7 minutes, scatter the onions around the lamb and return to the oven. Roast for 7 more minutes, baste the lamb again with another tablespoon of lemon juice, and pour the boiling water over the onions. Baste periodically with the remaining lemon juice and continue roasting until done, about 1½ hours, or until the thermometer reaches 140° F. for medium rare.

When done, transfer the lamb to a serving platter and wrap tightly in foil, then drape with a towel so the meat remains warm. Drain off some of the fat in the roasting pan if too much has rendered out, then add about 2½ cups of water, the tomato puree, and remaining teaspoon salt. Bring to a boil. Add the orzo slowly, cover, and cook over low heat for about 20 minutes, adding water as necessary to prevent it from sticking.

Carve the meat into thin slices and serve on hot plates, with a liberal portion of the orzo. Pass the grated cheese to sprinkle on top of the orzo.

NOTE: Orzo, a tiny rice-shaped pasta, is available at Italian or specialty food shops.

Stuffed Beef Tenderloin

The famous Union Stockyard, which opened in 1865, is no longer in operation; it closed down in 1971, as the meat-packing industry diversified and other yards sprang up closer to the farms and ranges where the animals were raised. Today only one yard still remains in Illinois—in Joliet.

However, there is no denying the Midwest's love affair with beef. People may be eating less of it, but the affection for it lingers on. For many, the ultimate showpiece cut is the beef tenderloin, so tender you can cut it with a fork. Stuffed with spinach, cheese, and garlic, then splashed with red wine and quickly roasted, it can be served either hot or at room temperature.

1 10-ounce package frozen chopped spinach
2 tablespoons balsamic vinegar
3 ounces Muenster cheese, grated
¼ cup dried currants
1 egg
1 garlic clove, minced
  Salt and pepper to taste
5½- to 6-pound beef tenderloin, trimmed and butterflied, at room temperature
½ teaspoon Midwestern Spice Blend (page 243)
⅓ cup dry red wine

Preheat the oven to 425° F. Defrost the spinach and squeeze out the extra moisture. Place in a large bowl and add the vinegar, cheese, currants, egg, garlic, and salt and pepper. Flatten out the tenderloin and arrange the filling in a 1-inch wide row down the center of the meat. Bring the long sides of the meat up over the filling and tie the meat with butcher's twine at about 1-inch intervals. Place in a shallow roasting pan and rub the roast with the spice blend. Pour the wine into the pan. Bake uncovered for 10 minutes, then reduce the heat to 350° F. and bake an additional 20 to 25 minutes for rare meat (135–140° F. on the meat thermometer), or 35 minutes for medium rare (150° F.).

Remove the meat from the oven and let it rest for 15 minutes before slicing it or, after it has cooled, cover tightly, refrigerate, and serve it at room temperature another day.

Cookout Hamburgers
———— ✳ ————
MAKES 4 SERVINGS

The fragrance of grilling hamburgers is a familiar one in the Midwestern suburbs and countryside during the summer months, and happening on it unexpectedly makes your mouth water. For the best-flavored hamburgers, ask your butcher for 70 to 85 percent lean ground beef chuck. Wrapping these patties with bacon gives them a nice smoky taste.

  1 **pound ground beef**
 ½ **teaspoon salt**
 ¼ **teaspoon freshly ground black pepper**
  2 **tablespoons chopped fresh basil**
 ¼ **teaspoon fresh or dried rosemary**
  2 **tablespoons catsup**
  2 **tablespoons water**
  4 **slices bacon**

Preheat the broiler or prepare a charcoal grill. In a bowl, lightly combine all of the ingredients except the bacon. Form the mixture into 4 patties, 3½ inches in diameter and 1 inch thick. Wrap a bacon slice around each and fasten with a small metal skewer or toothpick. Broil or grill the patties 5 inches from heat for 5 minutes on each side for medium.

Chicken with Peanut and Chipotle Sauce
———— ✳ ————
MAKES 4 SERVINGS

With a large Mexican population in Chicago, Mexican restaurants, groceries, and food enthusiasts abound. One of the most commonly used and appreciated chilies in this area is the chipotle, a smoked and dried jalapeño pepper that is available canned in tomato sauce at Mexican markets. Used sparingly, chipotle can add an unusual, sprightly flavor to many dishes.

  1 **tablespoon vegetable oil**
2½–2¾ **pounds chicken pieces**
     (I use 8 thighs)
 ½ **cup coarsely chopped onion**
 ¼ **cup coarsely chopped green pepper**
 ½ **cup chopped dry roasted peanuts**
  1 **canned chipotle chile, finely chopped**
  1 **(14 ounce) can tomatoes**
  1 **cup water**
     Scant tablespoon sugar
  1 **teaspoon chicken bouillon powder**
  1 **teaspoon chili powder**
 ¾ **teaspoon ground cinnamon**
  1 **tablespoon chopped fresh cilantro**

Heat the oil in a large skillet over medium-high heat. Add the chicken and sauté, skin side down, until brown, about 4 to 5 minutes. Turn and brown the second side, then remove from the skillet. Pour off all but 2 teaspoons of the drippings from the skillet, add the onion and pepper, and sauté over medium heat until the onion is golden, about 5 minutes. Add the peanuts, cooking and stirring 2 minutes longer. Add the remaining ingredients except the cilantro and combine well. Return the chicken to the skillet, spooning the sauce over it. Cover and cook over low heat for 30 minutes, or until the chicken is tender and the sauce is the consistency of thin gravy. (If necessary, remove the chicken to a platter and reduce the sauce over high heat.) Sprinkle with the chopped cilantro and serve with yellow rice.

✳ SPOON RIVER ✳

When *Spoon River Anthology* was published in 1915, the volume of free verse written by Chicago attorney Edgar Lee Masters created an uproar that catapulted the book to the top of the best-seller lists, a most unusual thing for a book of poetry.

"Where are Elmer, Herman, Bert, Tom and Charley/The weak of will, the strong of arm, the clown, the boozer, the fighter?" asks the poet in his first line, and then answers, "All, all, are sleeping on the hill." The scene is Lewistown and the Oak Hill Cemetery, with the real Spoon River winding its way lazily toward the Illinois. Masters, a native of Lewistown, wrote his poetic monologues in the form of epitaphs of 244 former inhabitants of "Spoon River," who are all now "sleeping on the hill."

Written with irony, compassion, and humor (some of it dour), the book helped usher in American literature's age of realism. Masters's house still stands and tombstones represent each of Masters's characters.

No trip to the Lewistown area is complete without a visit to the Dickson Indiana Mounds, a prehistoric earthworks. Observing this tangible remnant of an ancient civilization, with just the sound of the corn rustling in the nearby fields and an occasional cry of the quail, is a haunting sensation — the Indians seem very near, as do Masters's saints and sinners of Spoon River.

In Lewistown's Oak Hill Cemetery, the burial places of all the Spoon River Anthology characters are identified; though a tranquil spot, it is filled with memories of the people who lived in Lewistown and nettled Masters with their all-too-human foibles.

*Homemade ghouls and ghosts extend a spooky
Halloween welcome.*

Farfel Casserole

—————✳—————

MAKES 8 GENEROUS SERVINGS

*Farfel is a very small grated dry noodle that can be
found in the gourmet or Jewish food section of your
grocery. Sometimes labeled "barley shape," farfel is
actually made of wheat flour, though it does have a
texture similar to barley when cooked. I first ate this
dish when I was a guest at a Hadassah luncheon in
Chicago, and absolutely fell in love with it. I immediately requested the recipe and have served it many
times since. As a meat accompaniment it is unbeatable.
With great texture and flavor, it is an ideal dish for
entertaining and can be prepared and frozen before it
is baked.*

1½ cups (8 ounces) farfel
1½ cups rich Chicken Stock (page 239)

6 tablespoons (¾ stick) margarine
8 ounces fresh mushrooms, coarsely chopped
½ green bell pepper, chopped
1 small onion, chopped
2 celery stalks, chopped
1 egg, lightly beaten
½ teaspoon salt
¼ teaspoon freshly ground pepper
2 teaspoons Worcestershire sauce
½ cup minced fresh parsley

In a large saucepan, bring the farfel and chicken
stock to a boil. Lower the heat, cover, and simmer
until the farfel are just tender, about 15 minutes.
Drain in a colander but do not rinse.

Preheat the oven to 350° F. In an 11-inch sauté
pan, melt the butter over medium heat and add
the mushrooms, green pepper, onion, and celery;
sauté until the mushrooms begin to brown, about
10 minutes. Stir in the beaten egg. Add the remaining seasonings and mix. Add the farfel and combine well. Transfer to a greased shallow 2-quart
casserole. Cover and bake for 1 hour, or until the
farfel is completely heated through in the center.

Jansson's Temptation

— ✻ —

Scandinavian immigrants tended to set up their own societies in the new country, almost to the exclusion of outsiders. Today Swedish enclaves remain in several Midwestern states, including Iowa, Minnesota, and Wisconsin as well as Illinois. Bishop Hill in Illinois was settled in 1846 by a group of religious colonists, called Janssonists after their leader Erik Jansson.

This potato dish is familiar to Scandinavians but deserves wider exposure. Anchovies give these creamy potatoes a most delectable but unidentifiable flavor. It is a traditional smorgasbord offering and would be ideal for any buffet table, for it is very good served at room temperature.

- 3 tablespoons butter
- 2 medium onions, chopped
- 1 3-ounce can anchovies, drained and mashed with a fork
- 1 cup half-and-half, approximately
- 5 medium potatoes, peeled and thinly cut, like finely cut French fries
  Freshly ground black pepper

Preheat the oven to 350° F. In a medium skillet, melt the butter; add the onions and sauté until golden, about 10 minutes. In a small saucepan, combine the anchovies and 1 cup half-and-half, and cook together over medium heat until the mixture bubbles around the edges of the pan.

Grease a 9 x 13-inch baking dish and layer the potatoes and onions in it, grinding a bit of black pepper over each layer. Pour the warm cream mixture over all, distributing the anchovy bits equally among the potatoes. Add more half-and-half, if necessary, so the cream barely covers the potatoes. Bake uncovered for 1½ hours, or until the potatoes are tender and golden brown.

Bishop Hill Corn Fritters

— ✻ —

The Bishop Hill Colony, a communal Utopian community close to Galesburg, began disintegrating in 1861, when the colonists started dividing up the common property into individual holdings. The town declined but is now in the process of being restored by its 166 citizens, mostly descendents of the original settlers. It is no small task.

Delicate and cakelike, the Scandinavian corn fritters from the Bishop Hill Heritage Cookbook *are served dusted with confectioners' sugar and a pitcher of maple syrup. This old recipe rounds out a meal with real dash.*

- 2 eggs
- ¼ cup milk
- ¼ cup water
- 1 tablespoon butter, melted
- 1 16-ounce can whole kernel corn, drained (see Note)
- 2 cups all-purpose flour
- 2 teaspoons baking powder
- ¾ teaspoon salt
- ¼ teaspoon freshly ground pepper
- 1 tablespoon granulated sugar
  Vegetable oil, for frying
  Confectioners' sugar and maple syrup

In a mixing bowl, beat the eggs until light. Add the milk, water, and butter; blend. Stir in the corn and mix thoroughly. Add the dry ingredients and mix just to moisten.

Heat 2 inches of oil in an electric skillet or deep-fryer to 350° F. Drop the batter into the oil by tablespoonfuls and fry 2 to 3 minutes on each side or until nicely browned. Drain on paper towels and sprinkle immediately with powdered sugar. Serve with maple syrup.

NOTE: Instead of canned corn, 2 cups fresh or frozen corn can be substituted. The original recipe does call for canned corn, as fritters were considered a winter dish. And this recipe is much older than frozen food technology.

Violet Vinegar

——— ✳ ———

MAKES 2 PINTS

Early life in America was awesomely difficult for the women who helped settle the Midwest. Yet some of their letters to friends and family reflect the optimism that enabled them to persevere. I like to think that same optimism is still part of being a Midwesterner.

In a letter back to Sweden in 1847, an Illinois colonist wrote, "I need hardly to tell you how this land is flowing with milk and honey, for here we can take wild bees and honey right from the wilderness itself and also grapes and wild plums and apples and many kinds of berries and herbs. . . ."

Letters and journals also mentioned prairies of wildflowers stretching as far as the eye could see. The women, always resourceful, used the blooms of the flowers for sachets and fragrant vinegars, like this one, which makes a delightfully different dressing for fresh spring greens topped with violet or pansy blooms.

4 cups wild purple violets
4 cups rice vinegar (see Note)

Pack 2 pint jars tightly with the violets. Pour the vinegar (unheated) over the violets. Cover tightly and allow to stand in a sunny window for 4 or 5 days; the violets will bleach out and the vinegar become a marvelous pale lavender.

Strain and keep refrigerated.

NOTE: The original recipe called for cider vinegar, but to capture the delicate color and flavor of the violets, I use Japanese rice vinegar, which is not as strong or as dark as cider vinegar.

Creamy Salad Dressing

MAKES 4 SMALL SERVINGS

½ cup mayonnaise
1 tablespoon plus 1 teaspoon Violet Vinegar
1 teaspoon sugar
Fresh violet or pansy blossoms, for garnish

In a small bowl, combine all the ingredients except the flowers with a whisk. Pour over assorted spring lettuces and scatter blossoms over the top.

Communion Bread

——— ✳ ———

MAKES 100 SMALL PIECES

The Old German Baptist Brethren, sometimes called Dunkards, have several large congregations scattered about the Midwest and a main headquarters in Elgin. Dunkard women dress simply and wear head coverings similar to those of conservative Mennonite groups. During church services, the men sit on one side of the church, the women on the other. At communion, they serve a homemade unleavened bread, which resembles a thin buttery biscuit. Sometimes it is marked with a five-tined fork, symbolic of the five wounds of Jesus.

This is a delicious wafer, and frequently the women will make it as a special treat for the children. It is a very old recipe and not too sweet to serve as a soup accompaniment, which is how I use it.

1½ cups all-purpose flour
2 tablespoons sugar
½ teaspoon salt
½ cup (1 stick) cold butter (no substitutes)
½ cup milk

Preheat the oven to 425° F. In a large bowl, combine the flour, sugar, and salt. Add the butter and cut it in with a pastry blender or pulse 3 or 4 times in a food processor until it resembles fine crumbs. Add the milk and combine until a stiff dough forms.

Turn out on a floured cloth and roll out very thin, until the dough forms a rectangle 17 x 13 inches. The rolled-out dough should be thinner than pie crust and uniformly thick throughout. With a pizza cutter, even the edges. Transfer the dough to a greased cookie sheet and cut into ten 1-inch-wide strips with the pizza cutter. With the tip of a fork mark a design, about every inch, along all the strips (I only have four-tined forks, so I add an extra mark with the tip of a knife).

Place on the lower shelf of the oven and bake for 6 to 7 minutes. The outer edges will be quite brown. You can remove the outer strips from each side and continue baking the center ones a bit longer. For communion, these strips are broken into 1-inch pieces, but if serving with a meal, leave them in longer pieces.

Marshall Field's Cinnamon Crunch Muffins

MAKES 36 MUFFINS

Marshall Field's department store in downtown Chicago has been a landmark for more than a century. With its thirteen-story inner court on one side and a six-story rotunda topped by a Tiffany dome on the other, it has been a traditional meeting place for several generations of shoppers.

In December, taking the children to Marshall Field's to see the Christmas tree and then to lunch in the Walnut Room is a holiday highlight for innumerable Midwestern families. These soft, cakelike muffins with a crunchy and spicy topping are frequently on the menu there. Part of the crunchy topping is folded into the muffin batter, and the rest is sprinkled on top.

- 7 tablespoons butter, softened
- 7 tablespoons margarine, softened
- 2⅔ cups sugar
- 3 eggs, lightly beaten
- 1½ cups sour cream
- 1 teaspoon baking soda
- 6 cups sifted cake flour
- 1½ teaspoons salt
- 1½ teaspoons baking powder
- ½ teaspoon freshly grated nutmeg
- 6 cups Cinnamon Crunch (recipe follows)

Preheat the oven to 350° F. In a large bowl, cream the butter and margarine. Add the sugar and cream until fluffy; blend in the eggs. In a bowl, combine the sour cream and baking soda; set aside.

Sift the flour, salt, baking powder, and nutmeg together. Add the flour mixture and sour cream mixture alternately to the sugar mixture, beginning and ending with the flour mixture. Do not overmix. Fold in 2¾ cups of the Cinnamon Crunch. Spoon into paper-lined muffin tins, filling them a little over half full. Sprinkle the tops of the muffins with the remaining Cinnamon Crunch. Bake for 25 minutes or until golden brown.

Cinnamon Crunch

MAKES APPROXIMATELY 6 CUPS

- 13 tablespoons butter, softened
- 2 cups brown sugar
- 3⅓ cups chopped pecans
- 1¼ cups all-purpose flour
- 3¼ tablespoons ground cinnamon

Preheat the oven to 350° F. In a large bowl, work the ingredients with a pastry blender (or do in food processor) until the mixture resembles a coarse streusel mix. Spread on a cookie sheet. Bake for 5 to 8 minutes or until golden brown. Let stand for several hours or overnight to dry. Break into chunks and store in an airtight container.

"Under the clock at Field's," LEFT, is still a traditional rendezvous in downtown Chicago. The "el" or elevated trains, BELOW, provide daily transportation for thousands.

Swedish Rice Pudding with Two Fruit Sauces

— ✳ —

MAKES 6 SERVINGS

Rice pudding is served at Swedish Christmas tables, topped with fruit sauce or lingonberry sauce, made from the fresh berries or commercially canned sauce (see Source List). This one, adapted from the Bishop Hill Heritage Cookbook, *is lovely, with a deep creamy custard on top.*

Sometimes an almond is added to the pudding, according to the belief that the boy or girl who finds it in his or her dish will be the first in the family to marry.

½ cup long-grain rice
4 cups milk
3 eggs
⅔ cup sugar
2 teaspoons vanilla extract
2 tablespoons (¼ stick) butter, melted
¼ teaspoon salt
  Ground cinnamon
  Fruit sauces (recipes follow)

In the top of a double boiler, combine the rice and 1 cup of the milk. Cover and cook over simmering water until the rice is tender, about 45 minutes. Transfer to a greased oval gratin dish, approximately 11 x 8 x 3 inches.

Preheat the oven to 375° F. In a mixer bowl, lightly beat the eggs until frothy. Add the sugar, vanilla, butter, salt, and remaining milk and combine. Pour over the rice and sprinkle cinnamon liberally over the top; do not stir in.

Place dish in a pan of hot water and bake for 50 to 60 minutes, or until the pudding slightly puffs and is firm on top. Remove from the hot water and cool on a rack. Serve at room temperature or chilled with a fruit sauce.

NOTE: The dish size is important if you are to have the thick layer of custard on top. Don't use a shallow one.

Grape Juice Sauce
(Kram)

MAKES 4 CUPS

4 cups grape juice
½ cup sugar
¼ cup cornstarch

In a large saucepan, heat 3½ cups of the grape juice and sugar until boiling. In a small bowl, combine the cornstarch with the remaining ½ cup of juice. Add to the grape juice and sugar mixture and whisk, cooking until the mixture thickens. Cool to room temperature.

Lingonberry Sauce
(Lingonsylt)

MAKES 3 CUPS

1 quart fresh lingonberries (see Note)
1¾ cups water
1½ cups sugar
2½ tablespoons cornstarch

Place the berries and 1½ cups water in a medium saucepan. Cover and bring to a boil, lower the heat and simmer for 15 minutes, then set aside. In a small bowl, combine the sugar and cornstarch, then add the remaining ¼ cup water. Add to the berry mixture, stirring constantly. Return the pan to the heat and bring the mixture again to a boil. Cover and remove from the heat. Cool to room temperature.

NOTE: Lingonberries are dark red and similar to cranberries, but not as tart. Raspberries or strawberries may be substituted for the lingonberries.

Bread and Butter Pudding Cake with Caramel Sauce

from Terczak's Restaurant

———— ✳ ————

MAKES 10 SERVINGS

John Terczak calls the food he prepares in his homey, unpretentious Chicago restaurant "haute mom cuisine." We would call it "like we used to have at home" —that is, if our mothers were truly good cooks. Yet the crowds come for his pot roast, potato pancakes, chicken with dumplings, and cobblers, as well as for this bread and butter pudding. It is called a cake, for it is prepared in a cake pan, and is a tad more elegant than the bread puddings you've eaten before. One bite, and you'll be smitten.

PUDDING

- ¾ cup (1½ sticks) unsalted butter, well creamed
- 20 slices white bread, crusts on
- 2 cups plus 2 tablespoons granulated sugar
- ½ teaspoon ground cinnamon
- 1 vanilla bean, split, or 1 tablespoon vanilla extract
- 6 cups milk
- 6 whole eggs
- 4 egg yolks
- ¼ teaspoon salt

CARAMEL SAUCE

- ¼ cup (½ stick) unsalted butter
- 1⅓ cups granulated sugar
- 2½ cups half-and-half
  Confectioners' sugar

Preheat the broiler. Butter one side of each slice of bread and toast them, buttered side up, under broiler, watching carefully so they don't burn. Stand bread slices upright to cool so they do not become soggy; do not stack together. When the toast is cool and dry, trim off the crusts and cut into triangles. Arrange the pieces spiral fashion, points outward, in a deep 10-inch cake pan; there will be an empty space in the center of the pan. Sprinkle the toast with 2 tablespoons of the granulated sugar and the cinnamon. Set aside.

Preheat the oven to 400° F. Split the vanilla bean and scrape the seeds into a large saucepan. Add the rest of the bean and the milk and scald over medium-high heat. (If using vanilla extract, scald the milk alone.)

In a large mixer bowl, beat the eggs, yolks, remaining sugar, salt, and vanilla extract if used, until smooth and lemon-colored, about 1 minute. With the mixer on low, add the scalded milk in a steady stream. With a ladle, skim off the froth created from the beating.

Remove the vanilla bean and pour as much custard as you can into the center of the toast pan, being careful to limit the flow to this one spot. Do not saturate all bread points with custard. You may need to let the toast stand for a few minutes before adding the rest of the milk mixture; the toast does eventually absorb all of the liquid. Bake in a hot-water bath (I use a 14-inch flat round casserole) for about 40 minutes or until the pudding is firm, slightly puffed, and lightly browned. Remove from the oven and cool on rack.

While the pudding cools, prepare the sauce. Place the butter in a heavy saucepan and pour the sugar on top; do not stir. Over medium heat, allow the sugar and butter to caramelize slowly, about 10 minutes. Begin stirring when the mixture is brown and bubbling. Continue cooking until the caramel appears to begin scorching. Whisk in small amounts of half-and-half until the caramel is thick like a syrup. Strain through a fine sieve and keep warm in a hot-water bath until ready to serve.

When the cake is at room temperature, carefully cut it into 10 pie-shaped portions, using a bread knife and rubber scraper to avoid losing the custard. Dust 10 dessert plates with confectioners' sugar, place a slice on each, and spoon caramel sauce around each slice.

✳ NAUVOO ✳

Once the largest city in Illinois, this tiny town west of Peoria has a colorful history. During the mid-1800s, Mormon leader Joseph Smith moved his followers to this spectacular pastoral setting on the limestone bluffs in a gentle bend of the Mississippi River. Though these ambitious Mormons built 8,000 houses, their great temple was never completed, and by 1845, anti-Mormon feeling eventually brought the settlement to its knees despite its large population.

The town declined until a group of Euro-

pean settlers called Icarians attempted to start a communal village in Nauvoo in 1849. It too failed, another of the 450 American utopian experiments that flourished briefly during the eighteenth and nineteenth centuries.

In the wake of the Icarians, German and Swiss immigrants arrived and took over the cheese and wine-making industries. These are still the major products of Nauvoo, and today the Mormon settlement is being restored as a National Historic Site.

Nauvoo Rhubarb Pie

✳

MAKES 6 SERVINGS

The descendents of the Icarians meet annually in Nauvoo on the third weekend of July. At the Saturday lunch, a "French stew" is always served, followed by a green salad; the meal ends with rhubarb pie. The type of pie never varies; it was the Icarians who first brought rhubarb to Nauvoo, and it is served in their memory. This is a creamy-spicy version of an old country favorite.

    Nauvoo Country Pie Pastry (recipe follows)
3 eggs
1 cup granulated sugar
½ cup brown sugar
1 tablespoon all-purpose flour
¼ teaspoon ground cinnamon
¼ teaspoon ground allspice
¼ teaspoon ground cloves
¼ cup half-and-half or evaporated milk
3½ cups diced rhubarb

Red food coloring (optional)
2 tablespoons (¼ stick) butter, cut in pieces

Line a 9-inch pie pan with pastry and set aside. Preheat the oven to 350° F. In a large mixer bowl, beat the eggs. Add the sugars, flour, and spices; blend. Mix in the half-and-half, then the rhubarb. If desired, add enough red food coloring to tint the mixture a deep pink. Pour into the prepared shell and dot with butter. Roll on the top crust, crimp the edges, and slash the top to let the steam escape. Bake for 45 to 50 minutes, or until the crust is golden and the filling is bubbling up in the center. Remove from the oven to a rack to cool.

*ABOVE: **The Sunstone from the Nauvoo Temple.** RIGHT: **Nauvoo, meaning "a beautiful place," was settled by the Mormons in 1839 at this sheltered curving bend in the Mississippi. Water birds still find it a quiet place to congregate among the lily pads and raise their young quite undisturbed.***

Nauvoo Country Pie Pastry

———— * ————

It is hard to beat a pie crust made with lard; this old recipe came from a local Nauvoo church cookbook. I know lard pie crust isn't fashionable anymore, but somebody should record such a recipe somewhere, just for posterity. And maybe someday, somewhere, someone will decide to live a little and occasionally make a crust the old-fashioned way. I can't imagine it will actually decrease one's life span any more than the occasional martini does. So here is the recipe—just for posterity, of course.

> 3 cups all-purpose flour
> 1 cup cold lard
> 1½ teaspoons salt
> 1 egg
> 5 tablespoons cold water
> 1 teaspoon cider vinegar

In a food processor bowl, process the flour, lard, and salt until the mixture resembles coarse flakes.

In a small mixing bowl, beat the egg, water, and vinegar, then pour over the flour mixture. Pulse until the dough begins to mass together to form a ball. Turn out onto lightly floured surface and work dough into a round shape.

Roll out immediately, or dough can be refrigerated for 2 weeks. (If refrigerated, allow the dough to soften for 20 minutes before rolling out.)

Greek Honey Cake
(Karidopita)

———— * ————

Chicago's large Greek community is an active one and its food traditions flourish! Greek dishes have been happily assimilated into Midwestern kitchens for several reasons—we are familiar with the cuisine through excellent Greek restaurants, the ingredients are available locally, and the recipes are not hard to duplicate at home.

This Greek Honey Cake is a perfect ending to a Greek meal, or any other meal, for that matter. It is very, very moist; a honey sauce, similar to baklava syrup, is poured over the cake while it is still warm. A very rich and delicate cake, it should be cut into little pieces.

SYRUP
> ½ cup sugar
> ¾ cup water
> 1 cup honey
> 2 tablespoons lemon juice

CAKE
> ¾ cup softened butter, no substitutes
> ¾ cup sugar
>   3 eggs
>   1 cup all-purpose flour
> 1½ teaspoons baking powder
> ¼ teaspoon salt
> ½ teaspoon ground cinnamon
> ¼ cup milk
> ½ teaspoon grated orange rind
>   1 cup walnuts, chopped

Combine the ½ cup of sugar, water, and honey for the syrup in a deep saucepan. Bring to a boil and simmer for 5 minutes. (Be careful as this can boil over easily and make a gooey mess.) Skim and add the lemon juice. Simmer for another 2 minutes. Set aside to cool while you prepare the cake.

Preheat the oven to 325° F. In a mixer bowl, cream the butter for 2 minutes; add the sugar and beat for 3 minutes more. Add the eggs, one at a time, beating well after each addition. Sift together the flour, baking powder, salt, and cinnamon, and blend quickly into the butter mixture; do not overbeat. Add the milk and orange rind; blend. Fold in the nuts.

Pour into a greased 8 x 8 x 2-inch square baking dish and bake for 30 minutes, or until the top is a deep golden brown and the cake shrinks slightly away from the sides of the pan. Remove and immediately cut into 36 pieces. Drizzle the cool syrup over the hot cake. Refrigerate and allow to stand for at least 6 hours.

NOTE: This recipe can be doubled and baked in a 12 x 17-inch pan, which will make 120 pieces. It can be made several days in advance, and it also freezes well.

Blueberry Cream Cheese Roll

————— ✳ —————

MAKES 8 TO 10 SERVINGS

This is really a jelly roll, only it is filled with a tempting combination of cream cheese and a thickened blueberry mixture instead of jelly. The idea of rolling a cake around a filling might seem intimidating, but actually it is quite simple. When you roll the very pliable flat sponge cake up in a towel as soon as it comes out of the oven, you give the cake a pattern for re-rolling.

It is a very attractive dessert.

CAKE

    1 cup sifted all-purpose flour
    1 teaspoon baking powder
    ½ teaspoon salt
    3 eggs at room temperature
    1 cup granulated sugar
    1 teaspoon vanilla extract
    ⅓ cup hot water
    2 tablespoons confectioners' sugar

FILLING

    3 ounces cream cheese, softened
    2 tablespoons milk
    ½ cup granulated sugar
    3 tablespoons cornstarch
    1 teaspoon grated lemon rind
    ¼ teaspoon salt
    1 (14-ounce) can blueberries with its liquid
    1 tablespoon butter
    1 tablespoon fresh lemon juice
    ⅛ teaspoon ground mace

Preheat the oven to 375° F. Sift together the flour, baking powder, and salt. In a large mixer bowl, beat the eggs at high speed until lemon colored. Gradually add the sugar a tablespoon at a time, beating constantly; add the vanilla. Reduce speed to slow and add the flour mixture to the egg mixture, beating only until blended. Add the hot water all at once and beat to a smooth batter.

Line a 15 x 10-inch jelly roll pan with wax paper and grease. Spread the batter evenly over the pan. Bake for 12 to 14 minutes, or until the cake is golden and springs back when you touch it lightly with your finger. Loosen the cake carefully from the sides of the pan with a spatula. Sift powdered sugar over the cake, cover with a dish towel, and invert the cake onto the towel. Peel off the wax paper and quickly trim off the crisp edges with a sharp knife. Beginning at a short end, roll the cake and towel together into a firm roll. Cool on a rack while you prepare the filling.

In a mixer bowl, beat the cream cheese with the milk until smooth and fluffy. Set aside.

In a saucepan, combine the sugar, cornstarch, lemon rind, and salt. Place a strainer over the pan and drain the juice from the blueberries into the mixture, setting the berries aside. Cook over medium heat until thick, stirring constantly. Remove from the heat and stir in the butter, lemon juice, and mace. Carefully fold in the blueberries. Chill.

Carefully unroll the cake and spread the cream cheese mixture thinly over the entire surface. Spread the blueberry mixture over the cream cheese to within ½ inch of the edges, and reroll the cake. Place the roll seam side down on a rectangular tray and refrigerate until 30 minutes before serving. Cut into 1-inch slices and serve.

The Sinatra Room at Debevic's is filled with amusing memorabilia from the singer's heydey.

Peach Cobbler

from Ed Debevic's Restaurant

—— ✳ ——

MAKES 6 TO 8 SERVINGS

The food and decor are retro, and the service is sassy and, well, sometimes bizarre, but eating at Chicago's Ed Debevic's is just plain fun. And the food is good, too. Meat loaf, macaroni and cheese, generous sandwiches, and very good desserts are on the menu. It's a place to take your kids and out-of-towners, as well as yourself when you nostalgically yearn for a cherry phosphate or a Green River.

Peach cobbler here really is just like you had at home. Sometimes it even sports a little American flag.

  3 cups fresh sliced peaches
 ½ cup granulated sugar
  1 tablespoon cornstarch
 ¼ cup brown sugar
 ½ cup cold water
  1 tablespoon butter melted
  1 tablespoon fresh lemon juice

CRUST
  1 cup flour
 ½ cup sugar
1½ teaspoons baking powder
 ½ teaspoon salt
 ½ cup milk
 ¼ cup margarine, softened

 ¼ teaspoon grated nutmeg
  2 tablespoons sugar

Combine the peaches and granulated sugar in a medium bowl and mix gently. Transfer to a saucepan with the cornstarch, brown sugar, and water. Cook and stir over medium heat until thick. Add butter and lemon juice. Pour into an oiled 12 x 7 baking dish. Set aside while you prepare the crust.

Preheat the oven to 350° F. Sift the dry ingredients into large mixer bowl. Add the milk and margarine all at once and beat just until smooth. Drop the batter by heaping tablespoonsful over the peaches. Combine the nutmeg and sugar in a small bowl and sprinkle over the batter. Bake for 30 minutes. Serve with milk.

Frango Mint Cheesecake

Marshall Field's department store has made Frango mints for decades—small, intense chocolate mint squares that are a most wonderful candy and are also used in several recipes served in the store's dining rooms. Frango Mint Cheesecake was developed by Field's kitchen and is served in the Walnut Room of the Chicago store. Chocolate, mint, and cheesecake— what an unbeatable combination! I have changed the original graham cracker crust to this chocolate wafer crust, which freezes without getting soggy. See Source List to order Frango mints by mail.

CRUST

- 8 ounces thin chocolate wafer cookies
- 4 tablespoons (½ stick) butter, melted

FILLING

- 1 cup chopped Frango mints
- 3 8-ounce packages cream cheese, softened
- 1 cup sugar
- 2 large eggs
- ⅓ cup heavy (whipping) cream
- 1 teaspoon vanilla extract

TOPPING

- ¼ teaspoon unflavored gelatin
- 1 tablespoon cold water
- 4 Frango mints
- ½ cup sour cream
  Pinch of salt

In a food processor bowl, pulverize the cookies. Add the butter and mix. Turn the mixture into a 10-inch springform pan and press onto the bottom to form a ¼-inch-thick crust and set aside. Preheat the oven to 350° F.

Melt the chopped mints in a pie pan set in an electric skillet heated to 325° F., or in the top of a double boiler over hot water. Cool.

In a large mixer bowl, beat the cream cheese until smooth. Add the sugar and cream for 3 minutes. Add the eggs at low speed, continuing to beat at low speed until mixture is well blended. Add the melted mints, cream, and vanilla. Blend well.

Pour the batter over the prepared crust and bake for 35 minutes. The center will be shaky, but will firm up as it cools. Cool on a rack for 1 hour.

While the cake is cooling, combine the gelatin and cold water in a small bowl. Chop the mints and melt over hot water; stir in the gelatin mixture and cool slightly. Blend in the sour cream and salt. Spread the topping over the cooled cheesecake and chill in the refrigerator.

Black Walnut Angel Food Cake

The first thing you notice about this outstanding cake is its chocolate–black walnut fragrance. The texture is much moister than most angel food cakes—it doesn't even appear done when you take it out of the oven after its allotted time. For those who are on a low-cholesterol regime, this cake will be a delight.

- 1½ cups (approximately 16) egg whites, at room temperature
- 1 tablespoon water
- 1 teaspoon vanilla extract
- ¼ teaspoon salt
- 1½ teaspoons cream of tartar
- 2 cups sugar
- 1 cup sifted cake flour
- ½ cup unsweetened cocoa powder
- 1 cup ground black walnuts
  Quick Chocolate Frosting (page 245) or Crème Anglaise flavored with Grand Marnier (page 246)

Preheat the oven to 375° F. In a large mixing bowl, beat the egg whites, water, vanilla, and salt until frothy; add the cream of tartar and beat until stiff but not dry. Beat in 1 cup of the sugar gradually, about 2 tablespoons at a time. Sift the flour, the remaining 1 cup sugar, and the cocoa together 3 times. Fold the dry ingredients into the egg white mixture with a rubber spatula.

Pour about one-third of the batter into an un-greased 10-inch tube pan. Sprinkle with half the nuts. Cover with another one-third of the batter and add the remaining nuts, then pour over the remaining batter. Place the pan on a baking rack in the lower third of the oven. Bake for 45 minutes, or until the cake shrinks away from the sides of the pan and is golden brown. Invert to cool (see Note). Coat with chocolate frosting or serve with Crème Anglaise.

N O T E : It is imperative that you immediately invert the cake in its pan to cool. Place the cake pan upside down over an inverted funnel or a full wine bottle (so it won't tip over). Let the cake hang for at least 1½ hours so it is thoroughly set. If you leave the cake pan right side up to cool in the conventional manner, it will collapse. Gravity is essential here!

Roast Pear with Pumpkin Sauce

from Printer's Row

———— ✳ ————

MAKES 8 SERVINGS

Chicago chef Michael Foley plans his menus around seasonal specialties, and in the autumn you might be lucky enough to find this distinctive dessert of whole pears surrounded by a rich pumpkin Crème Anglaise. The pears are baked in individual foil pouches and remain perfectly shaped.

Foley accompanies this dessert with a spicy cinnamon pound cake. Simply add a finely cracked cinnamon stick to any conventional pound cake recipe.

8 ripe pears, unpeeled
4 tablespoons (½ stick) butter
¼ cup pear nectar, white wine, or water

SAUCE
1¼ cups sugar
7 egg yolks
1 quart milk
1 teaspoon vanilla extract
1 cup pumpkin puree

To prepare the fruit: Preheat oven to 400° F. Scoop out the core of each pear from the bottom to eliminate seeds and stem center; cut a slice off the bottom of each pear to make it stand up evenly, if necessary. Place each unpeeled pear in the center of a 12 x 12-inch piece of aluminum foil. Add ½ tablespoon butter and liquid to each pear and neatly seal the pears by bringing up the edges until they meet; fold tightly. Transfer to a cookie sheet.

Bake for 30 minutes to an hour—the length of time will depend on the type and ripeness of the pears. Test by inserting a metal skewer through the foil into the pear—when it slides in easily, the pears are done. Leave wrapped until ready to serve, up to 1½ hours. (They are best served slightly warm.)

To prepare the sauce: In a mixer bowl, beat the sugar and egg yolks until ribbons form when the beater is lifted up from the mixture. In a large saucepan over medium-high heat, scald the milk and vanilla—bubbles will form around the edge of the pan. Add the milk to the egg yolks in a thin stream, and just combine; do not overbeat. Return to the pan and cook, stirring constantly, over medium-low heat until it coats the spoon, about 12 minutes. Strain and cool slightly, then whisk in the pumpkin.

To assemble: Ladle ¼ to ½ cup (I favor the ½ cup—this is wonderful sauce!) onto a dessert plate. Unwrap the pears, and peel away the skin with a knife, leaving the stem on. Place the pears on top of the sauce. Serve with cider, coffee, or sparkling wine.

The town of Galena, just across the border from Iowa and Wisconsin, is perched on rolling hills near the Mississippi River. With its Currier and Ives look—85 percent of the town's buildings are on the National Historic Register—every building, every winding stairway invites you to explore its fascinating history. Practically every school of American architecture is represented here—Greek Revival, Italianate, Gothic—and the houses dazzle.

Antiques shops and restaurants have made it a popular visiting place, and some of the restored homes can be visited during the June Open House Tour. We were entertained there one evening by a local hostess, who served an appealing strawberry sorbet plus a silver tray filled with assorted cookies. The wicker-lined broad front porch of her house overlooked the turn-of-the-century garden filled with cloudy white spirea, blowsy pink peonies, and fragrant American Beauty roses.

The gentle clink of the iced tea glasses, the soft muted conversation, and the winking of the fireflies on the lawn kept the twentieth century at bay, at least for a little while.

Strawberry Ice

——— ✳ ———

MAKES 2 QUARTS

This stunning pink dessert is the very essence of June—and an updated version of sherbet. I freeze strawberry puree when the berries are in season, and then fix this in the dead of winter—it is exquisite. Be sure to serve it in crystal goblets to show the color to best advantage. Drizzle a little Chambord (raspberry liqueur) over the top, if you are so inclined.

7 cups fresh strawberries, hulled
2 cups sugar
1¼ cups fresh orange juice
1 cup fresh lemon juice

Puree the strawberries in a blender or food processor, working in batches if necessary. In a large bowl, combine the puree with the sugar, orange juice, and lemon juice and allow to stand at room temperature for 2 hours. Pour into a 9-inch square pan and place in the freezer.

When the mixture is frozen about 1 inch on all sides of the pan (about 1 hour), transfer to a mixer bowl and beat until mushy. Return the mixture to the pan and freeze again until it is slightly frozen, about 45 minutes. Beat one more time, return the mixture to the pan, and freeze until firm.

To soften the sorbet before serving, puree it for a few seconds in a chilled food processor bowl. Serve immediately.

NOTE: You can also make this in an ice cream machine, following the manufacturer's instructions.

LEFT: If you want a quiet place to live, Blue Grass might be ideal. RIGHT: Shaded porches are pleasant spots for summer afternoons.

Sour Cream Sugar Cookies

— ✳ —

MAKES 60 COOKIES

There probably isn't a Midwesterner alive who doesn't have memories of large, soft sugar cookies eaten at Grandmother's house. Sometimes they were plain, sometimes they were studded with huge black raisins. Either way, they seem most delicious when served with glasses of cold milk.

  1 cup (2 sticks) unsalted butter
  2 cups sugar
  3 eggs
  2 teaspoons vanilla extract
1¼ cups sour cream
  1 teaspoon baking soda
  4 cups all-purpose flour
  2 teaspoons baking powder
 ½ teaspoon salt
 ¼ teaspoon ground cinnamon
 ¼ teaspoon ground nutmeg

Preheat the oven to 350° F. In a large mixing bowl, cream the butter for 3 minutes. Add the sugar and cream thoroughly 3 minutes longer. Add the eggs one at a time, beating thoroughly after each addition; add the vanilla and blend. In a small bowl combine the sour cream with the baking soda. Sift together the flour, baking powder, salt, cinnamon, and nutmeg. Add the dry ingredients alternately with the sour cream mixture, beginning and ending with the flour mixture.

Drop the dough by tablespoons onto pieces of greased aluminum foil cut to fit cookie sheets—12 cookies to a sheet; the cookies should be about 1½ inches apart. Bake for 8 to 10 minutes, alternating the sheets from top to bottom racks once during baking. The cookies should not be brown on top. Cool on paper-lined racks.

Sorghum Caramel Corn

— ✳ —

MAKES 6 QUARTS

Sorghum molasses has a distinctive flavor all its own, and though botanically the plant is classified as a grass, it resembles cornstalks. It was an important sweetener in the nineteenth century, but fell from grace when cane sugar' became available after World War II. Many Amish farmers still raise sorghum and use its syrup in many of their desserts and candies.

6 quarts popped popcorn
2 cups brown sugar
½ pound (2 sticks) butter
½ cup sorghum molasses
1 teaspoon salt
2 teaspoons vanilla extract
¾ teaspoon baking soda

Preheat the oven to 250° F. Divide the popcorn between 2 very large bowls. Generously grease 2 lipped cookie sheets and set aside.

In a deep saucepan, combine the brown sugar, butter, and sorghum and boil for 5 minutes. Add the salt and vanilla and insert a candy thermometer. Bring the mixture to a boil and cook over medium heat for approximately 5 minutes, or until the thermometer registers 260° F. (hard ball stage).

Remove from the heat and quickly stir in the baking soda—the mixture will foam up. Pour immediately over the 2 bowls of popped corn and mix quickly so all the popcorn is coated. Turn out onto the baking sheets and spread evenly. Bake for 30 minutes, stirring every 10 minutes. Cool thoroughly on the sheets, then break into pieces and pack into a container as soon as cool. (The corn keeps crisp if kept in airtight containers).

Carl Sandburg's Fudge

MAKES APPROXIMATELY
45 PIECES

Sandburg was the child of immigrant parents and grew up in Galesburg, Ohio, where his father worked in a railroad round house, repairing locomotives.

Later Sandburg married Paula Steichen, the sister of photographer Edward Steichen. The young Sandburgs moved to Chicago, and in 1916, he published his first book, Chicago Poems. *Celebrating the land and the common wisdom of the working people, he caught the rhythm of their speech and their passions.*

Carl's daughter, Helga, graciously shared some family recipes with me. Making candy was a Sandburg family recreation in the early 1900s. Everyone would take his or her turn beating the fudge, which takes a strong arm.

Cold months are best for candy making—the air should be cool and dry. Don't double this recipe, for it will cook unevenly. A candy thermometer is necessary for best results.

2 cups sugar
2 squares (2 ounces) unsweetened chocolate, coarsely chopped
⅛ teaspoon salt
1 cup heavy (whipping) cream
1 tablespoon butter

In a deep heavy saucepan, combine the sugar, chocolate, salt, and heavy cream. Cook over medium heat, stirring only until the sugar is dissolved. Don't stir any of the crystals up onto the side of the pan back into the mixture. When the mixture boils, attach a candy thermometer, cover the pan, and cook over the lowest heat until the fudge reaches 240° F. (soft ball); it will take 15 to 18 minutes. Do not stir the candy during this period.

Remove from heat, add the butter, and place the pot in a deep pan filled with ice cubes and some water. With a wooden spoon, beat the mixture vigorously until it becomes creamy and begins to lose its gloss—that is the signal that it is done. Immediately pour out onto a buttered dinner plate. Cool and cut into 1-inch pieces.

Oma's Dandelion Wine

MAKES APPROXIMATELY 8 PINTS

In his only novel, Remembrance Rock, *Sandburg describes the garden in the back of the family's Galesburg house, now a museum. The four pointed cedars still stand there, "from which all the winds of destiny and history blow." His ashes are buried under a large boulder, which he named "Remembrance Rock." The garden is tranquil, tidy, and quite spacious. It is nice to imagine the Sandburg family, conservative and hard working, allowing themselves the luxury of sitting outside in the dappled Sunday afternoon sunshine, enjoying a glass of Grandmother Steichen's dandelion wine. Gather the dandelion blossoms on a dry day.*

2 quarts dandelion blossoms
1 gallon water
2 oranges, coarsely chopped
2 lemons, coarsely chopped
4 pounds sugar

Remove the dandelion stems and the outer ring of leaves around the blossoms. Place the blossoms in a large bowl or crock. Bring the water to a boil and pour over the blossoms. Cover with plastic wrap and allow to stand for 36 hours, stirring once or twice.

Strain the liquid through a cheesecloth-lined colander and return to the crock. Add the oranges, lemons, and sugar and cover again with plastic wrap. Store in a cool place, and let the mixture "work," or ferment, for 2 weeks. (This mixture is called the "must.") Strain again and return to the crock to ferment and bubble further. When the bubbling stops and the wine is clear, it is ready to be drunk or bottled. How long this fermenting takes varies considerably—it can be several weeks more. Siphon into clean clear bottles and cork with new corks, not old ones—plastic ones are ideal.

It was like this once: sprinklers mixed
our marigolds with someone else's phlox
and the sidewalks under maple trees
lacy with August shade,
and whistles called at eight and fathers walked
to work, and when they blew again,
men in tired blue shirts followed
their shadows home to grass.
This is how it was in Indiana.

Towns fingered out to country once,
where brown-eyed daisies waved a fringe on orchards
and cattle munched at clover, and
fishermen sat in rowboats and were silent
and on gravel roads, boys and girls
stopped their cars and felt the moon and touched,
and the quiet moments ringed and focused
lakes   moon   flowers.
This is how it was
in Indiana.

PHILLIP APPLEMAN
From "The Memo to the 21st Century," 1976

■   ■   ■

At the heart of the Heartland, Indiana is a study in contrasts, full of the ambiguities of custom and life-style that typically are found throughout most of this sprawling region. ✶ The lower part of Indiana's bootlike shape is Southern in attitudes, values, and food heritage. Its woods and hills echo those that lay southward across the Ohio River; its first settlers came from Virginia, the Carolinas, and Kentucky. We find the native persimmon here, hickory-smoked honey hams, and glorious cantaloupes, as big as the basketballs that are tossed into the hoops that hang on every barn.

The northern part of the state often wears the character of the settlers who came to its more open terrain from Congregationalist New England, New York, Pennsylvania, neighboring Ohio and, after 1848, Germany. This is the place for sauerkraut and cheese, turkeys and ducks, and fields of pungent mint that escapes into the roadsides and marries with orange lilies and brown-eyed Susans.

Economically, Indiana developed first as farmland, but rapid industrialization occurred when oil was discovered. Indiana was no longer a sleepy agrarian state, but the image remains and there are those who prefer that no one knows the difference.

A traveler among the wooded hills north of the Ohio River can still sight isolated log cabins surrounded by split-rail fences, with smoke curling from their stone chimneys on chilly mornings. Yet nearby is Columbus, a town of 36,000 people that is called "the Ath-

ens of the Prairie," having more than fifty visually stunning buildings designed by the world's most renowned architects, including Saarinen, Venturi, and Pei.

In the center of it all is Indianapolis, the state capital, a sprawling, vibrant, sassy industrial metropolis. Yet there is a feel of small-townness and security—the streets are wide, tree bowered, and lined with Victorian houses, and the arts flourish. It is possible to have a humanistic life in this city.

Auburn, farther north in apple and corn country, lies in a landscape dotted with chicken farms. Auburn produced three of the glitziest and most elegant cars the world has ever seen—the Auburn, the Cord, and the Duessenberg. They were built for the Flapper Age, and nothing quite like them has been designed since. And yet another contrast—a few miles from town—black Amish buggies dot the back roads, for this is also the site of the third largest Amish population in the country.

Indiana simply accepts and enjoys these contrasts in the north and south, in history and attitudes. It also happily accepts its varied cuisine. At Conner Prairie you can enjoy a hearthside dinner of pioneer foods by candlelight in an 1836 kitchen, or you can eat at

any number of restaurants where chefs turn out the most contemporary of dishes using the best of Indiana's ingredients. The character and quality of a region are revealed in its foods: Hoosiers cook with knowledge and love, with a dash of imagination. ✫

APPLE PECAN PANCAKES ✫ SAUTÉED SALT PORK WITH MILK GRAVY ✫ CHEESE PENNIES ✫ COUNTRY PÂTÉ ✫ STRAWBERRY SOUP ✫ SWEET POTATO BISQUE WITH SHERRY ✫ SPICY BUFFALO SAUERBRATEN WITH GINGERSNAP SAUCE ✫ BAKED CHICKEN BREAST WITH PECAN DRESSING ✫ GAME BIRD PIE ✫ SAUTÉED PERCH FILLETS WITH FRESH CUCUMBER RELISH ✫ ACORN SQUASH WITH MAPLE SYRUP AND BACON ✫ FRESH TOMATOES AND ONIONS WITH CREAM ✫ THE CHECKERBERRY INN SALAD ✫ MOLDED PINEAPPLE CHEESE SALAD ✫ 4-H FAIR OATMEAL BREAD ✫ TOMATO BREAD ✫ BANANA AND PECAN MUFFINS ✫ SUNFLOWER SEED BREAD ✫ ELEPHANT EARS ✫ STRAWBERRIES WITH CREAM MERINGUE ✫ BLUEBERRY SLUMP ✫ SOUTHERN CURRANT TARTS ✫ GINGERBREAD CAKE WITH RAISIN SAUCE ✫ THREE-APPLE PIE WITH CIDER RUM SAUCE ✫ INDIANA SUGAR PIE ✫ THE VERY BEST BROWNIES ✫ SNICKERDOODLES ✫ BASIL ORANGE COOKIES ✫ PERSIMMON ICE CREAM ✫ SASSAFRAS TEA ✫ TOMATO BASIL PRESERVES ✫ SPICY APPLE AND GREEN TOMATO CHUTNEY

Apple Pecan Pancakes

———— ✪ ————

MAKES ABOUT 24 3½-INCH
PANCAKES, OR 8 SERVINGS

At the dawn of the nineteenth century, John Chapman, later called Johnny Appleseed, left Massachusetts to roam the wilderness with little more than a Bible and the clothes on his back. For the next five decades, he traveled from the Atlantic Ocean to the Mississippi, planting apple seeds that developed into young nursery stock for the arriving pioneers.

Chapman's favorite apple was the Rambo, a fall apple that is rather hard to find but is still available at some old orchards and specialized nurseries (see Source List). It would have been ideal in these pancakes, but you can substitute McIntosh or Golden Delicious.

- 2 cups all-purpose flour
- 1 teaspoon baking soda
- ½ teaspoon salt
- 2 tablespoons sugar
- 2 eggs
- 2 cups buttermilk, at room temperature
- 2 tablespoons (¼ stick) butter, melted
- 1 teaspoon vanilla extract
- 1½ cups very finely chopped peeled apples
- ½ cup finely chopped pecans
- Vegetable oil for frying
- Warmed maple syrup

In a large mixing bowl, combine the flour, baking soda, salt, and sugar. Preheat a griddle or electric skillet to 350° F. (You need this lower temperature so the apples will have time to cook through.) In a small bowl, beat the eggs. Add the buttermilk, butter, and vanilla and mix thoroughly. Gradually add the egg mixture to the dry ingredients and stir until well combined. Fold in the apples and nuts. Allow the mixture to stand for 15 minutes.

Pour about 2 teaspoons of vegetable oil onto the heated griddle. For each cake, drop a scant ¼ cup of batter onto the griddle. Bake until the surface of the pancake is covered with bubbles that do not break, about 2 to 3 minutes. Turn and brown the other side. Remove to a heated platter and repeat until all the batter is used up. Serve the pancakes with maple syrup.

Sautéed Salt Pork with Milk Gravy

———— ✪ ————

MAKES 4 SERVINGS

In the southernmost states, salt pork is called "poor man's chicken" or "fatback." It has become an underground dish, with all the emphasis we now have on low-fat foods. Yet it is an important ingredient in some recipes, such as cassoulet and baked beans.

Salt pork is fatty pork that looks very much like bacon, but it is only salted, not smoked. When buying salt pork (you may have to order it), try to get a piece that has a lot of lean meat running through it.

This is eaten as a breakfast dish with pancakes, eggs, or grits, or as an entrée accompanied by gravy that is served with mashed potatoes or hot biscuits. The pork, which is blanched first to remove the salt and some of the fat, is crisp and highly flavored.

- 1 pound salt pork, thinly sliced
- ¼ cup cornmeal
- ¾ cup all-purpose flour
- 2 tablespoons vegetable oil
- Freshly ground black pepper

GRAVY

- 3 tablespoons all-purpose flour
- 2 cups milk
- ¼ teaspoon hot red pepper sauce

Place the salt pork in a saucepan, cover with water, and bring to a boil. Then pour off the water and drain the meat. In a flat baking dish, mix the cornmeal and ¾ cup of flour. Dip the salt pork slices in the cornmeal mixture, dredging the meat liberally on both sides. In a heavy skillet, heat the oil until hot, reduce heat to low, and add the salt pork. Fry 2 to 3 minutes, turn, sprinkle liberally with pepper, and fry an additional 2 to 3 minutes, or until golden brown and crisp. Drain on paper towels and place in a warm oven while making the gravy.

To make the gravy, pour off the drippings, leaving about 2 tablespoons in the frying pan. Add the 3 tablespoons of flour and cook and stir until golden brown. Add the milk and red pepper sauce, whisking and cooking until the gravy thickens.

The center of egg production in Indiana, the town of Mentone (population 973) proudly salutes the egg with this 3,000-pound monument, as well as the Mentone Egg Festival the first weekend of every June. After being sorted by size, eggs roll via conveyor belt toward the packing cartons.

Cheese Pennies

MAKES 8 DOZEN

Indiana Amish cheese makers sell at local groceries the rich yellow cheese they make primarily from the milk of Holstein cows, and it can also be bought at the factories that are scattered about Indiana. The cheese is eaten as a snack, or used in creamy macaroni casseroles and with potatoes.

A little cheese whimsy that I like are these Cheese Pennies, nice to serve with cocktails or as a soup accompaniment. Make a triple batch and freeze some so you will have a good supply on hand.

½ cup (1 stick) softened butter
2 cups grated extra-sharp cheese
1 teaspoon minced garlic
½ teaspoon cayenne pepper
¾ cup finely chopped pecans
1½ cups all-purpose flour

Preheat the oven to 375° F.

In a large mixer bowl, cream the butter and cheese until well blended. Add the garlic, cayenne, and pecans and mix well. Stir in the flour.

On a lightly floured surface, form the dough into 4 rolls, approximately 9 inches long—they will be a little smaller than a quarter in diameter. Wrap in plastic and refrigerate overnight.

Slice thinly, about ⅜ inch thick, and bake on ungreased shiny (not nonstick) cookie sheets for about 10 minutes. Do not let the tops or bottoms brown, or the penny will have a "browned" taste. Cool, and serve or freeze until needed.

Country Pâté

MAKES 10 TO 12 SERVINGS

With the ready availability of pork in Indiana, excellent recipes for using this meat abound, and meat loaves and coarse country pâtés using ground pork are popular. Pâtés are ideal for entertaining, for they can be made in advance, hold up well, and, most important, people like them!

When cut, this well-seasoned pâté has a prune filling in each slice. Bacon lines the loaf pan, which gives the finished pâté a fine smoothness from its fat and a bit of a smoky flavor. Make two of these while you are at it, and freeze the extra one, unbaked, for another time. Serve this with Spicy Apple and Green Tomato Chutney (page 63).

¼ cup brandy
8 moist pitted prunes
1 pound lean bacon
1 large onion, quartered
1 garlic clove
4 tablespoons minced fresh parsley
⅓ cup dry vermouth or dry white wine
1 teaspoon mixed herbs (thyme, savory, and oregano)
½ teaspoon salt
½ teaspoon grated nutmeg
½ teaspoon freshly ground pepper
½ teaspoon powdered sage
1½ pounds ground pork
1 pound ground veal

In a small saucepan, heat the brandy. Place the prunes in a small bowl and pour hot brandy over them; macerate for 30 minutes.

Preheat the oven to 375° F. Reserve 7 strips of bacon and place the rest in a food processor bowl with the onion and garlic. Process until smooth. Add the remaining ingredients except the meat, stir in the brandy from the prunes, and blend well. In a large bowl, mix the pork and veal together, and then pour in the bacon mixture. Mix well, using your hands if necessary.

Line a 9 x 5-inch loaf pan horizontally with the reserved bacon strips, letting the ends hang over the edges. Place half the meat mixture in the pan, patting it into the corners firmly. Run a row of prunes vertically down the middle of the loaf. Add the remaining meat, pressing it firmly over the prunes. Fold the overhanging bacon up over the top of the loaf. Cover with foil (pâté can be frozen at this point), place in a pan of hot water, and bake for 1 hour 45 minutes.

Remove pâté from the oven, drain off the juices, and cool. Rewrap in foil and refrigerate overnight; for full flavor, wait 2 days before serving. Remove the bacon strips, slice, and serve.

NOTE: The pâté will keep for 1 week in your refrigerator.

Strawberry Soup
─── ☆ ───
MAKES 8 1-CUP SERVINGS

June is strawberry month across the Midwest, and if we don't have a few growing in our own yard, we head to the U-Pick-It places or truck farms to gather some. To kneel in sandy rows out in the quiet fields under indigo summer skies is a nostalgic treat. And the sun-ripened berries do have a superb texture and flavor never matched by supermarket berries.

Many of the strawberries end up in shortcakes or ice cream, but also in cold fruit soups, which are not uncommon in the Midwest. A touch of cider and port adds a fillip to this one.

1 pound fresh strawberries, washed and hulled
1 cup apple cider or juice
¼ teaspoon ground cinnamon
2 tablespoons honey
1 tablespoon sugar
⅛ teaspoon grated nutmeg
1 cup heavy (whipping) cream
3 tablespoons port wine
Strawberry slices and sour cream, for garnish

In a food processor, puree the strawberries thoroughly. Add the cider, cinnamon, honey, sugar, and nutmeg. Just prior to serving, whisk in the cream and wine. Serve in chilled clear glass bowls and garnish with strawberry slices and sour cream.

Sweet Potato Bisque with Sherry
─── ☆ ───
MAKES 8 SERVINGS

This recipe for a cold soup that is truly elegant comes from Nancy Sideris, a Warsaw caterer noted for her innovative dishes. It reflects the Southern influence in Indiana's cuisine.

Laced with a bit of cumin and a splash of sherry, it can be made two days in advance of serving and refrigerated. Served in glass bowls, its deep orange color makes it most attractive.

2 tablespoons (¼ stick) butter
1 small onion, chopped
½ cup chopped celery
1¼ pounds fresh sweet potatoes, peeled and diced
2 cups Beef Stock (page 239)
Salt to taste
½ teaspoon freshly ground white pepper
½ teaspoon ground cumin
Dash of hot red pepper sauce
1 cup heavy (whipping) cream
2 tablespoons dry sherry
Milk, as needed
Chopped fresh chives or coarsely ground pumpkin seeds, for garnish

In a small saucepan, melt the butter over moderately high heat. Add the onion and celery and sauté until soft but not browned, about 4 or 5 minutes. Set aside.

Place the potatoes and the stock in a large saucepan and bring to a boil. Cover and cook over medium-low heat until very tender, about 25 minutes. Cool slightly. Transfer the potatoes and stock to a food processor bowl. Add the onion mixture and puree until very smooth. Cool to room temperature.

When cool, stir in the pepper, cumin, hot pepper sauce, cream, and sherry. If necessary, thin with additional milk to reach the consistency of a thin white sauce. Chill until very cold, and serve in punch cups or bowls, garnished with chives or pumpkin seeds.

★ BUFFALO RANCHING ★

There are more buffalo grazing in the fields now than there have been since the 1800s, when the demand for their pelts and tongues, considered a delicacy by the white man, nearly wiped them out. By 1910, only 254 buffalo existed in the entire world, and one of those was in a zoo in Calcutta.

Today there are about 100,000 of these shaggy, big-chested, black-maned, impressive beasts, once the symbol of the West as they grazed about the country. They were the center of life for the Plains Indians, providing them with food, shelter, and much of their culture. Today we are rediscovering buffalo as a source of meat that is lower in fat (it has half the calories of beef) and cholesterol. It is touted as "all natural," meaning no chemical injections or antibiotic feed procedures are used on the herds.

Buffalo, properly called bison, are being raised by a growing number of ranchers and farmers, and the meat is available in some grocery stores and by special order (see Source List). Since it has a lower fat content than beef, it should be cooked at lower temperatures than beef or it will become tough; the words to remember when cooking buffalo are "slow and low."

Spicy Buffalo Sauerbraten with Gingersnap Sauce

——— ☆ ———

MAKES 6 SERVINGS

German sauerbraten recipes lend themselves superbly to buffalo roasts; the four-day marinating period tenderizes and seasons the meat, and crumbled gingersnap cookies thicken the cooking juices. This is a highly flavored, substantial dish.

MARINADE

- 1 teaspoon salt
- ½ teaspoon freshly ground pepper
- 2 medium onions, sliced
- 1 medium carrot, sliced
- 1 celery stalk, chopped
- 2 bay leaves
- 4 whole cloves
- 8 whole allspice
- 1 teaspoon dry mustard
- ½ teaspoon celery seed
- ½ teaspoon dried thyme
- ½ teaspoon mace
- 2 cups red wine vinegar

MEAT

- 4 pounds boned and rolled buffalo rump roast
- 1 tablespoon vegetable oil
- 6 tablespoons (¾ stick) butter or margarine
- 2½ tablespoons all-purpose flour
- 2 tablespoons sugar
- 5 to 7 crushed gingersnaps
- 2 tablespoons light molasses
- ½ cup raisins

In a medium bowl, combine the marinade ingredients. Place the meat in a 2-gallon plastic sack and pour the marinade over the roast. Close the bag tightly and place in a flat glass dish. Refrigerate for 4 days, turning occasionally.

Preheat the oven to 300° F. Remove the meat from the bag, reserving the marinade. In a large roasting pan, heat the oil and 1 tablespoon of the butter or margarine over medium heat. Add the meat and brown on all sides, about 15 minutes. Pour the reserved marinade over the browned roast, cover, and bake for 4 hours.

Remove the meat to a heated platter. In a large saucepan, melt the remaining 5 tablespoons of butter or margarine. Add the flour and cook until the mixture bubbles, then pour in the pan juices and whisk until smooth.

Stir the sugar, gingersnaps, molasses, and raisins into the sauce; cook and stir until blended—the sauce will be fairly thick. Carve the meat into thick slices and serve with the sauce.

Baked Chicken Breast with Pecan Dressing

from the Red Geranium

——— ☆ ———

MAKES 6 SERVINGS

The Red Geranium Restaurant in New Harmony, with its attractive brick-walled dining room overlooking Paul Tillich Park, is just down the street from the Atheneum (though, conveniently, everything is "just down the street" from the Atheneum) and serves regional Southern Midwest specialties.

One of the Red Geranium's most often ordered entrées is an oval of well-seasoned dressing made with pecans from nearby Missouri and topped by an Indiana chicken breast. Baked in the oven, it is then served with a chicken gravy with a hint of lemon.

DRESSING

- 5 cups soft white bread crumbs
- 2 cups medium chopped pecans
- ½ cup finely chopped carrots
- ½ cup finely chopped celery
- ½ cup finely chopped onion
- ⅓ cup Chicken Stock (page 239)
- 2 tablespoons poultry seasoning
- ½ teaspoon celery salt
- ½ teaspoon coarsely ground black pepper

- 6 large chicken breast halves, skin on, boned
- ⅓ cup butter
- 1 tablespoon fresh lemon juice
  Paprika

In the very corner of Southwest Indiana nestles the historically significant and enchanting town of New Harmony, population approximately 1,000. It has never been a metropolis, but it had a lasting impact on American society.

First settled by the Rappites, a dissident German Lutheran group, Harmonie became an efficient and cosmopolitan village. The residents were industrious and hard-working, and more than twenty of the town's products were shipped all over the United States and abroad. Their trademark insignia, the Rappite Rose, was a guarantee of quality on the frontier.

Ultimately, fearing they were too prosperous and would be affected by their good life and lack of challenges, the Rappites moved to Pennsylvania, where they founded a colony appropriately named Economy.

They sold Harmonie to Robert Owen, a wealthy Welsh-born social reformer whose ambition it was to create a utopian community where free education and abolition of class and personal wealth would abolish human misery. His dream served as the setting for the novel *Raintree County*, by Russ Lockridge, who wrote, "The noble experiment lasted for two years and collapsed in the usual picturesque wreckage of innate human selfishness and inefficiency."

The urban-bred scholars and intellectuals brought in by Owen were mostly unable to adjust to the rough frontier town, and many left. But those who stayed developed an impressive list of "firsts": the first kindergarten, the first free library, the first civic dramatic club, the first seat of the U.S. Geological Survey, and the first women's club.

By the time of the Civil War, New Harmony was just another sleepy southern Indiana farm community, but recently the two distinct utopian communities have undergone breathtaking restorations. As an introduction and physical bridge to the old town is the Robert Mier–designed Atheneum, a dynamic post-modern white-ramped building perched like a great bird on the banks of the Wabash.

Philip Johnson designed the Roofless Church, created in the shape of the Rappite Rose and sheltering a sculpture by Jacques Lipchitz. But one of the most enduring symbols of the past is the Golden Raintree. Lining the streets of New Harmony, its golden panicles dropping yellow pollen on the sidewalks on warm afternoons in June, the tree is also a symbol of the future.

CHICKEN GRAVY

- 4½ tablespoons butter
- 4½ tablespoons flour
- 2 cups rich chicken broth
- 1 teaspoon fresh lemon juice
- 1 tablespoon finely minced fresh parsley

Preheat the oven to 350° F. Line a 12 x 17-inch flat baking pan with foil and grease it well. In a large bowl, combine all the dressing ingredients; the mixture will be rather crumbly. In the prepared pan, form the dressing into 6 oval mounds, approximately 4 inches by 2½ inches.

Place a halved chicken breast on top of each mound, tucking any escaping dressing under the chicken. In a small saucepan, melt the butter and lemon juice together and brush each breast liberally with the mixture, using it all up. Sprinkle the breasts with paprika. Cover the pan with foil and bake for 45 minutes, then uncover and bake until the breasts brown on top, about 10 minutes longer.

Meanwhile, prepare the gravy. In a medium saucepan, melt the butter. Add the flour and cook over medium-low heat for 2 minutes; do not allow the roux to brown. Add the broth all at once, increase the heat to medium, and continue cooking, whisking and stirring, for 5 minutes. Add the lemon juice and parsley. Keep warm until ready to serve. Place each mound of chicken and dressing on a dinner plate and pass the gravy separately.

Game Bird Pie

from Peter's Restaurant

———— ★ ————

MAKES 8 SERVINGS

Indiana-born and restaurant-raised Peter George presents some of the state's most contemporary cuisine at his establishment in Indianapolis. The chic minimalist dining room is accented with contemporary art. The menu changes every two weeks, offering such delights as tangy goat cheese pie, walleyed pike with mustard sauce, or roast pork with fig butter. Peter's choices are always based on the best of the Heartland's seasonal ingredients and are presented in unforgettable new combinations.

¼ cup (½ stick) butter
1 cup finely chopped onions
1 cup finely chopped celery
¾ pound boneless uncooked duck breast or thigh meat, cut in ½-inch dice (see Note)
¾ pound boneless uncooked pheasant breast or thigh meat, cut in ½-inch dice (see Note)
½ cup all-purpose flour
½ cup dry white wine
1 cup pheasant stock or Chicken Stock (page 239)
½ teaspoon dried thyme, or 1 tablespoon fresh, minced
¼ teaspoon ground cinnamon
   Pinch of ground allspice
   Pinch of grated nutmeg
2 bay leaves
   Salt and pepper to taste
   Never-Fail Pie Crust (page 244)

Preheat the oven to 400° F. In a large sauté pan, melt the butter; add the onions and celery and sauté for 3 minutes. Add the duck and pheasant and cook until meat has browned, about 6 to 8 minutes. Stir in the flour, reduce the heat, and cook 5 to 7 minutes, stirring occasionally until the mixture is bubbling in the center of the pan and a roux has formed.

Stir in the wine and stock. Bring to a simmer and add the thyme, cinnamon, allspice, nutmeg, bay leaves, and salt and pepper. Cook, stirring occasionally, for 10 to 15 minutes.

Line a 9-inch pie pan with the pastry. Pour in the pie filling and cover with the top crust. Crimp the edge with your fingers or a fork and slash the top crust so steam can escape. Bake 50 to 60 minutes, or until the juices are bubbling up through the middle of the pie. Remove from the oven and cool for 10 to 15 minutes before cutting into wedges.

NOTE: If duck and pheasant meat are not available, other poultry, such as chicken or turkey, can be substituted. The duck breasts can be ordered by mail (see Source List).

Plump ducks at Maple Leaf Farms, BELOW. OPPOSITE: *Because the Amish will not have phones in their homes, they use public phones in emergencies.*

Sautéed Perch Fillets with Fresh Cucumber Relish

from the Oyster Bar

———— ☆ ————

MAKES 8 TO 10 SERVINGS

Indiana is dotted with freshwater lakes, and fishing from a rowboat or off a cottage pier in the quiet dawn or at a strawberry sunset is a happy summer pastime for Hoosiers. Pan-frying is the usual way to prepare these local fish.

The Oyster Bar in Fort Wayne does fish a little differently. The restaurant resembles a French bistro, with its narrow space, red-checked tablecloths, and a changing daily menu of innovative regional foods presented on a blackboard. Owner Steve Gard and chef John Boch combine their talents to come up with new interpretations of old dishes, such as this sautéed perch. The fresh cucumber relish tartly and deliciously recalls Indiana's generous vegetable gardens.

CUCUMBER RELISH

1 medium cucumber, peeled and seeded
1 red bell pepper
1 small red onion
3 celery stalks
1 egg
Juice of 1 lemon
¼ cup rice wine vinegar
1 cup olive oil

FISH

2 quarts peanut oil
2 cups all-purpose flour
2 cups bread crumbs
2 tablespoons minced fresh dill
1 tablespoon minced fresh thyme
½ cup grated Parmesan cheese
1 teaspoon ground white pepper
2 eggs, lightly beaten
2 cups milk
3½ pounds lake perch fillets

Finely dice the cucumber, red pepper, onion, and celery and place in a medium bowl. Whisk together the egg, lemon juice, and vinegar; slowly add the olive oil, whisking constantly. Pour over the diced vegetables and toss. Allow to stand at

room temperature for 2 hours. (Refrigerate the mixture if made more than 2 hours in advance, but for full flavor, bring the mixture to room temperature before serving.)

Heat the oil to 350° F. in a 4-quart deep-fat fryer or deep skillet. Combine the flour, bread crumbs, dill, thyme, cheese, and white pepper. In a separate bowl, beat together the eggs and milk. Working in batches (4 is about right), dip the perch fillets first into the egg wash and then into the flour mixture; repeat the process again so the fillets are breaded twice. Drop the fillets into the hot oil and deep-fry until golden brown, about 3 to 5 minutes. Place the fried perch on a warmed platter and spoon the cucumber relish liberally over the fillets.

Acorn Squash with Maple Syrup and Bacon

———— ☆ ————

MAKES 4 SERVINGS

Sometime during the month of March in the Midwest, the word that "the sap is running" goes out, signaling an exodus to rural maple groves, where the syrup is still cooked down over wood fires in small batches and sold to grateful buyers.

Two of Indiana's favorite seasonings—maple syrup and bacon—dress up acorn squash with real style.

2 medium acorn squash, halved, with seeds and fibers removed
2 cups hot water
¼ cup brown sugar
½ teaspoon ground cinnamon
¼ teaspoon ground coriander
¼ teaspoon grated nutmeg
¼ teaspoon salt
⅛ teaspoon ground cloves
⅛ teaspoon freshly ground pepper
¼ cup (½ stick) butter
4 tablespoons maple syrup
2 bacon slices, cut in half

Preheat the oven to 450° F. Line a 9 x 13-inch baking dish with aluminum foil and arrange the squash cut side down on the foil. Pour the hot water around the squash and bake for 45 minutes. Meanwhile in a small bowl, combine the brown sugar and spices.

Remove the pan from the oven, drain off the water, and turn the squash cut side up. Spoon equal amounts of the sugar-spice mixture into the hollow of each squash. Pour a tablespoon of maple syrup over the spices and place half a bacon slice in each squash. Return the squash to the oven and bake 15 minutes longer, spooning the sauce over the cavity of each squash once or twice. The squash should be very tender.

Fresh Tomatoes and Onions with Cream

──── ✫ ────
M A K E S   4   T O   8   S E R V I N G S

This is another one of those old recipes that came to me with just a list of ingredients, including one specific instruction—"use a teacup of cream." This lovely nostalgic dish should be made only in the summertime when tomatoes are at their peak. Don't bother trying it with those orange things that pass for tomatoes at the supermarket in the winter; it won't be the same.

> 3 to 4 tablespoons olive or vegetable oil
> 2 large onions, thinly sliced
>   Salt and pepper
> 4 large tomatoes, peeled and halved
>   horizontally
> ¾ cup heavy (whipping) cream
>   Brown sugar
>   Finely minced fresh parsley and basil, for
>   garnish

Heat the oil in a skillet or sauté pan. Add the onions, cover, and cook over low heat for about 4 minutes. Uncover, stir, and sprinkle with a bit of salt and pepper to taste. Place the tomatoes, cut side up, on top of the onions. Cover and cook 5 minutes longer, or until the onions are tender and golden. Sprinkle the tomatoes with more salt and pepper and pour the cream over all. Sprinkle a bit of brown sugar on top of the tomatoes and con-

tinue cooking, uncovered, for 3 to 4 minutes longer, or until the cream and tomatoes are heated through. Do not overcook—the tomato halves should be intact. Sprinkle with salt and pepper and serve immediately in sauce dishes, with the parsley and basil sprinkled on top.

The Checkerberry Inn Salad

──── ✫ ────
S E R V E S   4

The Checkerberry Inn outside of Goshen is a sophisticated oasis in the middle of Amish country, with twelve stylish and uncluttered guest rooms each named after a wildflower. The dining room, which is also open to the public, serves equally stylish food with French overtones. The house salad is always a treat, consisting of assorted greens, fresh seasonal fruit, and this feisty creamy salad dressing.

Be sure to have all the ingredients at room temperature, or the dressing will not emulsify. It can be stored in the fridge for up to a week.

D R E S S I N G
> 1 egg yolk
> 2 tablespoons cider vinegar
> 2 tablespoons fresh lemon juice
> ¼ cup Dijon mustard
>   Pinch of salt
> ⅛ teaspoon ground white pepper
> 2 teaspoons sugar
> 1½ cups peanut oil

S A L A D
> 1 quart mixed greens, such as spinach and
>   green leaf lettuce
> 2 cups sliced or cubed seasonal fruits, such as
>   apple, pear, pineapple, raspberries

Place the egg yolk, vinegar, lemon juice, mustard, salt, pepper, and sugar in a blender jar and combine. With the motor running, slowly add the oil. The mixture will thicken like mayonnaise.

Combine the greens in a chilled salad bowl. Add the dressing and toss lightly. Transfer to 4 chilled plates and top each serving with ½ cup of fruit.

Molded Pineapple Cheese Salad

Molded gelatin salads get a bad rap most places, and certainly a green thing with pineapple rings suspended in it is not all that appetizing. Yet some, like this unusual salad with its tart dressing, can be both elegant and refreshing.

These salads have a rather posh history; the Victorians in England called them "jellies," and cooks in affluent private households during that period were often judged by the height of their jellies. The molds that remain from that time are extravagantly shaped, and the desserts created in them would have indeed made an impression when presented at the table.

SALAD

- 3 envelopes unflavored gelatin
- 1 cup orange juice
- 3 13-ounce cans crushed pineapple, drained and juice reserved
- ½ cup fresh lemon juice
- 2 tablespoons balsamic vinegar
- 1 cup sugar
- 1 cup grated cheddar cheese
- 1 cup heavy (whipping) cream
- 2 teaspoons grated orange rind

DRESSING

- 1 cup mayonnaise
- 2 tablespoons finely minced onion
- 2 tablespoons finely minced celery
- 2 tablespoons finely minced green bell pepper
- 2 tablespoons finely minced red bell pepper

Sprinkle the gelatin over the orange juice and let soften for 10 minutes. In a medium saucepan, bring 2 cups of the reserved pineapple juice, the lemon juice, balsamic vinegar, and the sugar to a boil over medium heat. Stir in the dissolved gelatin mixture, transfer to a large bowl, and chill in the refrigerator until syrupy, about 1½ to 2 hours.

Add the cheese and the reserved pineapple to the gelatin mixture and combine. Whip the cream until stiff peaks form, add the orange rind, and fold into the pineapple mixture. Pour into a 2½-quart mold that has been coated with vegetable cooking spray. Refrigerate for 6 hours or overnight.

Just before serving, combine all of the dressing ingredients in a small bowl. Unmold the salad and serve with the dressing.

Peppy cheerleaders from the Edgewood Middle School in Warsaw get into formation. RIGHT: A secluded spot in a Hoosier garden.

4-H Fair Oatmeal Bread

—————☆—————

MAKES 2 LOAVES

Bread baking is a skill 4-H cooks are taught in Division 5, their fifth year of the program, after they have mastered cakes, quick breads, and muffins.

This close-textured bread, sweetened with honey, would be a snap for any 4-H'er, or anyone else for that matter. It has only one rising.

> 2 cups boiling water
> 1 cup quick-cooking oats
> 2 packages active dry yeast
> ⅓ cup lukewarm water
> 1 tablespoon salt
> ½ cup honey
> 2 tablespoons (¼ stick) butter or margarine, melted
> 4 to 5 cups unbleached all-purpose flour
> 1 egg beaten with 2 tablespoons water

In a large mixer bowl, pour the boiling water over the oats and let the mixture rest until the oats are completely softened, about 30 minutes. In a small bowl, combine the yeast with the water and allow to stand 10 minutes. To the oat mixture, add the salt, honey, and melted butter or margarine; combine, then stir in the yeast. Gradually add enough flour to make the dough kneadable. Knead for 10 minutes, adding more flour as needed. The dough should be elastic, soft, and smooth.

Place the dough in a large oiled bowl, turning to coat the surface. Cover with a damp towel and place in a warm place to rise for about an hour.

Preheat oven to 325° F. After the dough has doubled in bulk, punch it down and divide into 2 parts. Shape into loaves and place in two 8 x 4-inch loaf pans that have been sprinkled with rolled oats.

There is no need for further rising. Brush the loaves with the egg wash and sprinkle some additional oats on top. Bake for about 50 minutes, or until golden brown. Tip bread out onto a wire rack to cool.

Tomato Bread

—————☆—————

MAKES 2 LOAVES

Tomatoes are an important crop in Indiana, and local cook Michelle Rich makes her own tomato juice and sauce from her exuberant garden. She devised this perfectly marvelous bread as a way to use up her canned goods. It is a very fragrant bread, and if there are any leftovers the bread makes outstanding croutons when tossed with olive oil and Parmesan cheese, then toasted. And use this bread as a basis for any poultry stuffing —it gives a real lift to a conventional stuffing recipe.

✳ 4-H CLUBS ✳

The 4-H program in Indiana, as all over the country, was devised originally to teach rural young men and women, ten years and older, how to be farmers and homemakers. This voluntary program encourages youngsters to develop the life skills and form attitudes that will help them become self-directed, productive citizens. The program now encompasses town and city youth as well, emphasizing practical skills and nurturing leadership qualities with the involvement of parents, volunteer leaders, and Extension professions. The county and state fairs are where the young people display their skills, crafts, and animals, and they are judged by professionals. The thrill of seeing a blue ribbon or the purple grand champion ribbon on a pie or cake is heady stuff!

2 cups tomato juice
½ cup canned tomato sauce
2 tablespoons olive oil
6 to 6½ cups all-purpose flour
2 packages active dry yeast
3 tablespoons brown sugar
1 teaspoon salt
½ teaspoon dried basil
¾ teaspoon dried oregano
¼ teaspoon ground rosemary
¼ teaspoon ground fennel
¼ teaspoon freshly ground pepper
2 small garlic cloves, crushed

Lightly grease a large bowl and two 9 x 5-inch loaf pans with olive oil. Set aside. In a small saucepan, heat the tomato juice, sauce, and olive oil to 120° F. In large mixer bowl, combine 3 cups of the flour with the yeast and the remaining ingredients. Pour in the tomato mixture and beat thoroughly for 3 minutes. Gradually add the remaining 3 to 3½ cups flour, mixing by hand if necessary until it holds together enough to turn out onto a floured surface. The dough is quite sticky and you may need to add a tad more flour, but don't add an excessive amount or you will have a dry bread.

Knead for about 5 minutes until the dough smooths out. Place the dough in the greased bowl, cover, and let it rise until doubled in size, about 1 hour.

Punch the dough down, let it rest for 15 minutes, then shape into 2 loaves and place in prepared pans. Cover the pans and let the dough rise an additional 45 minutes or until doubled in size.

Preheat the oven to 375° F. Bake the loaves for 10 minutes, reduce heat to 350° F., and bake 30 to 40 minutes more. The bread is done when the loaves sound hollow when thumped with your knuckle. Tip the loaves out immediately onto wire racks to cool.

Banana and Pecan Muffins
——— ☆ ———
MAKES 24 MUFFINS

Cooking schools still flourish in the Midwest with students requesting information about how to use a food processor, what wines should be served with certain foods, and how do you make bread and muffins, if you please? Pat Keenana of Fort Wayne answers all these questions and more at her cooking classes, which are popular wedding gifts. This spicy and aromatic muffin is one of her many creations. Don't overmix the batter—you'll get tunnels in the muffins instead of a nice cakelike texture.

2 cups sifted all-purpose flour
1¼ cups sugar
2 teaspoons baking soda
2 teaspoons ground cinnamon
2 teaspoons ground nutmeg
2 teaspoons ground cardamom
4 teaspoons ground ginger
½ teaspoon salt
4 egg whites, lightly beaten
1 cup vegetable oil
2 teaspoons vanilla extract
1 tablespoon lemon juice
1 tablespoon banana liqueur (optional)
1 cup coarsely chopped pecans
2 cups banana chunks

Preheat the oven to 350° F. Line 24 muffin tins with paper liners. In a food processor bowl, blend all of the dry ingredients. Add the egg whites, oil, vanilla, lemon juice, and banana liqueur and process just to blend.

Pour into a large mixing bowl; blend in the nuts and bananas. Fill the muffin cups two-thirds full and bake on the middle shelf for approximately 30 minutes, until a toothpick inserted in the center comes out clean. Serve hot and with butter.

NOTE: The muffins can be frozen and reheated.

Sunflower Seed Bread

from the Columbus Inn

———— ★ ————

MAKES 2 LOAVES

Columbus, with its wealth of contemporary architecture, is a mecca for architecture buffs and tourists alike. Many will take time out to enjoy a traditional English tea at the restored Romanesque City Hall that has sashayed into the twentieth century as a spiffy bed-and-breakfast called the Columbus Inn.

This is a delightful bread; nutty flavored and studded with sunflower seeds, it does need three risings, so plan accordingly.

1¼ cups lukewarm water
1 package active dry yeast
2 tablespoons sugar
¼ cup maple syrup or honey
½ cup buttermilk
¼ cup vegetable oil
1 teaspoon salt
2 cups whole wheat flour
2 cups unbleached all-purpose flour
1 cup toasted sunflower seeds

The tea table at the Columbus Inn is quite irresistible with its homemade goodies.

In a large mixer bowl, combine the water, yeast, and sugar; let the mixture stand for 10 minutes. Stir in the maple syrup or honey, buttermilk, oil, and salt. Add the flours and the sunflower seeds and combine well. The mixture will be sticky and moist. Cover with a tea towel and let rise in a warm place for 1 hour.

Punch down and turn the dough onto a floured surface and knead for 10 minutes (or use the dough hook attachment on your mixer). Form into a ball. Oil the bowl and the top of the dough. Return the dough to the bowl, cover with a tea towel, and let rise again for 30 to 45 minutes.

Punch down and divide the dough into 2 equal parts, form into loaves, and place in two 8¾ x 4¾-inch greased bread pans. Cover with a tea towel and let rise for 45 minutes. Preheat the oven to 375° F. Bake loaves for about 30 minutes, or until they sound hollow when tapped and the crusts are a deep golden brown. Allow to stand for 5 minutes, then tip out onto a rack to cool.

Elephant Ears

★

MAKES 18 PASTRIES

Whenever any kind of a fair comes to town, we all trot off to get in line with the kids for an elephant ear. This large, flat, irregularly shaped piece of piping-hot fried bread dusted with sugar and cinnamon is indeed shaped like an elephant ear and could be likened to a funnel cake that chose not to be funneled. One of these pastries constitutes a whole meal.

In the early years on the farm or in logging camps, cooks made Elephant Ears for a breakfast dish, but the dough was cut in small rectangles, and they went by the whimsical name "jiggers."

1½	cups milk
1	cup plus 2 tablespoons sugar
1½	teaspoons salt
6	tablespoons vegetable shortening
2	packages active dry yeast
4	cups all-purpose flour
	Vegetable oil, for frying
2	teaspoons ground cinnamon

In a medium saucepan, combine the milk, 2 tablespoons sugar, salt, and shortening; heat until the shortening is melted—the mixture should not boil. Cool to lukewarm. Add the yeast and whisk until the yeast dissolves. Stir in the flour, 2 cups at a time, beating until smooth after each addition. Put in a greased bowl, cover with plastic wrap, and let rise until double, about 30 to 45 minutes.

In a deep-fryer or deep electric skillet, heat at least 3 inches of oil to 375° F. Lightly punch down the dough with floured hands and tip out on a floured surface. With a sharp knife, divide the dough into 18 pieces—the chunks will be about the size of golf balls. Roll and stretch each ball into a thin 6- to 8-inch circle. Drop the stretched dough pieces, one at a time, into the hot oil. With tongs, straighten out the dough. Fry about 45 to 60 seconds; turn over and fry the second side an additional 45 to 60 seconds. They will be lightly browned. Drain on absorbent paper and sprinkle one side generously with the remaining sugar and the cinnamon. Eat immediately (not that you need that advice).

Seeing a grand champion ribbon on one's exhibit is a thrill.

Strawberries with Cream Meringue

———— ✪ ————

MAKES 4 TO 6 SERVINGS

My grandmother loved and collected beautiful dishes, many of which have come to me. Among them is a berry set—one large shallow bowl covered with cabbage roses (a design dear to a Victorian lady's heart) plus six matching individual serving dishes. I serve these cream-covered strawberries in her berry bowls every June.

4 cups hulled and halved fresh strawberries
¼ cup almond paste
⅓ cup fresh orange juice
2 tablespoons Cointreau
½ cup sugar
2 egg whites
½ cup heavy (whipping) cream
¼ cup sour cream
  Shaved sweet chocolate, for garnish

About 4 hours before serving, place the berries in an attractive serving bowl. In a small mixing bowl, combine the almond paste, orange juice, Cointreau, and 2 tablespoons of the sugar. Pour the mixture over the strawberries, mix lightly, and then refrigerate.

Up to 2 hours before serving (no earlier, for the cream won't hold up) beat the egg whites until foamy, gradually adding the remaining 6 tablespoons sugar. Continue to beat until the meringue is thick and glossy. In a separate bowl, whip the cream until it forms stiff peaks; fold the whipped cream and sour cream into the meringue. Spoon the mixture evenly over the berries, and garnish with shaved chocolate.

Blueberry Slump

———— ✪ ————

MAKES 10 TO 12 SERVINGS

This recipe is from Mary Lib Stewart, an Indiana friend who is a fine cook as well as a fine gardener. She served this slump at tea one perfect April afternoon when she had invited her other gardening acquaintances to view the "host of golden daffodils" that blooms in her woods and number in the thousands.

The slump is a delicate yellow cake punctuated with blueberries and the lemon sauce is the perfect accompaniment. Both the daffodils and the cake were unforgettable.

CAKE

½ cup (1 stick) butter, softened
1 cup granulated sugar
1 teaspoon vanilla extract
2 eggs
1¾ cups all-purpose flour
1¾ teaspoons baking powder
¼ teaspoon salt
½ cup milk
1 to 1½ cups blueberries, fresh or frozen

LEMON SAUCE

½ cup granulated sugar
2 tablespoons brown sugar
3 tablespoons cornstarch
¼ teaspoon salt
¼ teaspoon ground mace
1 cup water
2 tablespoons (¼ stick) butter
2 teaspoons grated lemon rind
3 tablespoons fresh lemon juice

Preheat the oven to 350° F. In a large mixer bowl, cream the butter, granulated sugar, and vanilla until well blended. Add the eggs and beat until light and fluffy. Sift together the flour, baking powder, and salt. Add the dry ingredients to the butter mixture alternately with the milk, beginning and ending with the dry ingredients. Fold in the blueberries.

Pour into a well-greased 10-inch Bundt pan and bake for 30 to 35 minutes, or until the top is golden brown and the cake springs back when touched with your finger. Allow to stand 10 minutes in the pan, then turn out onto a wire rack to cool.

While the cake is cooling, prepare the sauce. In a medium saucepan, mix the sugars, cornstarch, salt, and mace. Stir in the water. Bring to a boil and simmer until the sauce is clear and thick enough to coat the spoon. Add the butter, lemon rind and juice, and keep warm. Cut the cooled slump in wedges and top with hot lemon sauce.

Southern Currant Tarts

───── ★ ─────

MAKES 48 TARTS

Whenever I am in southern Indiana, I always stay with my friend, Elinor Fox. We are a generation and miles apart, but we share an affection for gardening and cooking and the arts that transcends years and geography. One time I arrived at her home late in the afternoon after a long drive, and waiting for me was a tray of these sharply lemon currant tarts and hot tea served in antique Quimper. I thought I had never tasted anything quite so delicious. These are a fine addition to a tea table, or could be served as a "little" dessert. And they are sturdy enough to be carried to a picnic.

½ recipe Never-Fail Pie Crust pastry
     (page 244)
1 cup dried currants
½ cup water
1 cup sugar
   Zest of 1½ lemons
   Juice of 1½ lemons
2 tablespoons (¼ stick) butter, melted
1 egg
¾ teaspoon vanilla extract
   Pinch of salt

On a floured surface, roll out the pastry until very thin. Using a scalloped cutter, cut out 48 rounds that are 2½ or 3 inches in diameter and place in shallow tart tins. Set aside.

Preheat the oven to 350° F. In a small saucepan, simmer the currants and water for 1 minute; drain well. In a food processor bowl, pulse 3 tablespoons of the sugar and the lemon zest until the peel is very finely minced. Add the rest of the sugar, the lemon juice, and the melted butter. Pulse once or twice to combine.

In a large bowl, beat the egg until frothy. Add the sugar mixture, the drained currants, vanilla, and salt. Mix and place 1 teaspoon of filling in each 2½-inch tart shell, a little more in a 3-inch shell. Bake the tarts for 12 to 15 minutes, or until bubbly and golden.

Remove from the oven, and while still warm, loosen each tart gently with the tip of a knife. Cool and remove from the tins. These can be frozen, with wax paper separating the layers of tarts.

Gingerbread Cake with Raisin Sauce

— ☆ —

Everywhere across the country there is renewed interest in our heirloom recipes. At the 1836 Conner Prairie Settlement in Nobelsville, just outside of Indianapolis, small hearthside candlelight dinners are served during the winter months at the Conner House. Using only the recipes and foods available in 1836, the guests help costumed interpreters prepare dinner—churning butter, kneading bread, and having a hi-ho time getting acquainted with fellow diners.

Gingerbread has been a popular American dessert since colonial days, and the version served at Conner Prairie is a soft, thick, and finely textured cake. Sometimes it is served with whipped cream or lemon sauce, but I prefer a nutmeg raisin sauce.

CAKE

- 3 cups all-purpose flour
- 2 teaspoons ground ginger
- 2 teaspoons ground cinnamon
- 1 teaspoon ground cloves
- ½ teaspoon salt
- ½ teaspoon baking powder
- ¼ teaspoon grated nutmeg
- 2 eggs
- ¼ cup (½ stick) butter, softened
- ¼ cup lard, softened
- 1 cup granulated sugar
- 1 cup dark molasses
- 1 cup buttermilk
- 1 teaspoon baking soda dissolved in ¼ cup boiling water

RAISIN SAUCE

- 3⅓ cups water
- ⅔ cup dark raisins
- ⅓ cup granulated sugar
- ¼ cup brown sugar
- 3 tablespoons fresh lemon juice
- ½ teaspoon grated nutmeg
- Pinch of salt
- ¼ cup (½ stick) butter
- 3 tablespoons cornstarch

Preheat the oven to 350° F. Sift the flour with the ginger, cinnamon, cloves, salt, baking powder, and nutmeg and set aside. In a small bowl, beat the eggs and set aside. In a large mixer bowl, beat the butter and lard together; add the sugar and blend well, about 3 minutes longer. Add the beaten eggs and molasses and blend. Add the flour mixture alternately with the buttermilk, beginning and ending with flour; do not overmix. Blend in the baking soda and water.

Pour the batter into a greased 9-inch square pan and spread it out evenly. Bake for 30 minutes, or until the top of the cake springs back when touched lightly with your finger.

While the cake bakes, combine 3 cups water, raisins, sugars, lemon juice, nutmeg, and salt in a medium saucepan. Simmer uncovered for 15 minutes. Add the butter and stir until it melts. In a small bowl, combine the cornstarch and remaining ⅓ cup water. Add it to the bubbling sauce and cook until the sauce thickens. Serve hot over squares of warm gingerbread.

NOTE: Both the gingerbread and sauce can be reheated in a microwave oven.

*OPPOSITE: **The gingerbread is inserted into the five-foot-deep beehive oven with a wooden paddle.** BELOW: **Sun bonnets are still available at country stores.***

Three-Apple Pie with Cider Rum Sauce

———— ★ ————

MAKES 8 SERVINGS

My mother-in-law's family was named Chapman. They have traced their roots back to John Chapman, the legendary Johnny Appleseed. His story has always enchanted me, and when I discovered the family connection, I began in earnest to collect Johnny Appleseed stories, as well as apple recipes.

This one is an exceptional pie, combining three different kinds of apples, an old country secret for a truly fine filling that creates a symphony of flavors. The Cider Rum Sauce, while not a new idea, was generally served over gingerbreads or steamed puddings; combined with the pie it is a most up-to-date dessert.

PIE

- 3 cups apple cider
- 8 cups sliced, peeled apples, a mixture of 3 kinds such as Ida Red, Rome, and Jonathan
- 2 tablespoons dark rum
- ½ cup granulated sugar
- ¼ cup brown sugar
- 2 tablespoons all-purpose flour
- ½ teaspoon ground cinnamon
- ¼ teaspoon ground cardamom
- ¼ teaspoon grated nutmeg
- Pinch of salt
- Never-Fail Pie Crust pastry (page 244)
- 2 tablespoons (¼ stick) butter, in pieces
- Vanilla ice cream, optional

CIDER RUM SAUCE

- ½ cup dark rum
- ¼ cup brown sugar
- 1½ tablespoons cornstarch
- 1 teaspoon grated lemon rind
- ¼ teaspoon ground cinnamon
- Pinch of ground cardamom, grated nutmeg, and salt
- 2 tablespoons (¼ stick) butter

In a medium saucepan over medium heat, boil the cider, uncovered, for 25 minutes, or until reduced to 1½ cups. Remove ¼ cup and reserve the rest for the sauce.

Place the apples in a large sauté pan and pour the ¼ cup of reduced cider and 2 tablespoons of rum over the top. Cook, covered, for 3 to 4 minutes, or until barely tender. Combine the dry ingredients in a small bowl, then mix gently into the apples with a rubber spatula.

Preheat the oven to 375° F.

Line a 9-inch pie pan with pastry and pour in the filling. Dot with the butter, then top with the second crust and crimp to seal the edges. Bake the pie for 1 hour, or until the filling bubbles up in the center. Cover with foil if the top begins to get too brown. Let cool to lukewarm.

Make the sauce. In a medium saucepan whisk together the remaining 1¼ cups reduced cider, the rum, brown sugar, cornstarch, lemon rind, cinnamon, cardamom, nutmeg, and salt. Over medium heat bring to a boil, add the butter, and cook for 2 minutes. Keep warm until ready to serve.

Cut the pie into wedges and serve with a scoop of vanilla ice cream and a dollop of hot cider sauce.

Indiana Sugar Pie

Of all the recipes in my first cookbook, the one that elicited the most affectionate response was the brown sugar pie, which is an old Pennsylvania Dutch favorite. Sometimes called a milk pie or poor man's pie, these sugar pies were generally made from the scraps of leftover pie pastry, filled with milk or cream and some sugar, and thickened with flour. It was such a casual pie that it was prepared right in the shell.

The letters poured in about that pie. Many remembered the pie just as it is in the cookbook, while others included their own versions. Some remembered white sugar pies and wondered if I might have the recipe for that kind.

Charlanne Dixon from Florida was raised in southern Indiana, where white sugar pies are popular. After much experimenting, she wrote, she re-created the sugar pie of her memories. It is a very good pie.

½ recipe Never-Fail Pie Crust (page 244)
4 tablespoons all-purpose flour
2 tablespoons (¼ stick) cold butter
1 cup sugar
 Pinch of salt
1 cup heavy (whipping) cream
1 cup milk
1 teaspoon vanilla extract
 Grated nutmeg, for garnish

Preheat the oven to 300° F. Roll pie dough out on a floured surface and use to line a 9-inch pie pan. Set aside. Blend the flour, butter, sugar, and salt in a food processor until well combined and smooth, about 5 seconds. Pour into the pie shell. Add the cream and mix gently with your fingers, being careful not to break through the bottom crust.

In a measuring cup, combine the milk and vanilla; pour over the top of the cream mixture, but do not stir in. Sprinkle lavishly with nutmeg. Bake for 1½ hours. (This seems too long, but it does require long baking.) The center of the pie will be bubbly and still a little wiggly. Cool completely at room temperature before cutting.

The Very Best Brownies

I've tried lots of brownie recipes throughout the years; this one still remains a favorite. It came to me from my friend Betsy Chapman, who, knowing my concern about where recipes originate from, said it really wasn't her recipe, she'd gotten it from someone in her tennis group, who'd gotten it from her doctor's wife. I think. Anyway, this recipe has been around and passed the test of time and good cooks. And that is because it is an exceptional brownie. It's cakelike but also a tad chewy, with that deep allure of chocolate that keeps you reaching for more of them. And more.

1 cup (2 sticks) butter, melted
2 cups sugar
7 tablespoons cocoa
4 eggs
1 cup flour
1 teaspoon baking powder
2 teaspoons vanilla extract
½ cup coarsely chopped pecans or English
 walnuts

Preheat oven to 350° F. In a large mixer bowl, combine the melted butter, sugar, and cocoa. Add the eggs, one at a time, blending after each addition. Add the remaining ingredients and mix just until combined. Pour into a greased 9 x 13-inch glass dish and bake for 20 to 25 minutes or until the top is firm to the touch. Do not overbake or the brownies will be dry. Allow to stand 15 minutes, then cut into 32 squares.

Snickerdoodles

———★———

MAKES 4½ TO 5 DOZEN COOKIES

James Whitcomb Riley was one of the most accurate interpreters of Middle-American life of the last century. The happy families he describes in his poetry were the epitome of all that we like to think of as typical and truly American. Many of us are familiar with his "Little Orphant Annie" and, of course, the favorite "When the Frost Is on the Punkin and the Fodder's in the Shock."

His favorite cookie was the Snickerdoodle, and each year on his birthday—October 7—this sweet crispy cookie is served to all visitors who come to his Lockerbie Street home in Indianapolis. The house is considered one of the best Victorian restorations in the country.

Lemonade and snickerdoodles in the front parlor of the James Whitcomb Riley house.

1	cup (2 sticks) margarine, softened
1¾	cups sugar
2	eggs
2¾	cups all-purpose flour
2	teaspoons cream of tartar
1	teaspoon baking soda
½	teaspoon salt
4	teaspoons ground cinnamon

Preheat the oven to 400° F. In a large mixer bowl, cream the margarine. Slowly add 1½ cups sugar, then the eggs. Mix the flour, cream of tartar, baking soda, and salt, and gradually add to the creamed mixture. Chill the dough overnight.

Combine the remaining sugar and the cinnamon on a small plate. Divide the dough in half, keeping one half refrigerated until needed. Shape the dough into balls the size of walnuts, and roll the balls in the cinnamon sugar. Place 2 inches apart on an ungreased baking sheet and bake just until golden—check the bottoms to make sure they are not getting too brown—about 8 minutes. The cookies will puff up first, then flatten out with crinkled tops. Cool on racks and store in a tightly covered container.

Basil Orange Cookies

———★———

MAKES ABOUT 7 DOZEN COOKIES

A painstakingly restored pre–Civil War summer kitchen is the center of Oris Hippensteel's herb garden, close to North Manchester. The post-and-beam log cabin is her retail shop and classroom, where she gives lectures on herbs and prepares meals for small groups by reservation. She raises over 200 varieties of herbs, laying out her garden as an artist does a canvas, with an eye to color and texture. The plants find their way into her handsome wreaths and flower arrangements.

Oris sometimes serves this soft yellow cookie, adding dried basil as a flavoring. The herb flavor becomes more pronounced as the cookies ripen; they taste best at room temperature, though they freeze very well.

★ HEARTLAND HERBS ★

Outsiders tend to think of Midwestern food as bland and unseasoned, but herbs are, and always have been, heavily used throughout the region. Migrating eighteenth- and nineteenth-century European cooks grew thyme, savory, woodruff, dill, garlic, parsley, rosemary, and sage in order to duplicate recipes from home. Herbed preserves, vinegars, and condiments were common during the Victorian period, and after World War II, when returning GIs wanted dishes like those they had sampled abroad, dried basil, marjoram, and oregano became readily available commercially and were embraced with enthusiasm. And as the Midwest's Mexican and Asian populations grow, herbs like cilantro and vegetables like chilies are taking hold as well. Today even the plainest of cooks raises a small assortment of herbs outside the kitchen door or in pots on the patio.

Oris Hippensteel's herbal creations delight the eye and the palate.

COOKIES

- 1½ cups granulated sugar
- 1½ cups vegetable shortening
- 2 eggs
- 1 cup milk
- 5 cups all-purpose flour
- 2 teaspoons baking soda
- 1 teaspoon salt
- ⅔ cup orange juice
- 3 tablespoons grated orange rind
- 1 teaspoon vanilla extract
- ¼ cup dried basil

FROSTING

- 2 cups or more confectioners' sugar
- 1 tablespoon butter, melted
- 2 to 3 tablespoons milk
- ½ teaspoon orange extract
- Pinch of salt
- Chopped pistachio nuts, for garnish

Preheat the oven to 350° F. In a large mixing bowl, cream the granulated sugar and shortening for 3 minutes. Add the eggs and continue beating until blended; add the milk, mixing thoroughly. Sift together the flour, baking soda, and salt; add to the mixture. Add the juice, rind, and vanilla, then stir in the basil by hand. Drop by heaping teaspoonfuls onto greased cookie sheets, approximately 2 inches apart. Bake for 10 to 12 minutes, or until the top springs back when touched with your finger. Remove to a rack to cool.

To make the frosting, combine all of the ingredients except the pistachio nuts in a mixer bowl, and beat until smooth. The frosting should be rather thick; add more sugar as needed.

Spread a generous smear of frosting on each cookie and sprinkle on some pistachio nuts. Pack the cookies in tins or plastic containers, using wax paper to separate each layer.

Persimmon Ice Cream

Madison, on the banks of the Ohio River and just across from Kentucky, has a Southern ambience that is evident in its menus as well as in the architecture. The town of 20,000 is a nineteenth-century Federalist Williamsburg. The concentration of architectural styles—Federal, Classic, Revival, Gothic Revival, Italianate, French Second Empire—takes your breath away.

Pork had a lot to do with Madison's affluence and its now beautifully restored homes; there were many slaughter houses here, for this was a place where settlers bought supplies to take with them into the wilderness by paddleboat, including barrels of salt pork.

Surrounding the town are banks of redbuds and the native persimmon tree, which grows well in the soil around Madison. The sweet pulp of the persimmon fruit is used in many ways and, to my way of thinking, this is one of the best.

        3 eggs
      ½ cup sugar (see Note)
      ½ teaspoon ground cinnamon
      ½ teaspoon ground allspice
          Pinch of salt
        2 cups half-and-half
        1 pound canned sweetened persimmon pulp
        1 tablespoon Cointreau

In the top of a double boiler, beat the eggs with a hand-held electric mixer just until broken up. Add the sugar, spices, and salt, and beat until well blended; add the half-and-half. Cook over simmering water until the mixture is thickened and coats a spoon, about 6 to 7 minutes. Don't let it boil. Remove from the heat and cool, then refrigerate to chill thoroughly, overnight if you like.

Add 1 cup of the persimmon puree to the chilled custard and blend. Transfer the mixture to the chilled cannister of an ice cream freezer and freeze according to manufacturer's directions.

Combine the remaining ½ cup of puree with the Cointreau and drizzle a little over each serving of ice cream.

NOTE: Canned persimmon pulp (available by mail, see Source List), comes sweetened. If you use unsweetened pulp, increase the sugar to ¾ cup.

Sassafras Tea

In the country, early spring used to be synonymous with fragrant pink sassafras tea, which was considered a tonic—it thinned the blood and took away the winter blahs. My grandfather had a grove of sassafras trees in the sheep meadow, and every spring, just as soon as the ground thawed, he would dig up some roots and bring them to the house, where they would be scrubbed clean, then soaked and dried. When I visited the farm, my grandmother would make the tea for me to drink and serve it in her best green-flowered Haviland cups. Sweetened with sugar, the rose-colored tea tasted like root beer.

        2 teaspoons dried sassafras shavings
        8 cups boiling water
          Fresh lemon juice
          Sugar

Place the tea in a tea strainer, put the strainer in a large teapot, and pour the boiling water over it. Cover and steep 5 minutes or longer. It should be rose-colored, but the tea will become a deeper red as it steeps. Serve with lemon and sugar. It is also delicious iced.

Tomato Basil Preserves

☆

This is a very unusual jam, both sweet and savory with its piquant cinnamon and basil flavoring. It is a real treat when presented with Hot Biscuits (page 4) or toasted English muffins. Make it in August, when basil is prolific in everyone's garden.

> 5–6 large ripe tomatoes
> Large bunch of fresh basil, stems included
> Rinds of 1 lemon and 1 orange
> 6½ cups sugar
> ¼ cup fresh lemon juice
> 2 tablespoons Worcestershire sauce
> ½ teaspoon ground cinnamon
> ½ teaspoon butter
> 1 pouch liquid pectin

Core, peel, and crush the tomatoes; measure 3 cups into a large kettle. Add the basil and bring to boil, then reduce heat and simmer uncovered over medium-low heat for 10 minutes; discard the basil. Add the rest of the ingredients except the pectin and bring to a hard boil. Boil hard for 1 minute, stirring constantly. Remove from the heat, add the pectin, then quickly skim off the foam.

Ladle at once into hot sterilized half-pint jars, leaving ¼-inch headspace. Wipe the jar rims and adjust the lids. Process in a boiling hot-water bath for 15 minutes after the water returns to a boil. Store in a dark place; the jam may take several weeks to thicken.

Spicy Apple and Green Tomato Chutney

☆

MAKES 12 PINTS

In the fall, just at frost time, the cherry tomato vines are loaded with little green tomatoes that resemble the lovely aggie marbles of our youth. It really hurts to think those tomatoes won't ever have time to ripen, but this chutney enables us to enjoy them anyway. It is a great mélange of flavor.

> 10 cups apples, unpeeled, cored and chopped coarsely
> 10 cups green cherry tomatoes
> 2 tablespoons ground cinnamon
> 1 tablespoon ground cloves
> 1½ teaspoons ground turmeric
> 1½ teaspoons freshly ground black pepper
> 2⅛ teaspoons salt
> 3½ cups cider vinegar
> 5 cups sugar
> ½ cup water

Preheat the oven to 350° F. Combine all of the ingredients in a large roaster, and bake, uncovered, for 2 to 3 hours, stirring occasionally. The time needed for cooking depends on the amount of water in the fruits, so it will vary. The mixture will be dark and thick and wonderfully fragrant when done.

Ladle the chutney into hot sterilized 1-pint jars to ¼ inch from the top and seal at once. Process in a boiling-hot water bath for 15 minutes. The mixture can also be frozen, if you prefer.

There is a corner of America where the spring is lovely beyond belief, the land rolling and intensely green like the center of France, the rivers small between oak-covered bluffs and crossed by quiet bridges where boys still sit with pole and line, hook and worm. Of course, generation after generation, the young mature and go away to the big and crowded cities. But their hearts never seem to leave this place and today, they tell me, more and more drift back here in their older years, striving, I hope not vainly — to find the magic talisman of peace.

ERIC SEVAREID

■ ■ ■

Grant Wood captured the image of Iowa in his canvases—the rolling groomed landscapes, its agricultural bounty, modest farm buildings, and a no-nonsense people who care for the land and live by enduring social values. There is a distinct feeling that this is the "middle land," unchanging and stable. But don't be deceived. Underneath the calm surface of daily life, Iowa teems with energy. ✱ Iowa's first settlers came across Illinois from Pennsylvania, Ohio, and Indiana, packing pots and pans and family recipes. Some came by river from the South, while immigrants from Germany, Norway, Sweden, and Holland arrived to work in the mines and to farm the giving soil. A later migration of Amish found the state an ideal place to live their private lives on the good land.

Just ahead of the arriving settlers, government surveyors worked east to west, marking off uniform sections of land, planning the checkerboard of parcels that gives Iowa its orderly look. The incoming settlers bought the land at federal land-grant offices or from land-grant railway companies for bargain prices. The land was settled without confusion or conflict, which is what you would expect from Iowans. With a railroad spanning the state by 1867, Iowa was ready to help feed the rest of the country.

Cornfields blanket the state, a never-ending sea of green rustling like taffeta in the summer winds. On both sides of the straight country roads, pork and sheep producers, surrounded by freshly painted white buildings and taut fences, keep their eye on the weather. In the summer, there are white mists in the morning that burn off by noon, leaving hot days of golden sunlight that dry the windrows of sweet alfalfa hay. The evening sunsets are orange, then fade to peach and salmon, and the nights are noisy with crickets and tree toads. And in the fall, the corn turns the color of dark honey.

But Iowa isn't a totally agricultural state. It produces everything from microwave ovens to motor homes. Farm implements, major appliances, and plastics are exported all over the world from here. Who hasn't heard of Maytag?

A favorite Indian hunting ground, this was the home of the warrior Blackhawk. It was also the birthplace of Buffalo Bill Cody. And we mustn't forget Meredith Willson and his "Seventy-six Trombones," or the Rodgers and Hammerstein movie *State Fair,* which captured all the rural values of another period that we now remember with fondness and nostalgia.

The state has always been prosperous and peaceful. Stabilizing influences were Protestantism, Republicans, and *McGuffy Reader* principles, which rooted its people in a warmly complicated web of religion, country, and family. Iowans earnestly attend to public education, religion, and social and political issues. And food. It's farm and flag cuisine, reflecting the richness of the land and the taste of its conservative and inquisitive citizens.

In the Grant Wood lithographs, we have a far wider view of the state than just *American Gothic.* Wood documented seasonal rhythms of agriculture and the activities that go on year round, and his well-known mural *Dinner for Threshers* leaves with us the enduring image of hard work, plenty, and indeed, beauty. ✶

CORNED BEEF HASH ★ NORWEGIAN PANCAKES ★
SAVORY BLUE CHEESE TART ★ OVEN-BAKED SPLIT
PEA SOUP ★ ROASTED RED PEPPER SOUP ★ STEWING
HEN WITH CORNMEAL PARSLEY DUMPLINGS ★ SPICY
CORNED BEEF ★ STUFFED PORK LOIN WITH CIDER
SAUCE ★ OLD-FASHIONED SUNDAY POT ROAST WITH
VEGETABLES AND BROWN GRAVY ★ BAKED PARSNIPS
GLAZED WITH MAPLE SYRUP ★ MASHED TURNIPS
AND POTATOES ★ TOMATO CAKES ★ SPICED
RED CABBAGE ★ GRILLED SWEET ONIONS ★
LA CORSETTE'S CORN CUSTARD ★ METHODIST
MACARONI AND CHEESE ★ CREAMY POTATO SALAD
★ CORN PATTIES WITH CHEESE ★ SOUR CREAM
CORN MUFFINS ★ AMISH FRIENDSHIP BREAD ★ AMISH
DATE OATMEAL CAKE ★ OLD-FASHIONED VINEGAR
PIE ★ PEARS À LA CARVER ★ LEMON-FROSTED
OATMEAL RAISIN COOKIES ★ CHOCOLATE CAKE
DOUGHNUTS ★ CORNCOB JELLY

Corned Beef Hash

MAKES 4 SERVINGS

Beets are not added to the Midwestern interpretation of hash as they are to the red flannel hash of New England. Midwestern hash is simply a savory mixture of leftover Spicy Corned Beef (page 74), potatoes, and a few seasonings. Do not chop the meat and potatoes in the food processor—the pieces should be just a bit coarser than what a food processor would produce.

The secret of good hash is long, slow sautéing so there is a good, crisp outer crust. Serve this as a hearty breakfast dish, with poached eggs on top.

 3 cups chopped cooked corn beef
 2 cups chopped cold boiled potatoes
 1 small onion, finely chopped
 3 tablespoons flour
 ¼ cup milk
 1 tablespoon catsup
 1 tablespoon Worcestershire sauce
 ½ teaspoon ground pepper
 ½ teaspoon dried thyme, or 2 tablespoons minced fresh thyme
 2 tablespoons vegetable oil
 4 poached eggs

In a large bowl, combine all the ingredients except the vegetable oil and eggs in the order given. Mix well.

Heat the oil in a large skillet over medium heat. Spread the meat and potato mixture evenly in the skillet, allowing space around the edge, pressing it down firmly to make a thick patty. Sauté over low heat for 30 minutes, turning every 10 minutes with a spatula. Serve crust side up, on a heated plate, topped with the poached eggs.

Norwegian Pancakes

MAKES 16 TO 18 PANCAKES, OR 4 TO 6 SERVINGS

The Midwest has a love affair with pancakes. My husband, Dick, and I ate so many different interpretations of them when we traveled researching this book that we lost count. But we are not complaining!

Some of the very best pancakes we sampled were in Decorah, in northeast Iowa. Many Norwegians immigrated there, we were told, because the landscape and winters reminded them of home. I am delighted they brought this superb recipe with them; the pancakes are rich, very thin, sweet, buttery—similar to a crepe. Serve them with Grape Juice Sauce (page 18) as a dessert, or with maple syrup for breakfast.

 3 eggs
 1 cup sugar
 ¼ teaspoon salt
 1 teaspoon grated lemon rind
 1 cup (2 sticks) butter, melted
 1 cup half-and-half
 1 cup all-purpose flour

In a large bowl, beat the eggs until light, about 3 minutes. Add the rest of the ingredients in the order given and beat together. The batter will be very thin.

Heat a heavy iron skillet or crepe pan and grease very lightly, just barely rubbing the sides and bottom with a bit of butter. Pour in ⅓ cup batter, tipping the skillet so batter runs up the sides. When the pancake loses its gloss, loosen sides gently and turn. When brown on the second side, fold into fourths and place in a heated casserole. Repeat until all the batter is used.

A lonely but still-operating windmill is a poignant reminder of pioneer days before the Midwest was settled.

Savory Blue Cheese Tart

Forget Stilton, forget Roquefort; look for Maytag Blue Cheese if you are seeking a blue cheese that surpasses all European competitors. Developed and made in Newton, Iowa, by the Maytag family of washing machine fame, the cheese was created as a way to use the milk of the Holstein-Friesian cows owned by one of the Maytag sons. It is available via mail order (see Source List).

Cut this appetizer pie in small wedges and serve as a well-flavored hors d'oeuvre.

- ½ recipe Never-Fail Pie Crust (page 244)
- ½ cup toasted chopped pecans
- 6 ounces cream cheese, at room temperature
- 2 eggs
- 4 ounces Maytag Blue Cheese
- ½ cup half-and-half
- 1 teaspoon cornstarch
- ¾ teaspoon Worcestershire sauce
- ¼ teaspoon coarsely ground black pepper
  Chopped fresh chives and blossoms, for garnish

Preheat the oven to 350° F. Roll out the pastry dough on a floured surface and use to line a 9-inch pie pan. Sprinkle the nuts in the bottom of the pie shell. In a food processor bowl or blender, combine the cream cheese, eggs, blue cheese, half-and-half, cornstarch, and seasonings until smooth. Pour into the crust and bake 35 to 40 minutes, or until the center is fairly firm. Cool and chill 2 hours, then cut into 12 wedges and arrange on a platter. Garnish top with the chopped chives and arrange chive blossoms around the edge of the platter.

Oven-Baked Split Pea Soup

Better Homes and Gardens magazine is located in Des Moines. From the middle of the country, this magazine and the library of cookbooks it has published have doubtlessly influenced American cookery more than any other food publication. This is an adaptation of one of their recipes from Food Editor Nancy Byal. It is a flavorsome and satisfying winter supper meal and, best of all, it can be made in the oven and left to cook unattended. Turkey kielbasa can also be used in this soup.

- 1 pound split peas
- 8 cups water
- 1½ cups diced carrots
- 1½ cups diced celery
- ½ cup diced onion
- ½ cup parsley sprigs
- 2 teaspoons dried thyme
- 1 teaspoon celery seed
- 1 teaspoon salt
- ¼ teaspoon freshly ground pepper
- 1 bay leaf
- 1 pound fully cooked smoked kielbasa, coarsely chopped in food processor
- ½ teaspoon bitters

Preheat the oven to 350° F. Rinse the split peas in cold water, then place in a large kettle with all the remaining ingredients except the sausage and bitters. Bake, covered, for 2 hours. Remove from oven and cool.

Discard bay leaf and puree the soup in food processor, working in batches, until smooth. Return to kettle. Add the chopped sausage and bitters. Bake 30 minutes longer, or until the sausage is heated through.

Roasted Red Pepper Soup

During August, Midwestern roadside market stands are piled high with handsome fruits and vegetables. This is the time to buy enormous red bell peppers at the unheard of price of "4 for a dollar." Red and green peppers can be chopped and frozen to use all winter, or extra peppers can be roasted and stored in the refrigerator. But first, try this handsome red soup with its sweet delicate flavor. It can be presented hot or cold. Serve it with Sage Cornbread Madeleines (page 167).

2 large Roasted Red Bell Peppers (page 243)
1 cup Chicken Stock (page 239)
1 cup peeled, seeded, and chopped tomatoes
½ cup diced raw potatoes
1 garlic clove, mashed
¼ cup sour cream
   Dash of hot red pepper sauce
   Salt and pepper to taste

Coarsely chop the peppers and place them in a medium saucepan. Add the stock, tomatoes, potatoes, and garlic. Bring to a boil, lower heat, cover, and simmer for 25 minutes.

Remove the pot from the heat and allow the mixture to cool slightly. Transfer to a food processor bowl and process until smooth. Add the sour cream, hot pepper sauce, and salt and pepper; blend. Add more stock if the soup seems too thick.

Stewing Hen with Cornmeal Parsley Dumplings

MAKES 4 SERVINGS

The improved and succulent flavor of a mature stewing hen will more than compensate for having to order it special. Some cooks prefer to thicken the boiling broth slightly with a cornstarch and water mixture before adding the dumplings; that is entirely up to you and how thick you want the broth. Start with 3 tablespoons of cornstarch and ½ cup water and go from there.

1 (3–4 pound) stewing hen, cut into serving pieces
1 celery stalk with leaves, cut into thirds
1 carrot, peeled and quartered
1 medium onion, peeled and quartered
1 bay leaf
½ cup parsley sprigs
6 peppercorns

DUMPLINGS
1 cup water
½ cup yellow cornmeal
½ teaspoon salt
½ teaspoon freshly ground black pepper
1 egg, lightly beaten
½ cup all-purpose flour
1 teaspoon baking powder
1 (7-ounce) can whole kernel corn, drained
2 tablespoons finely minced fresh parsley

Place the hen in a large stewing pot. Add the celery, carrot, onion, bay leaf, parsley, peppercorns, and water to cover, and bring to a boil. Reduce the heat to a simmer and cook, covered, until the chicken is tender, about 1½ hours. Strain the broth and discard the vegetables, then return the broth and chicken to the pot and bring back to a boil while you prepare the dumplings.

In a medium saucepan, combine the water, cornmeal, salt, and pepper, and bring to a boil. Cook and stir until thickened; remove from the heat. Stir some of the hot mixture into the beaten egg, then stir the egg mixture back into the hot cornmeal. In a medium mixing bowl, combine the flour and baking powder. Add the cornmeal mixture and beat well, and then stir in the corn and parsley.

Drop the dumpling batter by tablespoons into the boiling broth. Cover the pan tightly and simmer for 12 to 15 minutes without peeking.

Serve the chicken and dumplings on a deep platter or in a shallow tureen with some of the broth spooned over.

*OVERLEAF: **Amish boys and girls alike enjoy a game of softball at recess.***

Spicy Corned Beef

★

MAKES 6 SERVINGS

This is a perfect dish for entertaining for it can be made several days in advance. After cooking in a spicy broth and slicing, the beef is then glazed with a to-mato–brown sugar sauce. Any leftovers can be used in Corned Beef Hash (page 68) or in sandwiches.

1 (4–5 pound) piece of corned beef
¼ teaspoon dried rosemary
1 bay leaf
1 teaspoon dill seed
6 whole cloves
1 cinnamon stick
1 garlic clove
1 medium onion, cut in chunks
2 celery stalks, cut in chunks
½ orange, unpeeled, cut in chunks

GLAZE
½ cup chili sauce
1 cup water
½ cup brown sugar

In a large stockpot, combine all of the ingredients except the glaze and cover with warm water. Bring to a boil and simmer, covered, over medium-low heat for 40 minutes per pound, approximately 2½ hours. The meat should be tender, but not falling apart.

Remove the beef from the broth, cover, and cool, then refrigerate overnight. While the meat is cold, slice it very thinly and place in a 9 x 13-inch serv-ing dish. Cover and refrigerate.

To serve, preheat the oven to 350° F. Make the glaze by combining the chili sauce and water; pour just enough glaze over the beef to moisten it well —it should not cover the meat entirely. Sprinkle the brown sugar over the top and bake the beef, uncovered, for 30 minutes, or until the meat is heated through and the sugar is a bit crackly; you may want to turn up the heat to broil for a minute or two to achieve this effect.

Stuffed Pork Loin with Cider Sauce

★

MAKES 4 SERVINGS

Cider, dried tart cherries, apples, and cardamom all come together in this triumphant stuffing for an old-fashioned entrée: stuffed pork tenderloin. The sauce is a piquant accompaniment.

Dried cherries, though produced primarily in Mich-igan, are now readily available in most of our local supermarkets, or they can be ordered by mail (see Source List). Dried fruits of all kinds have always been a standby in the Midwest, dating back to the pioneer days when fresh and canned fruit was not available.

1 large pork tenderloin, about 1⅓ pounds

STUFFING
2 tablespoons dried tart cherries
¼ cup apple cider
1 cup crustless bread cubes, approximately 3 slices
1 tablespoon minced onion
¼ teaspoon celery seed
¼ teaspoon ground cardamom
¼ teaspoon dried thyme
⅛ teaspoon grated nutmeg
⅛ teaspoon freshly ground pepper

SAUCE
1 tablespoon vegetable oil
3¼ cups apple cider
4 small apples, preferably Jonathan, peeled, cored, and quartered
2 tablespoons dried tart cherries
2 tablespoons orange zest
1 tablespoon minced onion
1 bay leaf
¼ teaspoon dried thyme, or 2 tablespoons minced fresh
⅛ teaspoon ground cardamom
3 tablespoons cornstarch

Halve the tenderloin lengthwise with a sharp knife, then butterfly each long piece slightly so it is flattened out; set aside.

Plump the cherries in the cider in the micro-wave or in a small saucepan over low heat. In a medium bowl combine the rest of the stuffing ingredients and toss with the plumped cherries and their liquid; allow to stand until all the cider is absorbed by the bread cubes. Divide the stuffing between the 2 pieces of meat, patting it on firmly. Flip one stuffed loin on top of the other (this works; do not be concerned) so that the dressing sides are together. Tie with kitchen cord at 1-inch intervals.

Preheat the oven to 325° F. In a Dutch oven, heat the oil over medium heat. Brown the loin on all sides, about 10 minutes. Pour over 3 cups of the cider, add the apples, cherries, orange zest, onion, bay leaf, thyme, and cardamom, and stir. Cover and bake for 30 minutes, or until the onion is tender, or until the meat registers 160° F. on a meat thermometer.

In a small bowl combine the cornstarch with the remaining cider using a small whisk. Remove the meat to a carving board. Discard the bay leaf. Bring the cooking liquid to a boil over medium heat; whisk in the cornstarch mixture, and stir until thick and smooth. Carve the meat into slices and serve with a gravy boat of the sauce.

Old-fashioned Sunday Pot Roast with Vegetables and Brown Gravy

————— ★ —————

MAKES 6 SERVINGS

A traditional Sunday meal after church was pot roast. The meat would be browned and partially cooked on Saturday, the vegetables pared and refrigerated in water, and then, just before the family left for church on Sunday, the pot roast and vegetables would be combined and slipped into the oven. On their arrival home, the family would find a house filled with a mouth-watering aroma. Afterward, weather permitting, everyone played croquet in the afternoon.

3 pounds boneless beef rump, well trimmed
3 large garlic cloves, peeled and cut in thirds
2 tablespoons vegetable oil
1 cup coarsely chopped celery
1 cup coarsely chopped onion
3 large carrots, peeled and halved
4 cups Beef Stock (page 239)
2 bay leaves
½ green bell pepper
1 tablespoon catsup
¾ teaspoon dried thyme
½ teaspoon salt
½ teaspoon freshly ground black pepper
6 small potatoes, peeled and quartered
¼ cup (½ stick) butter, at room temperature
¼ cup all-purpose flour
⅛ teaspoon or more hot red pepper sauce

Preheat the oven to 325° F. Make 9 deep incisions in the meat and insert the garlic pieces. Heat 1 tablespoon of the oil in a heavy roasting pan; add the meat and brown on all sides over medium heat. Transfer the meat to a plate.

Add the remaining tablespoon of oil to the pan. Add the celery, onion, and carrots and sauté for about 5 minutes. Add the stock, bay leaves, green pepper, and catsup. Return the meat to the pan, cover, and bring to a boil. Transfer to the oven and bake for 2 hours.

Move the meat aside and stir in the thyme, salt, and pepper. (At this point, the meat can be stored in the refrigerator until the next day.) Place the potatoes on the bottom of the pan, and rearrange the meat on top. Re-cover, and bake 45 minutes longer, or until the meat and potatoes are tender.

In a small bowl, mash the butter and flour together until a smooth paste is formed. Transfer the meat to a large heated platter and, using a slotted spoon, remove the carrots and potatoes and arrange them around the meat. Discard the bell pepper, bay leaves, and celery. Bring the pan juices to a boil over high heat, then whisk in the butter mixture by tablespoonfuls. Cook over high heat until the mixture forms a gravy, then reduce heat and simmer for 3 minutes. Add hot pepper sauce to taste. Pour some of the gravy over the meat and pass the remainder with the meat and vegetables at the table.

ABOVE: *Mail Pouch Tobacco signs, once fixtures on the country landscape, are becoming relics of the past.*
OPPOSITE: *With the luxury of lawns comes the chore of mowing them, and it is usually a Saturday task.*

Baked Parsnips Glazed with Maple Syrup

★

MAKES 6 SERVINGS

This white root vegetable that is first cousin to the carrot has long been popular with Midwestern country cooks. Parsnips are an exceedingly hardy vegetable, and will winter over in the ground through even the harshest of Iowa seasons. In fact, frost or very cold weather improves their flavor, changing their starch content to sugar. Ideally, the parsnips should all be the same size so they will cook evenly in your pan, but Mother Nature rarely cooperates. Cut the larger parsnips into halves or fourths, and if they are really large, cut out the cores, for they will be woody.

The sauce, with its hint of marjoram, cooks down to a pleasing glaze. This is very nice with pork and game dishes and for Thanksgiving dinner.

2 pounds parsnips
2 tablespoons (¼ stick) butter
½ cup maple syrup
½ teaspoon dry mustard
½ teaspoon dried marjoram
   Salt and pepper to taste

Preheat the oven to 400° F. Peel the parsnips and slice them approximately ⅞ inch thick. Transfer the parsnips to a medium saucepan with water to cover. Bring to a boil and cook, covered, for about 5 minutes, or until just tender—don't let them get mushy. Drain the parsnips and transfer to a greased 1-quart casserole.

In a small saucepan, combine the rest of the ingredients and bring to a boil over low heat. Pour over the parsnips and bake uncovered for 40 minutes, or until the sauce is cooked down and the parsnips begin to brown.

Mashed Turnips and Potatoes

★

Many people are dubious about turnips, but once peeled, turnips look suspiciously like potatoes. Together, the two make a hearty dish that is especially good served with pork. Along with rutabagas, carrots, and potatoes, these long-keeping root vegetables were winter staples of the European immigrants who settled in the Midwestern states.

- 3 medium turnips
- 3 medium potatoes
- 1 bay leaf
- ½ teaspoon salt
- 1 teaspoon sugar
- ¼ teaspoon grated nutmeg
- ⅓ teaspoon ground white pepper
- 3 tablespoons butter
- 2 to 4 tablespoons heavy (whipping) cream
- 1 tablespoon or more butter and finely minced chives, for garnish

Wash, peel, and cut the vegetables into 2-inch chunks, keeping the potatoes and turnips separate. Place the turnips in a deep saucepan with water to cover plus the bay leaf and salt. Simmer, covered, for about 20 minutes. Add the potatoes and cook until the vegetables are soft, about 25 minutes longer. Drain well and discard the bay leaf.

Return the cooked turnips and potatoes to the saucepan and add the rest of the ingredients. Cook over medium-high heat until the cream bubbles up. Mash and beat the mixture smooth—I use a hand mixer. Taste to see if more salt or sugar should be added. Transfer to a serving bowl and make a well in the top of the mixture, then add the butter and sprinkle generously with chives.

Tomato Cakes

★

This recipe crops up in a lot of old cookbooks, including Amish ones. Crackers, along with sugar, were among the few things the early pioneer cooks bought at country stores. Everything else they raised or produced themselves, from sorghum molasses to vinegar. It's no wonder we find many "scalloped" dishes—those made with cracker crumbs—in the Midwest. It was a way to use a readily available ingredient in a new way, and sometimes to extend a handful or cup of vegetables so it would serve four people instead of two.

Out of necessity came some honestly good creations, such as this tender fritterlike dish, sharply flavored with tomatoes and seasoned with bits of onion, basil, and rosemary.

- 2 eggs, lightly beaten
- 1 28-ounce can crushed tomatoes in tomato puree
- 2 teaspoons sugar
- 1½ tablespoons chopped fresh parsley
- 3 tablespoons minced onion
- ½ teaspoon dried basil
- ½ teaspoon salt
- ¼ teaspoon crushed dried rosemary
- ¼ teaspoon freshly ground pepper
- 1½ cups soda cracker crumbs (approximately 38)
  Oil and margarine, for frying

In a large mixing bowl, combine all the ingredients except the oil and margarine in the order given. Allow the mixture to stand for 15 minutes. Heat an electric skillet to 340° F. Add 1 tablespoon oil and 1 tablespoon margarine. Pat rounded tablespoons of tomato mixture into 3-inch ovals about ¼ inch thick and drop into the hot fat. Sauté 2 minutes each side and transfer to a warm platter. Keep adding 1 tablespoon each oil and margarine to the skillet for each batch of cakes. Keep finished cakes in a heated oven while frying the rest of the mixture.

Spiced Red Cabbage
(Rodekool)

———— ★ ————

MAKES 6 SERVINGS

Several communities around the Midwest have large Dutch populations: Holland, Michigan; Otsburg, Wisconsin; Greenleafton, Minnesota; and Pella and Orange City, Iowa. All are immaculate towns with lace-curtained windows, and people observe the customary coffee breaks at 9 A.M. and 3 P.M.

In Pella, the earliest Dutch immigrants spent the cold first winter of 1847 in huts cut from the prairie sod and topped with roofs of woven straw, earning the town the nickname "Strawtown." The Strawtown Inn, built in the 1800s, stands on the site of those huts.

The best time to visit Pella, or any of the Dutch communities, is during their mid-May tulip festivals —tulips are whimsically referred to as the "mother flower." Street scrubbings, klompen dancing in wooden shoes, traditional costumes, and, of course, sturdy Dutch food are all part of the festivities.

The Strawtown Inn serves this zesty spiced cabbage dish on blue Delft china.

1 large head red cabbage, very finely sliced (about 5 cups)
1 cup chopped unpeeled apple, such as Jonathan, Winesap, or McIntosh
1 tablespoon whole allspice
½ teaspoon salt
¼ teaspoon grated nutmeg
¼ teaspoon ground cinnamon
¼ teaspoon freshly ground black pepper
¼ cup red wine vinegar
⅓ cup brown sugar
2 tablespoons (¼ stick) butter or more as needed

Place the cabbage in a large sauté pan, and add enough water to cover. Bring to a boil, lower the heat, and simmer, covered, until it is limp and soft, about 5 minutes. Drain off all but ½ cup water. Add the apple, toss, and continue cooking until the apple is tender, about 15 minutes.

Add the spices, vinegar, and brown sugar and continue cooking until the cabbage and apple mixture is very tender and most of the liquid is gone. Add the butter and serve.

Grilled Sweet Onions

———— ★ ————

MAKES 4 SIDE-DISH SERVINGS

Big sweet onions, sliced thick, basted with olive oil, prebaked slightly, and then finished up on the grill, are a quick and unusual meat accompaniment for barbecued beef and chicken. The onions become a bit charred, are very tender and sweet, and are altogether wonderful.

2 large sweet onions, 3 inches or more in diameter, peeled and sliced about ½ inch thick
½ cup olive oil
Chopped fresh marjoram or dried, to taste
Salt and pepper to taste

Preheat the oven to 400° F. Place the onions in a 9 x 13-inch baking dish in a single layer. Brush with the olive oil and sprinkle with marjoram, salt, and pepper. Bake the onions, uncovered, for about 25 minutes. (This precooking step makes the onions very sweet.)

Place the onions on a charcoal grill and cook 5 minutes on one side, then turn and cook 2 minutes on the other side. Remove carefully with a spatula and serve.

*OVERLEAF: **The complex farm machinery of the Midwest has the drama of a Calder sculpture.***

La Corsette's Corn Custard

──★──

In Newton, just east of Des Moines, the historic La Corsette Maison Inn is situated in a 1909 mission-style mansion. The mission oak woodwork, Art Nouveau stained-glass windows, and original furnishings make this a special place to stay as well as to eat. Innkeeper Kay Owen raises nearly all the vegetables and herbs that find their way into her beguiling recipes. Her savory corn custard with a hint of cornmeal is an outstanding dish.

    1 cup fresh corn kernels (about 2 to 3 ears)
    2¾ cups milk
    1 teaspoon salt
    1 cup yellow cornmeal
    ½ cup (1 stick) unsalted butter, cut into 1-inch
       pieces
    3 eggs, separated, at room temperature
    2 teaspoons sugar
    ¼ teaspoon freshly grated nutmeg
    4 to 5 drops hot red pepper sauce

Preheat the oven to 400° F. Generously butter a 2-quart charlotte mold or soufflé dish. Chop the corn kernels coarsely in a food processor using on/off pulses. In a medium saucepan, bring the corn, 2 cups of the milk, and salt to a boil over medium heat. Slowly stir in the cornmeal. Return the mixture to a boil and stir until very thick, about 1 minute. Remove from the heat. Immediately beat in the butter, then stir in the remaining ¾ cup milk. Blend in the egg yolks one at a time. Add the sugar, nutmeg, and hot red pepper sauce. (This can be prepared 4 to 6 hours ahead and set aside at room temperature.)

Beat the egg whites until stiff but not dry. Fold one-fourth of the whites into the cornmeal mixture, then fold in the remaining whites, blending gently but thoroughly. Pour into the prepared mold and bake for 10 minutes. Reduce the oven temperature to 375°, and continue baking until the custard puffs slightly and browns but center is still soft, about 55 minutes. Serve hot.

NOTE: The custard can also be baked in 8 individual ramekins. Bake 5 minutes at 400° F., then reduce the oven temperature to 375° F. and continue baking about 18 minutes longer. If the custard is prepared ahead, cover it with greased foil and reheat in a bain-marie in a 300° F. oven for about 20 minutes.

Methodist Macaroni and Cheese

──★──

Local church or temple cookbooks are treasure troves of regional recipes. In them you can find a cross section of ages and tastes, but current trends always emerge, as certain types of recipes are repeated. For instance, one such cookbook had three recipes for saffron tea. I had never seen those recipes before and haven't since.

In Iowa church cookbooks you find many casserole recipes, such as this rich and creamy macaroni and cheese, which is very well seasoned.

    ½ pound elbow macaroni
    3 tablespoons butter
    3 tablespoons finely minced onion
    ¼ cup all-purpose flour
    1 cup milk
    1 cup half-and-half
    1 tablespoon Worcestershire sauce
    ½ teaspoon celery salt
    ¼ teaspoon dry mustard
    ¼ teaspoon grated nutmeg
    ⅛ teaspoon ground white pepper
    8 ounces extra-sharp cheddar cheese, grated
       Paprika, for dusting

Preheat the oven to 350° F. In a large saucepan, cook the macaroni according to package directions until tender. Drain and set aside.

In a medium saucepan, melt the butter over medium heat. Add the onion and sauté until golden, about 3 to 4 minutes. Stir in the flour and continue cooking and stirring until the mixture bubbles all over the bottom of the pan, about 4 minutes. Add the milk and half-and-half all at once, raise the heat slightly, and whisk in the Worcestershire sauce, celery salt, mustard, nutmeg, and pepper. Continue cooking and whisking until the mixture bubbles in the middle and thickens, about 3 minutes.

Sprinkle in the cheese, whisking until the mixture is smooth and the cheese has melted. Transfer the drained macaroni to a greased 1½-quart casserole. Pour the cheese sauce over it and combine. Sprinkle the top with paprika. Bake, covered, for 25 minutes, then uncover and continue baking 10 minutes more.

N O T E : This can be made 2 days in advance and refrigerated or frozen.

Creamy Potato Salad

MAKES 10 SERVINGS

The secret of this well-seasoned potato salad is the vinaigrette that is poured over the warm potatoes. This is a most desirable dish—creamy, colorful, with lots of flavor—just like memories of the potato salads that used to be served at family reunions. The recipe looks like it calls for lots of ingredients, but none of them takes any preparation and they all add up to super eating.

    7 large red-skinned potatoes

VINAIGRETTE
    ½ cup vegetable oil
    ¼ cup cider vinegar
    ½ teaspoon salt
    ¼ teaspoon coarsely ground black pepper
    ¼ teaspoon dry mustard

SALAD
    1 cup chopped onion
    2 cups chopped celery
    ½ cup salad pickles (see Note)
    3 tablespoons prepared mustard
    3 tablespoons sugar
    ½ teaspoon salt, or more to taste
    ½ teaspoon coarsely ground black pepper
    ½ teaspoon dried basil, or 1½ tablespoons minced, fresh
    ½ teaspoon dried oregano, or 1½ tablespoons minced fresh
    1 teaspoon celery seed
    1 teaspoon celery salt
    3 hard-cooked eggs, peeled and chopped
    8 slices bacon, cooked, cooled, and chopped
    ½ cup minced fresh parsley
    2 cups mayonnaise

Peel the potatoes and place in a saucepan with water to cover. Cook over medium heat, covered, for approximately 25 minutes, or until they are just tender when pierced with a knife. Drain and transfer to a large bowl; when cool enough to handle, chop into 1-inch cubes.

Combine the vinaigrette ingredients in a small jar and shake to blend. Pour over the warm potatoes and toss, taking care not to break up the potatoes. Set aside.

In another large bowl, combine the salad ingredients. Pour the dressing mixture over the cooled potatoes, which should have now absorbed all of the vinaigrette. (If they haven't, let the potatoes stand a few more minutes.) Toss lightly but thoroughly. Chill for at least 4 hours before serving.

N O T E : Salad pickles are cubed chopped sweet pickles, not a fine relish, and are ideal for salads They are a most convenient product and can be ordered by mail (see Source List).

Corn Patties with Cheese

———— ★ ————

MAKES 6 SERVINGS

On warm summer nights, the Iowa farmers say you can hear the corn growing—and during the peak growing season, it does indeed grow 3 to 5 inches a day. When truckers drive through, the Iowa highways are lined with fields of corn so tall it looks as if they are driving through a green tunnel. Talking back and forth on their CB radios, they appropriately call this state the "corn patch."

I devised this dish to go with grilled duck breasts, but they could also be served as a first course, with a dollop of red pepper or tomato sauce on top.

2	tablespoons olive oil
¼	cup finely minced onion
3	cups Chicken Stock (page 239)
1½	cups yellow cornmeal
1½	cups grated Swiss cheese
⅓	cup minced cilantro (fresh coriander)
	Salt and pepper to taste
¼	cup grated Parmesan cheese
	Paprika, for dusting

In a deep kettle, heat the oil over medium heat and sauté the onion briefly, just until softened, about 2 to 3 minutes. Add the stock and bring to a full boil. Gradually sprinkle in the cornmeal, whisking briskly so the mixture does not lump. Reduce the heat to low, cover, and cook for 10 minutes, stirring and watching it carefully so it does not scorch. The mixture will be very thick. Add 1 cup of the Swiss cheese, the cilantro, salt, and pepper, and combine well.

Pour into a greased 8-inch square pan and allow to cool completely, uncovered. Then cover and refrigerate.

To serve, preheat the oven to 425° F. Turn the cornmeal square onto a work surface and cut in 9 squares. Cut each square in half to form 2 triangles, then transfer to a greased cookie sheet. In a small bowl, combine the remaining ½ cup Swiss cheese and the Parmesan cheese, and sprinkle over the tops of the triangles. Top each with a dusting of paprika. Bake for 10 minutes or until the cheese is melted and the tops are golden brown.

Sour Cream Corn Muffins

— ★ —

MAKES 12 MUFFINS

These are absolutely delightful corn muffins. Flat-topped like little golden cakes, they are fine-textured and delicately flavored. There is a hint of bacon, and the bottoms of the muffins are crunchy with cornmeal. The batter can also be spooned into preheated cornstick pans or baked in a heavy skillet for cornbread.

1 cup yellow cornmeal
½ cup all-purpose flour
2 teaspoons baking powder
2 teaspoons sugar
1 teaspoon salt
1 egg
¼ cup plus 2 tablespoons melted bacon fat
¾ cup buttermilk
1 cup sour cream
Additional cornmeal for the muffin tins

Preheat the oven to 425° F. Place a heavy 12-cup muffin tin in the oven. In a large mixer bowl, combine the cornmeal, flour, baking powder, sugar, and salt. Add the egg, ¼ cup of the bacon fat, buttermilk, and sour cream. Beat until smooth.

Remove the muffin tin from the oven, spray the sides and bottom with vegetable cooking spray, and add ½ teaspoon of bacon fat to each mold. Sprinkle some cornmeal, about ¼ teaspoon, into each mold. Spoon ¼ cup of batter into each mold and bake for 15 minutes (see Note), or until golden brown and the muffins are shrinking away from the sides of the molds.

NOTE: If using a cast-iron skillet, bake 18 to 20 minutes.

TOP: *The American flag is displayed prominently all over the Midwest, even appearing on top of all-American apple pie.* BOTTOM: *Hardware stores provide farmers and their gardening wives with working gloves year round.*

Amish Friendship Bread

————— ★ —————

Just as soon as the Amish TV cooking show began airing nationally, I was besieged by requests for Amish Friendship Bread, a delicious bread made with a sour dough starter. Because there are several recipes you can make from the starter recipe, everyone wanted that recipe the most.

It is my observation that having this starter around is like getting married—it is a real commitment and it is forever. And like that institution, it gets better with age.

Some rules to observe: Use nonmetallic bowls; use wooden utensils for stirring, not an electric mixer. Leave the starter outside the refrigerator, uncovered. This is so it can pick up from the air the natural yeast that is flying about your kitchen. If the open dish bothers you terribly, it can be covered with a single layer of cheesecloth. Do not use the starter the day you feed it; the bread will not rise as high. Do not refrigerate the mixture until Day 12. The starter really multiplies after the fifth day, so be sure your container is large enough; I use a 10-cup bowl. I also keep a paper and pencil next to it and write down what I do when, so I don't get off schedule.

Friendship Starter

2 cups unbleached all-purpose flour
2 cups warm water
1 package active dry yeast

2 cups milk
2 cups unbleached all-purpose flour
2 cups sugar

Day 1: In a glass or ceramic bowl, mix the first 3 starter ingredients thoroughly. Leave on the kitchen counter uncovered; don't refrigerate it.

NOTE: You may have received one cup of the starter from a friend. If so, you do not need to make the above culture and can go directly to the bread recipes that follow, unless you want to keep the starter going. If you do, then continue with the following directions.

Days 2, 3, and 4: Stir well with wooden spoon.

Day 5: Stir and add 1 cup milk, 1 cup flour, and 1 cup sugar. This is called "feeding the starter."

Days 6, 7, and 8: Stir with a wooden spoon.

Day 9: Stir and add another 1 cup milk, 1 cup flour, and 1 cup sugar. Stir well.

Days 10 and 11: Stir well.

Day 12: Ladle 1 cup of starter into each of 4 containers (I use glass jars with lids) and refrigerate. Use one to make one of the bread recipes that follow, keep one for your use another time, and give the two others to friends. Don't forget to include all the recipes (including the starter) for your friends.

You are ready to begin baking—at last! If you do not bake on this day, add 1 teaspoon sugar and refrigerate the mixture. The sugar will feed the yeast and keep it alive. Date the jars and every 10 days remove the starter from the refrigerator, transfer it to a bowl, and feed it the usual combination of 1 cup each of milk, flour, and sugar. Leave it outside the refrigerator uncovered for 2 days, then either bake it or divide it among friends, and always save some for yourself.

Friendship Bread I

MAKES 2 LOAVES

1 cup Friendship Starter, at room temperature
3 eggs
⅔ cup vegetable oil
3 teaspoons vanilla extract
2 cups unbleached all-purpose flour
1 cup sugar
2 teaspoons baking powder
1½ teaspoons ground cinnamon
1 teaspoon baking soda
1 teaspoon salt
1 cup chopped English walnuts or pecans
2 medium apples, peeled and finely chopped

Preheat the oven to 350° F. Grease two 9 x 5-inch loaf pans. In a large mixing bowl, beat together the starter, eggs, vegetable oil, and vanilla. Add the dry ingredients and blend. Fold in the nuts and apples and transfer the batter to the prepared loaf pans. Bake for 50 minutes and remove from the oven. Allow the bread to cool for 10 minutes, then tip out onto a rack to finish cooling completely.

NOTE: To make 24 muffins, spoon into greased muffin tins and bake for 25 to 30 minutes.

Friendship Bread 2

MAKES 12 LARGE SERVINGS

BATTER

- 1 cup Friendship Starter
- 3 eggs
- ⅔ cup vegetable oil
- 2 cups unbleached all-purpose flour
- 1 cup granulated sugar
- 2 teaspoons baking soda
- ½ teaspoon salt

TOPPING

- ⅓ cup melted butter
- ½ cup granulated sugar
- ½ cup brown sugar
- ½ cup quick-cooking oats
- 1 cup chopped English walnuts or pecans
- 1½ teaspoons ground cinnamon

Preheat the oven to 350° F. In a large mixer bowl, beat together the starter, eggs, and vegetable oil; add the rest of the ingredients and mix. Set aside. Combine the topping ingredients in a small mixing bowl.

Put half of the batter in a greased 9 x 13-inch pan. Sprinkle with half the topping. Cover with the remaining batter; sprinkle on the rest of the topping and bake for 35 to 40 minutes.

Amish Date Oatmeal Cake

——— ★ ———

MAKES 6 SERVINGS

In the little town of Kalona, a few miles south of Iowa City, there is a large Amish-Mennonite community. An Amish woman whom I met there had brought this recipe back from a family reunion in Kirchner, Canada. The Amish and Mennonites travel about a great deal; the Amish, who generally travel by horse and buggy, hire a van and a driver to take them to weddings, funerals, and reunions. And they always exchange recipes whenever they go out of town.

This is a very rich and heavy cake, as most date cakes are, but that is not a criticism—the cake is really luscious. No icing is needed, but I do like to serve it in a pool of Crème Anglaise (page 246).

- 1 cup boiling water
- 2 cups quick-cooking oats
- ¾ cup (1½ sticks) butter, at room temperature
- 2 cups brown sugar
- 2 eggs
- 1½ cups finely chopped dates
- 1 cup coarsely chopped pecans
- 1 teaspoon grated orange rind
- ½ cup all-purpose flour
- 1 teaspoon baking soda
- ½ teaspoon salt
- 1 teaspoon grated nutmeg
- 1 teaspoon ground allspice

Preheat the oven to 350° F. In a large bowl, pour boiling water over the oats, mix well, and allow to cool slightly. Blend in the butter, brown sugar, eggs, dates, pecans, and orange rind. Sift together the dry ingredients and mix into the oat batter. Pour into a greased 8-inch square pan and bake for 45 minutes, or until the center is firm when touched with your finger and the cake shrinks away from the sides of the pan slightly. Cool, cut into squares, and serve plain or with a cream sauce.

Old-fashioned Vinegar Pie

MAKES 6 TO 8 SERVINGS

Vinegar pies were popular all over the Midwest among those early cooks who had to prepare meals from the ingredients they had on hand. Lemons, in short supply and expensive, too, were luxuries many country women could ill afford, so it was not uncommon for the vinegar that was stored by the barrel in basements to be substituted for lemon's tart flavor.

This pie is opaque, quivery, and spicy, and the taste of vinegar is not overly pronounced. If you didn't know it contained vinegar, I don't think you would be able to discern it.

PIE

- 3 egg yolks
- 4 tablespoons all-purpose flour
- 1 cup brown sugar
- ⅛ teaspoon salt
- 1 teaspoon ground allspice
- ¼ teaspoon mace
- ¼ cup cider vinegar
- 2 cups warm water
- ¼ cup (½ stick) butter, at room temperature
  9-inch baked pie shell (½ recipe Never-Fail Pie Crust, page 244)

MERINGUE TOPPING

- 3 egg whites
- ¼ teaspoon salt
- 1 teaspoon cider vinegar
- 6 tablespoons granulated sugar
- 1½ teaspoons cornstarch

In the top of a double boiler, beat the egg yolks well. Combine the flour, sugar, salt, and spices and blend into the egg yolks. Add the vinegar and mix, then add the warm water. Simmer over boiling water for 25 minutes, or until the mixture is thickened; the water should just reach the bottom of the top pan. Stir in the butter and cool slightly, about 15 to 20 minutes, without stirring. Pour the warm filling into the baked shell; set aside to cool.

Preheat the oven to 325° F. In a large mixer bowl, beat together the egg whites, salt, and vinegar until soft peaks form. Gradually add the sugar, 1 tablespoon at a time. Continue beating until stiff peaks form; sprinkle in the cornstarch just before the beating is completed. The peaks should not topple over when the beater is raised.

Spread the meringue over the filling all the way to the edge of the pastry. Bake for 15 to 18 minutes, or until the meringue is golden brown. Cool the pie completely, then refrigerate.

Pears à la Carver

Iowa City lies amidst a Grant Wood landscape accented with white farmhouses and barns with tall dark cement silos. This pastoral region seems an unlikely setting for a writers' workshop of international renown. The Creative Writing Program at the University of Iowa has an impressive list of alumni that includes Tennessee Williams, John Gardiner, Flannery O'Connor, John Irving, and Gail Godwin. The instructors are equally as impressive: Philip Roth, Kurt Vonnegut, John Cheever, and Nelson Algren among others.

Poets and novelists must eat, though, and they have even recorded their favorite recipes in the Iowa Writers' Workshop Cookbook *(Fell Press). The following recipe for baked pears is from poet Tess Gallagher, created and named for her husband, the late fiction writer, Raymond Carver.*

Antique washboards lined up for a garage sale entice the passerby, OPPOSITE. BELOW: ***One of Iowa's fine corn-fed porkers sniffs the breeze.***

4 firm ripe pears
½ cup light corn syrup
½ cup light brown sugar
1 tablespoon vanilla extract
½ cup heavy (whipping) cream
¼ cup chopped toasted walnuts

Preheat the oven to 375° F. Peel the pears and core them from the blunt end, leaving the stems intact. In a medium saucepan, combine the syrup, brown sugar, and vanilla. Cook and stir 2 minutes over medium heat until the sugar is dissolved and the mixture thins.

In a buttered shallow 9-inch square baking dish, lay the pears on their sides, but not touching. Pour the syrup over the pears and cover. Bake 30 minutes, turning once with a spatula. Uncover and bake 20 to 30 minutes more, basting with the syrup every 10 minutes.

Transfer the pears to individual serving dishes. Pour the syrup back into the saucepan and reduce it over low heat until it is thick and dark and about ½ cup of syrup remains—about 5 minutes. Stir in the cream and cook 1 minute longer. Pour the syrup over the pears and sprinkle with the walnuts.

Lemon-Frosted Oatmeal Raisin Cookies

——— ★ ———

MAKES 6 DOZEN COOKIES

For those of you who have a craving for the soft, spicy, old-fashioned oatmeal raisin cookies of your youth, this one is for you. The recipe is from Clemons, Iowa, and dates back to the mid-1800s. The addition of lard is one reason these cookies remain moist for a long time after baking, though you could use all butter or substitute margarine for the lard if you prefer.

The frosting is my addition—the lemon adds some nice tartness, and I am prone to frost cookies anyway.

COOKIES

½ cup brown sugar
½ cup granulated sugar
½ cup (1 stick) butter
½ cup lard
2 eggs
1 teaspoon lemon extract
1 cup raisins
2 cups water
1 teaspoon baking soda
2 cups all-purpose flour
2 cups old-fashioned rolled oats
1 teaspoon ground cinnamon
1 teaspoon ground allspice
1 teaspoon ground cloves
¾ teaspoon salt

FROSTING

2 cups confectioners' sugar
1 tablespoon very soft butter
Pinch of salt
1 tablespoon fresh lemon juice
1 teaspoon grated lemon rind
½ teaspoon vanilla extract
3 tablespoons milk, approximately

Preheat the oven to 350° F. In a large mixer bowl, cream the sugars, butter, and lard. Beat in the eggs until well blended, then add the lemon extract and set aside. In a small saucepan, combine the raisins with the water and bring to a boil; lower the heat and simmer uncovered for 5 minutes. When cool, drain the raisins, reserving ⅔ cup of the cooking liquid. Add the baking soda to the reserved cooking liquid, letting it dissolve.

In a large bowl, whisk together the flour, oats, cinnamon, allspice, cloves, and salt; blend into the sugar mixture. Add the raisins and cooking liquid, and combine well. Drop by heaping teaspoonfuls onto greased baking sheets 2 inches apart and bake 10 to 12 minutes, or until golden and firm on top when touched with your finger. Transfer the cookies to a wax paper–lined rack to cool slightly.

In a mixer bowl, beat the confectioners' sugar, butter, salt, and lemon juice until smooth. Blend in the lemon rind, vanilla, and enough milk to make a smooth consistency. Spread ½ teaspoon frosting over each warm cookie.

Chocolate Cake Doughnuts

——— ★ ———

MAKES 30 DOUGHNUTS

Finding uses for leftovers like extra mashed potatoes is the mark of a frugal Midwestern cook. And adding them to doughnut batter assures that you will have a moist doughnut that never dries out. Take these on a tailgate picnic to the ball game or any other picnic. Store them without powdering them with the sugar— they look better freshly dusted.

2 eggs
1½ cups granulated sugar
1 cup cold unseasoned mashed potatoes
¼ cup (½ stick) butter, melted
1½ teaspoons vanilla extract
3 cups all-purpose flour
2 teaspoons baking powder
1 teaspoon salt
1 teaspoon grated nutmeg
½ cup unsweetened cocoa powder
½ cup milk
Vegetable oil, for frying
Confectioners' sugar, for dusting

In a large mixer bowl, beat the eggs well. Add the sugar, mashed potatoes, butter, and vanilla, and whip until creamy. Sift together the flour, baking powder, salt, nutmeg, and cocoa. Add alternately with the milk to the egg mixture and mix well. Chill the batter for 2 hours in the refrigerator.

Heat the oil in a deep-fryer to 375° F. Roll the dough to a ½-inch thickness on a lightly floured board. Cut with a doughnut cutter and slide into the hot oil with a metal spatula. Fry for 1½ minutes on each side, turning with tongs. Drain on paper towels. Sprinkle with confectioners' sugar before serving.

Corncob Jelly

MAKES 4 HALF-PINT JARS

I have had several requests for this recipe, for it is rarely seen in cookbooks anymore and people remember it from days gone by. Utilizing shelled corncobs from field corn as a jelly base was yet another way country women "made do" with what they had. The jelly has a very pleasing but subtle flavor; try it on Hot Biscuits (page 4) or buttered toast.

To find dried red corncobs, call the grain elevator in the nearest small town. Ordinarily, cobs are sold by the ton for about twenty dollars—they are used as mulch, for smoking meats, and as kindling. If you explain that you are making corncob jelly—be prepared for incredulity—and require just a dozen cobs, they will doubtless give you all you need.

12 dried red corncobs, kernels removed
1 box powdered pectin
1 tablespoon lemon juice
3 cups sugar
Few drops red food coloring, optional

In a stockpot, combine the cobs with enough water to cover. Bring to a boil over high heat. Reduce the heat to medium-low and simmer, covered, for 30 minutes. The corncobs will absorb quite a bit of the water.

Strain the mixture through a cheesecloth-lined sieve; there should be about 7 cups of corncob juice remaining. Transfer the liquid to a medium saucepan, and boil, uncovered, over medium heat for about 45 minutes, or until 3 cups of liquid remains. Add the pectin and lemon juice. Bring to a full rolling boil that you cannot stir down, then add the sugar. Return the mixture to a full rolling boil and boil for 1½ minutes longer. Remove the pan from the heat and, if you prefer, add enough food coloring to tint the jelly a deeper pink.

Pour hot into hot sterilized half-pint jars, leaving ¼-inch head room. Wipe the rims of the jars with a wet paper towel and put on the disc lid and ring. Process in a hot water bath for 5 minutes, allowing the water to return to a full rolling boil before you start timing it. Remove the jars from the water, cool, and store in a dark place.

★ CANNING ★

If you are considering canning or preserving foods, there are two books that you should own: *Putting Food By*, by Greene, Hertzberg, and Vaughan (Stephen Greene Press, paperback, $9.95) and *The Ball Blue Book*, published by the Ball canning jar people. The latter can be ordered by writing: The Ball Corporation, Consumer Products Division, 345 South High Street, Muncie, IN 47305; the cost is $3.50 postpaid.

Putting Food By, complete with recipes, is extremely well done, covering every possible preserving method you could imagine (including freezing), with reasons why some things will work and why some things won't. The book is updated regularly. The Ball book has very good recipes and is nicely illustrated, and I wouldn't be without it. Canning can be a practical and convenient way to preserve food, but ideas about canning processes change almost yearly—you should know what is going on and these books will tell you.

> FRIDAY "Fish Fry" 4 PM - 11 PM
> ALL You Can Eat "Walleye"
> $6.50
> SaTURDAY "NITE" SPECIALS
> SERVING LUNCH - DINNER 7 DAYS WK.

I would think of a trout stream I had fished along when I was a boy and fish its whole length very carefully in my mind, fishing very carefully under all the logs, all the turns of the bank, the deep holes and the clear shallow stretches, sometimes catching trout and sometimes losing them.

ERNEST HEMINGWAY
"Now I Lay Me," 1938

■ ■ ■

The immense untamed, unspoiled wildness of Michigan has always attracted travelers: the Indians, the French, the British, and the peripatetic tourists, including Hemingway, who immortalized it all in his "Up in Michigan" stories. ✳ Water gives Michigan its distinct shape—two separate peninsulas and two separate psychologies. Since their peninsula is shaped like a hand, southern Michiganians like to call it the "mitten" state. Theirs is the productive farmland that boasts acres of fruit orchards and vineyards, fields of wheat, potatoes, asparagus, and beans of every description under the sun. ✳ The Upper Peninsula, whose denizens call themselves "UPers," boasts vast forests of great white pine and hardwoods and thousands of clear, deep inland lakes filled with trout,

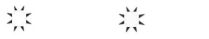
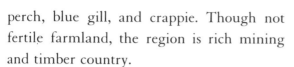

perch, blue gill, and crappie. Though not fertile farmland, the region is rich mining and timber country.

Michigan is also the home of the elusive morel, which attracts hunters by droves every spring in search of that woodsy-scented brown sponge mushroom. Tall white birch groves stretch for miles, reaching like poetry into the blue sky. In the month of April, their tiny leaves are still vulnerable to spring frosts; their tassly blossoms hang down like long earrings.

Michigan's first wave of growth came when the Erie Canal opened in 1825, and pioneers arrived from New England, bringing that region's culture, attitudes, and food ways. German settlements began in the 1830s around Ann Arbor and spread across much of southern Michigan and up to Frankenmuth, an unabashedly German town that still celebrates its German traditions— and Christmas—all year long.

The Dutch established cities called Zeeland and Holland, and the English and the Scots opted for the rural areas along the Indiana border. Irish immigrants landed in Detroit and Grand Rapids. The Welsh made the north their own, working the mines there and bringing their folded-over meat pies with them for lunch. The lore and the lure of the Cornish pasty continues unabated to this day.

Churches were the predominant cultural influence in all immigrants' lives, but the Germans, always a step ahead and well or-

ganized, emphasized music, social events, and their own language via German newspapers. Of all the immigrants coming to the Midwest, the Germans had the most influence, with their work ethic, their love of music, and, of course, their food.

By 1870, another wave of immigration provided workers for the lumber camps in the Upper Peninsula. The river system transported the logs to the lakes and then onto the Great Plains, to build the towns and cities that were rapidly developing in that part of the United States.

Dr. John Kellogg and Charles W. Post had already made Battle Creek "the cereal city." Seventh-day Adventists had come there in the 1840s, and their emphasis on health had led to Kellogg's establishing a sanitarium. Post came for treatment, and stayed on to become Kellogg's greatest competitor, a typical American story.

The third wave of immigrants added to the cooking broth when Henry Ford turned his assembly line at Highland Park into mass production for the twentieth century and put a Tin Lizzie in the garage of the average American. This time the immigrants were from all over the globe—Poles, Russians, Greeks, and the largest Arab-speaking population in North America, plus African-Americans from the South.

While Ford was standardizing production on his assembly lines, Michigan farmers were turning to specialized crops, including sugar beets, turkeys, peppermint, spearmint,

celery, blueberries, and estate-bottled wines; except for California, the state has the largest variety of agricultural products in the nation.

Still, it is the beauty of the land that people remember about Michigan. Traverse City in the north is the cherry city, and in May the hillside orchards that were lately colorless bloom into a billowing, rapturous white. At the mouth of the Boardman River on West Grand Traverse Bay, wedges of swans arrive like a burst of music. The annual cycle of agrarian grace has begun. ✳

APPLE FRITTERS * GRITZ * AUNT GRACE'S CHARD TART * MICHIGAN BEAN AND BUFFALO SAUSAGE SOUP * MICHIGAN PASTIES * VENISON ROAST WITH CARROT-ROSEMARY SAUCE * LOIN LAMB CHOPS WITH MINT PESTO * PORK LOIN ROAST WITH BROWN GRAVY * CHAR-GRILLED HERB CHICKEN WITH ROASTED NEW POTATO AND PEPPER SALAD TAPAWINGO * GRILLED DUCK BREAST WITH MOREL CIDER SAUCE * HEMINGWAY'S RECIPE FOR PAN-FRIED TROUT * PLANKED MICHIGAN WHITEFISH * GRILLED MICHIGAN COHO SALMON * MICHIGAN CASSOULET * AMERICAN SPOON HOLIDAY STUFFING * STIR-FRIED FIDDLEHEADS AND ASPARAGUS TAPAWINGO * ASPARAGUS WITH RED PEPPER SAUCE AND FRESH BASIL * APPLE-ONION CASSEROLE WITH CINNAMON * LOGGING CAMP FRIED POTATOES * BAKED CHERRY DUMPLINGS * SAILOR DUFF PUDDING * CARAMELIZED WALNUT TORTE * BOURBON BUTTERMILK PIE * ENGLISH TOFFEE COOKIES * SPICED TOMATO BUTTER

✳ ANTIQUE APPLES ✳

In the Southmeadow Fruit Gardens east of Lake Michigan, the land rolls away in hills ruffled with apple trees. This is the state's fruit belt, and Netherlands-born nurseryman Theo Grootendorst works amidst an orchard of 200 antique apple varieties that he helped develop. Their names are quaint and evocative: Carpentin, grown along the Rhine in 1798; the Cornish Gilliflower from England; the Ingrid Marie from Denmark.

America hasn't always been the province of the Golden Delicious. At the end of the nineteenth century, 8,000 varieties were still listed by the Department of Agriculture.

Alas, most of these rare apples are no more; their quirky appearance and sometimes short keeping qualities eventually led to their demise as less perishable varieties took their places.

The good news is that antique apples are having a renaissance. Scattered about the country, a handful of commercial growers like Grootendorst are reintroducing these nostalgic apple varieties to the public. Southmeadow Fruit Farm sells apple trees through mail order, and their catalog, which is a splendid compendium of detailed and fascinating descriptions, would make Johnny Appleseed weep with joy.

Apple Fritters

✳

MAKES 4 DOZEN FRITTERS, APPROXIMATELY 8 SERVINGS

Apple fritters appear in many forms in Michigan; this recipe calls for chopped apples, and the finished product is a small, round, fat cake, with a touch of cinnamon. Serve it for breakfast with maple syrup and crisp bacon.

1½ cups unbleached all-purpose flour
¼ teaspoon salt
2 teaspoons baking powder
1 teaspoon ground cinnamon
3 tablespoons sugar
1 egg
¾ cup milk
1 teaspoon vanilla extract
3 medium firm apples such as Golden Delicious or Granny Smith
3 teaspoons fresh lemon juice
Vegetable oil for frying
Maple syrup

Sift together the flour, salt, baking powder, cinnamon, and sugar; set aside. In a large mixer bowl, beat the egg lightly. Add the milk and vanilla and blend. Peel and core the apples, chop finely (use your food processor if you like), and toss with the lemon juice. Add the dry ingredients gradually to the milk mixture, then add the apples. Blend.

Heat an electric skillet to 365° F. Add enough oil to reach about ¼ inch deep. Drop the batter by heaping teaspoonfuls into the skillet, patting each fritter down a bit; they will be approximately 2½ inches in diameter. Fry until golden on one side then turn and brown the second side, about 3 minutes. Drain on paper towels, then transfer to a platter and keep warm in the oven while you fry the rest. Serve with warmed maple syrup.

RIGHT: Theo Grootendorst propagates antique apple varieties by grafting, not by seed.

Gritz

— ✳ —

This old Midwestern recipe, popular in Michigan, Indiana, and Illinois, has several names, including gritz, grits wurst, breakfast grit, or knipp, which means "snip" in German. Gritz started out as did Pennsylvania scrapple—a way to use up the last of the butchering scraps. The leftover pork or beef pieces (and sometimes the heart and tongue) were made into a meaty broth with grains added as a thickener. Unlike scrapple, which incorporates cornmeal, gritz is thickened with oatmeal and barley. When town folk who didn't butcher made gritz, they used a combination of beef and pork cuts, which I prefer.

Sauté slices of this well-seasoned, firm loaf and serve with maple syrup, just as you would fried mush. It is a savory breakfast dish, ideal for brunch entertaining.

1½ pounds boneless beef chuck, well trimmed
1½ pounds boneless pork shoulder, well trimmed
1 medium onion, quartered
1 bay leaf
1 teaspoon salt
6 whole cloves
1¼ cups old-fashioned rolled oats
1¼ cups quick-cooking barley
¾ teaspoon grated nutmeg
½ teaspoon ground allspice
¼ teaspoon salt
¼ teaspoon freshly ground black pepper
Cooking oil for frying
Maple syrup or sorghum molasses

Place the meats, onion, bay leaf, salt, and cloves in a large stockpot and cover with water. Cover and bring to a boil; lower the heat and simmer approximately 3 hours, or until the meat is tender, skimming occasionally. The pork might be done before the beef; if so, remove it, cover, and set it aside on a platter until it is cool enough to handle.

While the meats are still warm, cut them in chunks and pulse in a food processor until the texture is fine. Refrigerate the meats and the broth overnight. The next day, remove the fat and bay leaf from the broth and discard. Measure out 5 cups of broth and freeze the extra for soup stock.

Return the 5 cups of broth to the stockpot; add the oatmeal, barley, and remaining seasonings. Cover and bring to a boil, then lower the heat and simmer for 30 minutes, stirring occasionally. The consistency should be like thick cooked oatmeal. Add the meat and mix well. Transfer the mixture to a greased 9 x 5-inch loaf pan. Cool, cover with plastic wrap, and chill overnight.

To serve, cut the loaf into 12 slices. Heat a small amount of cooking oil in a heavy skillet and sauté the slices over medium heat for 2 to 3 minutes on each side. The outside should be crusty and golden brown. Serve hot with maple syrup or sorghum molasses.

NOTE: The loaf or slices can be frozen.

Aunt Grace's Chard Tart

from the Rowe Inn

— ✳ —

The Rowe Inn at Ellsworth in northern Michigan is a small country restaurant operated by the Westhovens, a couple who were among the first of the local restaurateurs to use and promote indigenous Michigan ingredients. Their dishes combine the old and the new, such as this appetizer tart that features chard, cheese, and egg. It is one of the favorite summer offerings at the inn, and is named for the woman who supplies the restaurant with fresh fruits and vegetables all season long.

CRUST
1 package active dry yeast
1 teaspoon sugar
¼ cup warm water
3 tablespoons sour cream
1 egg
2 cups all-purpose flour
2 tablespoons (¼ stick) butter, softened
½ teaspoon salt

2 tablespoons olive oil

1 large onion, thinly sliced

1 red bell pepper, cored, seeded, and thinly
   sliced

1 pound Swiss chard (preferably ruby chard)

1 egg

¼ cup chopped fresh basil leaves
   Freshly ground black pepper and salt to
   taste

¾ pound Colby or mild cheddar, grated

Combine the yeast, sugar, and water in a small bowl, and let sit until foamy, about 5 or 10 minutes. In a large bowl, combine the sour cream and egg, then stir in ½ cup of the flour and the butter and salt. Add the yeast mixture and mix thoroughly. Gradually add the remaining 1½ cups of flour until a soft dough is formed. Place the dough on a lightly floured surface and knead lightly until it is no longer sticky, adding a bit more flour if needed. Place the dough in a buttered bowl, turning to butter the entire surface. Cover and let the dough rise until doubled in size, about 1 hour.

For the filling, heat the oil in a skillet, and slowly sauté the onion until soft, about 5 minutes. Add the red pepper slices and sauté for 5 minutes longer. Preheat the oven to 350° F.

Bring a large pot of water to a boil. Carefully rinse and clean the Swiss chard and chop coarsely, including the stems. Cook the chopped chard and stems for 2 minutes in the boiling water. Drain the chard and squeeze out as much water as possible. Stir together the egg, basil, pepper, salt, and the cooked chard.

Grease a 10-inch tart pan with a removable bottom. Punch down the dough and roll out on a floured surface to form a 14-inch circle. Fit the dough into the tart pan, trimming the excess from the edges. Spread the onion and pepper slices over the bottom of the tart shell. Cover with the Swiss chard mixture, then top with the cheese. Bake for 45 minutes, or until the top is golden. Cut into wedges and serve hot.

Michigan Bean and Buffalo Sausage Soup

from the Rowe Inn

— ✳ —

MAKES 12 SERVINGS

Michigan is the world's largest producer of navy beans, with black beans, turtle beans, cranberry beans, red kidney beans, and snap beans not far behind. It seems appropriate to combine navy beans with buffalo, a lean delicate red meat that is making a comeback in the Midwest through domestically raised herds.

The sausage can be ordered by mail (see Source List), or a spicy firm kielbasa can be substituted.

1⅓ cups dried Michigan navy beans, sorted and
    rinsed

1 pound buffalo sausage or kielbasa, diced

2 cups diced onions

2 cups diced carrots

2 cups diced celery

1 28-ounce can plum tomatoes, undrained

2 quarts Chicken Stock (page 239)

2½ teaspoons dried thyme

2 bay leaves

1 teaspoon salt

½ teaspoon freshly ground pepper

In a large soup pot, soak the beans overnight. Drain and set aside.

In a large skillet, sauté the sausage over medium heat until cooked through. Remove from the pan with a slotted spoon and reserve. Add the onions, carrots, and celery to the pan drippings; sauté until the vegetables are softened but are still crunchy, about 8 to 10 minutes.

Seed and finely chop the tomatoes; add them with the juice to the sautéed vegetables, along with the sausage. Add the chicken stock, beans, and seasonings. Cover, bring to a boil, lower heat, and simmer for 2 hours, checking the beans now and then to determine when they are tender. Discard bay leaves. Taste and adjust seasonings, if necessary.

Michigan Pasties

Pasties are the ultimate Michigan snack food, no longer just a treat for those folk who live on the Upper Peninsula. I've always enjoyed eating pasties when visiting there, but when I attempted to duplicate them in my own kitchen, they never seemed to taste as good as they did in those country kitchens and restaurants.

After much research, close questioning of Michigan residents, and many testings, I offer the following recipe as a close relative to those hearty pasties so beloved by the hard-working miners in the Wolverine State.

> 1 pound boneless beef sirloin, cut in ½-inch cubes
> 1 pound boneless pork butt, coarsely ground
> ⅓ cup ground suet
> 2 medium carrots, finely minced
> 2 medium potatoes, cut in ¼-inch cubes
> 1 medium onion, finely chopped
> 1 teaspoon salt
> 1 teaspoon dried thyme
> ¼ teaspoon freshly ground black pepper
> ¼ teaspoon hot red pepper sauce
> 1½ recipes Never-Fail Pie Crust dough (page 244)
> ½ cup (1 stick) margarine, melted
> ½ cup hot water
> Chili sauce (optional)

Preheat the oven to 350° F. In a large bowl, thoroughly combine the meats, vegetables, and seasonings. With a knife, divide the mixture into 6 wedges, like a pie.

On a floured surface, divide the dough into 6 pieces. Roll out one piece at a time and, using a 9-inch plate or pot lid, cut each into a round with a sharp knife. Place one portion of the meat mixture on half of the round; fold the other half of the pastry over the meat, creating a plump half-moon.

Press the edges together firmly with your fingertips, then seal with a fork tine. Using a small ¾-inch decorative cutter (or a sharp knife), cut a piece of dough from the center of the pasty and discard. With a large spatula, transfer the pasty to 1 of 2 greased baking sheets; do not crowd them. Repeat until all the pie crust and meat mixture is used. The pasties can be frozen at this point.

Bake the pasties for 1 hour, placing a piece of foil over the top of the sheet if they begin to brown too much. Combine the melted margarine and water. Using a funnel or a pitcher, pour some of the liquid into each pasty and continue baking 10 minutes more.

Remove the pasties from the oven and place on a rack. Cover with a towel and allow to stand for 30 minutes before eating. Serve with chili sauce, if desired.

NOTE: To bake frozen pasties, preheat the oven to 375° F. Place the frozen pasties in the oven, lower the heat immediately to 350° F. and bake for 1 hour and 20 minutes. Add the margarine-water mixture and bake 10 minutes longer. If the pasties start to brown too much, cover with foil.

Manton Rangers Football team, Manton, Michigan (population 700), at practice.

* PASTIES *

A book could be written about the pasty; it has a long history with European roots. Pronounced PASS-tee, these pies were filled with hand-chopped, not ground, beef. Suet gave the pasty both flavor and juiciness.

Today some cooks add broth, gravy, cream, or butter to the filling, for the pasty can be dry in the hands of an inexperienced cook. But this is frowned upon by the purists, and I prefer using suet myself. Chopped potatoes and onions were always added, making the pasty a one-dish meal. There is a school of thought that prefers rutabagas to carrots, but the carrot does provide color. Early pasty makers might have put a whole meal into the crust, filling one end with meat and vegetables and the other end with fruit such as apples, cherries, or peaches — very clever, I'd say!

Because the pasty was a portable meal, the dough was not known for its tender flakiness. It was said that a really good pasty should be tough enough to withstand being dropped down the mine shaft. The men carried pasties to the mines in cotton pouches, or in their shirts to keep the pasty warm. Sometimes the pasties were reheated on a shovel over the candle the miner wore on his hat.

Venison Roast with Carrot-Rosemary Sauce

All of our Midwestern states have a rich Native American heritage, and those Indians were all fine hunters, subsisting primarily on game. Today game hunting is one of Michigan's most popular sports, and a wild deer is considered a prize trophy by hunters and cooks alike. Properly cooked venison, with its fine-grained flesh and distinctive flavor, is truly wonderful eating. Quite lean without much marbling, it tends toward dryness and lends itself well to braising and low-temperature cooking. To ensure tenderness, a venison roast should be marinated for at least four days; a slow cooker is ideal for the final preparation. Serve this dish with Rutabaga Casserole (page 137) or with Corn Patties (page 84).

       3- to 4-pound boneless venison roast,
          trimmed of fat
    1 cup dry red wine
 1¼ cups water
    3 garlic cloves, crushed
    6 medium carrots, cut in 1-inch pieces
    2 celery stalks, cut in 1-inch pieces
    1 medium onion, coarsely chopped
  ½ teaspoon dried rosemary, crushed
    1 teaspoon ground cumin
    2 bay leaves
    1 tablespoon fresh lemon juice
    1 teaspoon Worcestershire sauce
  ½ teaspoon salt
  ¼ teaspoon freshly ground pepper
    2 tablespoons cornstarch

Place the venison, wine, 1 cup water, and garlic in a big plastic bag, fasten the bag firmly, and lay it in a glass baking dish. (This is insurance against leaky messes.) Marinate the roast in the bag, refrigerated and turning occasionally, for 4 days.

Drain the marinade into a slow cooker. Preheat the broiler. Brown the roast on all sides under the broiler for about 20 to 30 minutes. Transfer it to the slow cooker and add the carrots, celery, onion, rosemary, cumin, and bay leaves. Turn the cooker to low and cook for 10 hours, or until the roast is fork-tender.

Remove the roast and keep it warm in a pre-heated 150° F. oven. Transfer the cooking liquid to a medium saucepan; add the lemon juice, Worcestershire, salt, and pepper. Bring the mixture to a boil. Remove bay leaves. In a small bowl, combine the cornstarch and remaining ¼ cup water and add to the cooking liquid. Continue cooking until the mixture thickens. Cut the meat into serving portions and ladle a generous amount of sauce over each serving.

Loin Lamb Chops with Mint Pesto

from the Rattlesnake Club

When a restaurant has a name like the Rattlesnake Club and is still one of the hottest places in eight states, you have to know the chef is doing something right—really right!

The engaging Jimmy Schmidt, a native Midwesterner, has had classical French training, which he uses to a fine turn. "I don't have any one set of culinary influences, though," he muses.

His loin lamb chops dressed with a mint pesto are simple yet elegant. Lamb farms abound in nearby Indiana, and fresh mint is readily available from Michigan mint farms that raise most of their crop to sell to Wrigley—and we all know where that mint ends up!

    6 cloves Roasted Garlic, peeled and minced
          (page 243)
  ¾ cup olive oil
    8 loin lamb chops, about 4 ounces each, about
          1½ inches thick
    1 cup chopped fresh mint
  ½ cup chopped fresh parsley
  ¼ teaspoon freshly ground black pepper
    1 tablespoon balsamic vinegar
       Salt
  ¼ cup whole mint leaves

In a small bowl, combine 2 cloves of the garlic and 2 tablespoons of the olive oil. Rub the mixture on all surfaces of the lamb chops. Preheat the grill or broiler.

In a blender combine the remaining roasted garlic and olive oil, chopped mint, parsley, and pepper. Puree and add the vinegar, blend, and adjust salt to taste. Set aside.

Place the chops on the grill and cook until well seared, about 4 minutes. Turn over and continue grilling until the desired temperature is reached (130° F. for medium-rare, 140° F. for medium), about 4 minutes on each side, depending on thickness. Transfer the chops, 2 each to a heated plate, and spoon the pesto over. Garnish with the mint leaves and serve immediately.

Pork Loin Roast with Brown Gravy

✳

MAKES 6 TO 8 SERVINGS

Sometimes there is nothing quite so satisfying as a pork roast. This one is quick to prepare, for it does not have to be browned first. The rosemary and marjoram give it added zip and the gravy has a broth base. All together, this is a very good dish, especially if served with mashed potatoes. And leftovers make wonderful sandwiches.

  4 pounds boneless rolled top loin of pork
  1 small onion, sliced
  ¼ teaspoon dried hot red pepper flakes
  ½ teaspoon dried marjoram, or 2 teaspoons fresh
  ½ teaspoon dried rosemary, or 2 teaspoons fresh
  2 tablespoons minced fresh parsley
  1¾ cups Chicken or Beef Stock (page 239)
  1 bay leaf
  2 tablespoons all-purpose flour
    Liberal dash of Worcestershire sauce
    Pinch of freshly ground black pepper (optional)

Preheat the oven to 325° F. With a sharp knife, make 7 horizontal slits down the center of the roast, approximately 2 inches long and 2 inches deep. Stuff each slit with a slice of onion. Combine the red pepper flakes, marjoram, rosemary, and parsley and stuff that in slits around the onion. Transfer roast to a Dutch oven, add ½ cup of the stock, any remaining onion, and the bay leaf.

Bake, covered, for 2 hours. Remove the lid so the roast will brown and continue baking for another 30 minutes. Remove meat to a cutting board or platter and cover with foil (and then I put a heavy towel on top of that) to keep it warm. Skim the excess fat off the pan juices (use paper towels) and remove the bay leaf; there will be about 2 cups of liquid.

Place the pan over high heat and reduce the liquid to about ⅓ cup; it will be a deep golden brown. Add 1 cup of stock and bring to a boil. Shake the remaining ¼ cup of stock and the flour in a small jar until smooth; whisk into the bubbling broth and cook, whisking until the mixture is smooth and thickened. Season with the Worcestershire and add a dash of black pepper, if desired.

Slice the meat thinly and serve with the gravy.

N O T E: Rolled boneless loins of pork can be ordered specially from your butcher; be sure that the pork is tied, not wrapped in a net bag.

✳ T A P A W I N G O ✳

Outside the little town of Ellsworth, forty miles from Traverse City, is Tapawingo, a restaurant devoted to serving Michigan's regional cuisine. Using locally produced fruits, vegetables, meat, and poultry, plus the best from Lake Michigan's waters, chef-owner Harlan Peterson, affectionately known as Pete, is creating new combinations from the classics of Michigan.

Whitefish, morels, fiddleheads, and cherries become sophisticated fare in the kitchen at Tapawingo. Peterson, a former industrial designer for the Ford Motor Company in De-troit, restored a sprawling gray-shingled farmhouse for his restaurant. Overlooking a small lake and flower gardens bright with color, the dining room is blond wood and chrome, but at one end of the room a fire burns — even on occasional cool summer evenings — in a Petoskey stone fireplace. Little pitchers of wildflowers and herbs adorn the top of each table.

In the Chippewa language, *tapawingo* means "place of peace." The restaurant is appropriately named, and appreciative diners find it a haven for good food.

Char-Grilled Herb Chicken with Roasted New Potato and Pepper Salad Tapawingo

— ✳ —

MAKES 4 SERVINGS

This well-seasoned combination of chicken and roasted new potatoes flavored with a bit of bacon and arranged on a bed of spinach is an intriguing combination of textures for an entrée salad.

This has quite a few ingredients, but all are readily available and the dish actually takes little time to prepare. Whole scallions, lightly brushed with olive oil and grilled, make a nice garnish.

MARINADE

1½ tablespoons Dijon mustard
1 tablespoon minced fresh garlic
2 tablespoons minced fresh rosemary
2 tablespoons minced fresh thyme
2 tablespoons minced fresh marjoram
¼ cup olive oil
½ teaspoon freshly ground pepper

2 large whole chicken breasts, boned, skinned, and split

SALAD

6 tablespoons extra-virgin olive oil
1 tablespoon minced fresh garlic
1 tablespoon minced fresh rosemary
1 teaspoon freshly cracked peppercorns
½ teaspoon salt
12 small red new potatoes, halved
6 strips of bacon
1 each small red and yellow bell peppers, roasted (page 243)
⅓ cup thinly sliced scallions, with some green tops
¼ cup chopped fresh parsley
Salt and freshly cracked peppercorns to taste

Grilled chicken salad shares center stage with a walnut torte and morel pizza on Chef Pete Peterson's table.

DRESSING

4 tablespoons balsamic vinegar
1 tablespoon Dijon mustard
2 egg yolks
1 teaspoon salt
½ teaspoon freshly cracked peppercorns
Cayenne pepper to taste
½ cup extra-virgin olive oil

Spinach leaves

Mix the marinade ingredients in a shallow dish. Add the chicken breasts and turn to completely coat with the mixture. Cover, refrigerate, and marinate overnight or at least for several hours.

To prepare the salad, preheat the oven to 400° F. In a large bowl, combine the olive oil, garlic, rosemary, pepper, and salt. Add the halved potatoes and toss. Spread in a 9 x 13-inch baking dish and bake for 30 to 45 minutes, or until the potatoes are just cooked and lightly browned. Stir at least twice during baking.

Preheat a charcoal grill or broiler. While the potatoes roast, cut the bacon into ½-inch squares and fry until crisp. Drain well. Slice the roasted peppers into ¼ x 1-inch pieces. Set aside.

To prepare the dressing, whisk together all the dressing ingredients in a medium bowl, except the olive oil. Slowly whisk in the oil, beating constantly until the dressing is homogenized.

When the potatoes are roasted, transfer them to a large bowl and add the bacon, scallions, roasted peppers, and parsley. Pour over the salad dressing and carefully toss the ingredients together. Season with salt and pepper, if necessary.

Remove the chicken breasts from the marinade; place on a hot grill or under a broiler and cook for 4 to 5 minutes on each side, depending on thickness of the breast. Transfer to a warm platter.

On 4 dinner plates, arrange a bed of fresh spinach leaves. Place ¼ of the potato salad on one side of the plate and a grilled chicken half-breast on the other.

Grilled Duck Breast with Morel Cider Sauce

——— ✳ ———

MAKES 4 SERVINGS

Redolent of Michigan morels and spiked with cider, this sauce can also be made with regular mushrooms, and it is equally good served with grilled steak. The cilantro gives it an added lift.

  6 slices bacon, cut in ½-inch pieces
 ½ pound fresh morels, or 1¾ ounces dried morels, reconstituted, coarsely chopped (see Source List)
1¾ cups apple cider
 ¼ cup dry red wine
  1 tablespoon balsamic vinegar
 ¼ teaspoon dried thyme
 ¼ teaspoon dried rosemary
  1 tablespoon cornstarch
     Salt and pepper to taste
  2 tablespoons minced cilantro (fresh coriander)
  2 6-ounce duck breasts

In a 10-inch sauté pan, cook the bacon over medium heat until crisp. Using a slotted spoon, transfer the bacon to paper towels to drain. Prepare the grill or preheat the broiler.

Pour off all but 2 tablespoons of fat from the skillet. Add the mushrooms and cook until their juices evaporate, about 5 minutes, stirring now and then. Add 1½ cups of the cider, the wine, vinegar, thyme, and rosemary. Cook over high heat for about 5 minutes, or until the sauce is reduced by half.

In a small bowl, combine the cornstarch with the remaining ¼ cup cider, and add to the hot cider mixture. Cook and stir until thick; add the cilantro and reserved bacon.

Grill the duck breasts over a charcoal fire or in the broiler until they are medium-rare, about 3 to 5 minutes. Slice thinly and arrange on warm plates. Top with a liberal portion of the sauce.

Hemingway's Recipe for Pan-Fried Trout

——— ✳ ———

MAKES 4 SERVINGS

In midsummer, upper Michigan's roadsides are lined with Queen Anne's lace and tall elderberry bushes, their froth of white blooms scenting the air. The untilled meadows filled with spotted star thistles give a dusky lavender look to the Traverse Bay landscape.

Northern Michigan has always been a lure to Midwesterners, including Ernest Hemingway, whose family summered there. "Horton Bay, the town, was only five houses on the main road between Boyne City and Charlevoix," he wrote in his short story, "Up in Michigan." The mystique and legends that surround Hemingway remain with you as you travel along the shorelines in this part of the country.

In a 1920 contribution to the Toronto Star, *Hemingway described his method of cooking freshly caught trout while camping out. You can use the same method in your kitchen.*

  4 slices bacon
  4 whole trout, approximately 8 ounces each, cleaned, heads on
 ⅓ to ¼ cup yellow cornmeal

In a heavy black iron skillet (the locals call them "spiders"), cook the bacon over medium heat until it is almost crisp. Remove and reserve. Dust the trout lightly with cornmeal on all sides. Place the trout in the drippings and put a slice of bacon on top of each. Sauté until golden brown, about 5 to 6 minutes on a side, turning once and putting the bacon back on top so the smoky flavor of the bacon bastes the fish. Serve immediately.

When we were first married, my husband and I moved into an old English Tudor house, and in the process I inherited some old pots, pans, and dishes. Among them was a thick oval wooden board, very dark, that seemed to have been burned or charred. I used it for years as a chopping board, never knowing in my youthful ignorance that I was really using a plank that had been created for baking whitefish, one of the Midwest's finest regional specialties.

That chopping board is long gone and I mourn its passing. Now I need it and want it. Fresh-fish enthusiasts agree that planking is one of the very best ways to prepare whitefish; the subtle flavor from the wood enhances the taste of the fish.

Planking is almost a lost art — a tradition passed down from cook to cook. The original recipe dates back to the Indians, who planked their fish by lashing the larger ones to any old piece of wet driftwood they found on the beach, and the wood with the fish on it was set upright in the sand, next to the fire, cooking vertically in the heat of the flames.

The twentieth-century version calls for an unfinished oak or maple plank; it should be about 2 inches thick and 13 to 14 inches long. (You can get this at your local lumberyard or fix-it shop.) Heat the plank in the oven or put it under hot water just before you are ready to begin cooking. The contemporary garnish for this is mashed potatoes, piped onto the plank and browned in the oven.

Planked Michigan Whitefish

✳

MAKES 4 SERVINGS

When I was a girl, trucks from Michigan packed with whole whitefish and ice drove up and down Midwestern country roads, selling their wares to eager landlocked farmers' wives. Those fish would end up on country tables, stuffed, fried, or planked. Combined with corn on the cob and sliced tomatoes, still warm from the garden, that was fine eating, indeed.

  1 cooking plank, warmed (see box)
  1 whitefish, approximately 3 pounds split, backbone and head removed
¼ cup (½ stick) butter, melted
¼ cup fresh lemon juice
    Salt
    Freshly ground pepper
    Paprika
    Seasoned hot mashed potatoes
    Lemon wedges and parsley sprigs, for garnish

Preheat the oven to 400 ° F. Oil the warmed plank and place the fish, skin side down, in the middle.

Combine the butter and lemon juice and brush the fish liberally with the mixture. Season with the salt, pepper, and paprika. Bake, basting occasionally with the butter-lemon mixture, for about 20 minutes or until the fish flakes when tested with a fork. When almost done, pipe the hot mashed potatoes from a pastry bag around the fish. Turn the heat up to broil to brown the potatoes, about 5 minutes. Garnish with lemon wedges and parsley.

NOTE: If the plank business seems too much of a fuss, you can bake the whitefish in a greased dish for 10 to 15 minutes. Some cooks place 3 or 4 bacon strips across the fish for extra flavor.

Grilled Michigan
Coho Salmon

—— ✳ ——

MAKES 6 TO 8 SERVINGS

The Coho salmon, native to the coastal waters and rivers of Alaska and the Pacific Northwest, has flourished in the Great Lakes since 1966, when it was introduced by conservationists. A protected sport fish, it is barred to commercial fishermen.

This simple way to prepare the salmon, with its hint of tarragon, is hard to improve upon. Grill the fish under the broiler or over charcoal. The remaining basting sauce of butter and lemon can be poured over the grilled fish or passed in a sauceboat at the table.

BELOW: *At Fresh Catch, in Petoskey, fishermen bring in their daily catch for smoking.* OPPOSITE: *Along Michigan's shore line, Victorian summer houses like these are impeccably maintained.*

BASTING SAUCE

1 cup (2 sticks) butter or margarine
3 tablespoons fresh lemon juice
3 tablespoons chopped fresh parsley
2 tablespoons minced fresh tarragon
½ teaspoon hot red pepper sauce
½ teaspoon lemon pepper or black pepper

6 to 8 Coho salmon steaks, 1½ inches thick
Salt
Paprika, for garnish

Melt the butter in a small saucepan. Stir in the remaining sauce ingredients and keep warm over low heat. Brush the grill with oil to prevent the fish from sticking. Arrange the salmon steaks on the grill, about 4 inches from the coals; sprinkle with salt and grill 5 to 7 minutes per side, basting frequently with the sauce, until a knife test shows the center has lost its transparency and the fish flakes slightly. Sprinkle with paprika and serve.

Michigan Cassoulet

——— * ———

Even the plainest of Midwestern cooks has been making a stripped-down version of cassoulet for years—what she calls ham and beans. And generally it is a rather good dish.

The beloved French provincial casserole of white beans and assorted meats and either duck or goose requires several days' labor and umpteen mixing bowls; this simplified version uses a slow cooker and requires no watching. Do not omit the salt pork—you need it to provide the unctuous smoothness that is the mark of a good cassoulet. The entire dish can be combined several days in advance and refrigerated.

NOTE: *Start the beans by soaking them the night before cooking, and be sure to save the bean cooking liquid.*

- 1 pound dried Michigan navy beans
- 1 celery stalk
- 2 bay leaves
- Handful of parsley sprigs
- ½ pound salt pork, rind removed, finely cubed
- ½ to ¾ pound boneless lamb shoulder, cut in 2-inch pieces
- ½ cup chopped celery
- ½ cup chopped onion
- ½ cup chopped carrot
- 1 teaspoon minced garlic
- 1 14-ounce can tomatoes, drained and coarsely chopped
- ½ cup dry white wine
- 2 tablespoons chopped fresh parsley
- ½ teaspoon dried thyme
- ¼ teaspoon dried savory
- ¼ teaspoon freshly ground black pepper
- 12 ounces fully cooked kielbasa, cut in 1-inch pieces
- 2 thick slices French bread
- 2 teaspoons finely minced fresh parsley

Place the beans in a large kettle with water to cover; soak overnight. The next morning, add the celery stalk, 1 bay leaf, and parsley to the beans, cover, and bring to a boil. Lower the heat and simmer, partially covered, for 30 minutes. Drain, reserving 2 cups of the cooking liquid. Discard the celery and herbs and transfer the beans to the slow cooker.

In a medium skillet, combine 2 tablespoons of the cubed salt pork and the lamb, and brown well over medium heat. Transfer all, including the drippings, to the slow cooker.

In the same skillet, combine 3 tablespoons of the salt pork with the chopped celery, onion, carrot, and garlic and sauté over medium heat until the onion begins to brown, about 3 to 5 minutes. Transfer to the cooker. Then add the remaining salt pork and the tomatoes, wine, parsley, and seasonings to the bean mixture in the cooker. Mix gently to avoid breaking up the beans. Add enough of the reserved cooking liquid to come within 1 inch of the top of the beans.

Cover, turn temperature to high, and cook for 1 hour. Add the kielbasa. Turn to low and continue cooking for 3 to 4 hours; do not stir while cooking. (The cooking time is imprecise, for this depends on the age of the beans, their growing locale, and even the hardness of the water. Do not let beans overcook and get mushy. If necessary, add more of the reserved cooking water to keep the water level at 1 inch below the top of the beans.)

Meanwhile, toast the bread in a flat pan in a 160° F. oven for 2 hours. Break into large pieces and process until fine crumbs are formed—you need a scant ½ cup. Stir in the parsley. About 30 minutes before the beans are done, sprinkle the crumbs on top and then, using a wooden spoon, gently push them deep down into the beans to thicken the juices. When the beans have reached the desired texture, turn off the cooker. Serve hot.

✳ AMERICAN SPOON FOODS ✳

In Petoskey, Justin Rashid gleans the best of Michigan's foodstuffs, both wild and home grown, to create condiments, jams, jellies, and other gourmet items that are the essence of summer in the Midwest. Rashid and Larry Forgione, the chef of An American Place in New York City and vocal exponent of regional American foods, are co-founders of American Spoon Foods. The company has grown from a little operation to a big one, but the small-kitchen quality of its goods remains unchanged. Items such as pumpkin butter, cherry-gooseberry relish, cranberry maple sauce, and thimbleberry preserves are offered by mail, along with the popular dried cherries, blueberries, and morels. Their barbecue sauce is also offered in the catalog.

"I remember real food," says the articulate Rashid. "We all do, but today there is so little of what we are able to buy that is real. A lot of people want authentic food again; good food triggers good memories," he says with a smile. "And that is what we try to make here — good food and good memories."

American Spoon Holiday Stuffing

———— ✳ ————

MAKES ENOUGH STUFFING FOR AN 18-POUND TURKEY

This stylish poultry stuffing is a marvel of flavor with Madeira-macerated dried cherries, toasted pecans, shallots, tarragon, thyme, and sage. Don't keep this one just for the Thanksgiving turkey—use it also with roast duck, goose, and crown roast of pork.

- 6 ounces dried tart cherries
- 1 cup Madeira
- 14 slices day-old dense-textured white bread, toasted and torn into small pieces (about 8 cups)
- 1½ cups toasted pecan pieces
- ½ cup (1 stick) unsalted butter
- 1 cup finely chopped onion
- 1 cup finely chopped celery
- ½ cup finely chopped shallots
- 3 crisp apples, peeled and coarsely chopped
- ½ cup golden raisisn
- ½ cup finely chopped flat-leaf (Italian) parsley
- 2 teaspoons dried tarragon, crumbled
- 1 teaspoon dried thyme
- 10 to 12 dried sage leaves, crumbled
- 1 teaspoon salt, or to taste
- 1 teaspoon freshly ground pepper, or to taste

In a small bowl, soak the cherries in the Madeira for several hours or overnight.

In a large bowl, combine the bread pieces with the pecans. Drain the cherries, reserving the Madeira, and add them to the bread mixture.

Melt the butter in a large skillet. Sauté the onion, celery, and shallots until the vegetables are softened, then add to the bread mixture. Add the apples, raisins, parsley, tarragon, thyme, sage, salt, pepper, and the reserved Madeira; toss the stuffing well. Cool, then stuff bird as usual.

*OVERLEAF: **The tantalizing selection of regional specialties at American Spoon Foods' retail shop,** LEFT. **The Victorian craftsmen produced ginger bread designs to adorn porches with whimsey and style,** RIGHT.*

MAPLE CREAM
kept in cooler $4.95
- please ask

Stir-Fried Fiddleheads and Asparagus Tapawingo

———— ✳ ————

MAKES 4 SERVINGS

Pete Peterson changes the menu daily at his restaurant, and in the spring, if you are lucky, you may be there when he prepares fiddleheads, those violin scroll–shaped fern tips that push their way up through the forest bracken of Michigan. These ferns can be of the ostrich, cinnamon, or brake fern variety and should be eaten as soon as they are picked. In Michigan they are available frozen in some supermarkets.

- ½ pound fresh fiddlehead ferns
- ¾ pound fresh asparagus
- ¼ cup (½ stick) butter, melted
- 1 teaspoon minced shallots
  Salt and freshly ground pepper

Rinse the fiddleheads under running water and remove any brown flecks. Snap off the tough ends of the asparagus spears, and cut them on the diagonal into 1½-inch pieces.

Heat the butter until almost smoking in a wok or large sauté pan and add the ferns, asparagus, and shallots. Toss the vegetables constantly until the pieces are crisp-tender, about 2 minutes. Season with salt and pepper and serve immediately.

Asparagus with Red Pepper Sauce and Fresh Basil

———— ✳ ————

MAKES 8 TO 10 SERVINGS

In the food world, rumors are flying about tiny white asparagus said to be grown in caves in Michigan. I finally tracked down this special vegetable.

This asparagus is pure white, tender, and harvested so young there are 160 spears per pound. It can be ordered by mail (see Source List) and will keep for ten days in the refrigerator. Its producers would neither confirm nor deny the cave rumor. I was told, however, that it is never exposed to light, which accounts for its creamy white color.

Michigan has always raised asparagus, and many will wonder how it can be improved upon. In this dish, the green of garden asparagus combined with the subtle red pepper sauce creates a beguiling and colorful salad, but it would be equally handsome using white asparagus.

- 6 red bell peppers, roasted and peeled (page 243)
- 2 shallots, coarsely chopped
- 3 tablespoons chopped parsley
  Scant 1 cup walnut oil
- 1½ tablespoons balsamic vinegar
- 1¼ teaspoons salt
- ½ teaspoon freshly ground pepper
- 3 pounds fresh asparagus
- ½ cup coarsely chopped fresh basil, for garnish

Place the peppers in a blender and add the shallots and parsley; puree until smooth. Add the oil, vinegar, salt, and pepper; blend and refrigerate. (The recipe can be prepared to this point up to 3 days in advance.)

Cut the tough stem ends off the asparagus and steam or microwave until tender but firm; time depends on thickness. Drain, place on a tray, and cool to room temperature.

Pour the sauce around the asparagus and sprinkle the basil over the top.

NOTE: This sauce is also good with crudités.

Apple-Onion Casserole with Cinnamon

MAKES 6 SERVINGS

This old country dish of layered apples and onions with just a hint of cinnamon is unexpected and quite delicate. It is a good side dish with any meat or fowl dish, and keeps well on the buffet. It must bake slowly for at least two hours, so plan accordingly.

The recipe would have been made originally with an old apple variety, such as Cox's Orange Pippin, Red Gravenstein, or Pitmaston Pineapple. Since they are not readily available, try this dish with other local varieties.

- 8 tablespoons (1 stick) butter
- 2 large mild onions, peeled, sliced ¼ inch thick, separated into rings.
- 6 large cooking apples, such as Northern Spy or Golden Delicious, peeled, cored, and sliced ¼ inch thick
- 2 tablespoons sugar
- 2 teaspoons ground cinnamon
  Salt and pepper to taste
- 30 round buttery crackers, crushed finely
- 1 cup apple cider or apple juice

Preheat the oven to 325° F. In a large skillet, melt 2 tablespoons of the butter over medium-low heat. Add the onions and sauté until golden, about 10 minutes, stirring occasionally. Remove the onions with a slotted spoon and set aside. In the same skillet, melt 3 tablespoons of butter over medium-low heat. Add the apples and cook until golden, about 12 to 15 minutes, stirring occasionally.

Butter a 1½-quart baking dish and spread half of the apples evenly over the bottom of the dish. Top with half of the sautéed onions; sprinkle with 1 tablespoon sugar, 1 teaspoon cinnamon, salt and pepper to taste, and half of the cracker crumbs. Repeat layering. Pour the apple cider or juice over the top and dot with the remaining 3 tablespoons butter. Bake, uncovered, until the casserole is bubbling up in the center, about 2 hours.

Logging Camp Fried Potatoes

MAKES 4 GENEROUS SERVINGS

It would be hard to improve on this potato dish— thinly sliced potatoes and onions cooked slowly in bacon fat in a heavy iron skillet until the potatoes are meltingly tender on the inside but crispy deep brown on the outside, with the smoky undertone of bacon and onion. This was a favorite way for the cooks in Michigan logging camps to prepare potatoes for the hungry loggers who needed hearty meals three times a day. Urbanites will be just as enthusiastic about this dish; it is a savory accompaniment to a Midwestern classic: charbroiled steak, preferably a 2-inch-thick sirloin.

- ¼ cup bacon fat or vegetable oil
- 4 medium potatoes, peeled and sliced ⅛ inch thick
- 1 large onion, sliced ⅛ inch thick and separated into rings
  Salt and pepper to taste
  Lots of minced fresh parsley

Preheat a cast-iron 9-inch skillet over medium heat for about 4 minutes, or until it feels hot to your finger when you touch it lightly (see Note). Add the fat and, when melted, add a layer of potatoes, onion, and a sprinkling of salt, pepper, and parsley; and repeat until all the potatoes and onion are used. Lower the heat slightly, cover, and cook over medium-low heat for 10 minutes. Turn the potatoes carefully with a spatula (you don't want to break them up) and continue cooking for 15 minutes longer, removing the cover for the last 5 minutes.

NOTE: To use an electric skillet, heat it to 300° F., add the fat, and proceed with the recipe as instructed.

Baked Cherry Dumplings

MAKES 6 SERVINGS

In the spring, the Michigan cherry trees in bloom are a stunning sight. Later, in July, Traverse City holds a cherry festival with parades and regattas. A one-acre cherry orchard planted here in the 1880s has blossomed into an industry that produces 78 million pounds of cherries a year. All the restaurants feature cherry desserts, such as this one, on their menu.

        4 cups tart red cherries, washed and pitted
        1 cup plus 2 tablespoons granulated sugar
      ¼ cup brown sugar
        2 tablespoons quick-cooking tapioca
      ½ teaspoon almond extract
    1½ cups all-purpose flour
        2 teaspoons baking powder
      ½ teaspoon salt
        6 tablespoons (¾ stick) cold butter
        1 egg
      ⅓ cup milk
      ½ teaspoon grated nutmeg

Preheat the oven to 400° F. In a shallow 2-quart casserole or 12 x 7-inch pan, combine the cherries, 1 cup of the granulated sugar, the brown sugar, tapioca, and almond extract. Allow this to stand while you prepare the rest of the dumplings.

In a large mixing bowl, sift together the flour, baking powder, and salt. Cut in 4 tablespoons of the butter until fine crumbs are formed. In a small bowl, beat the egg and add the milk. Combine with the flour mixture and stir until just blended. Dot the cherries with the remaining 2 tablespoons of butter. Drop the batter by heaping tablespoons on top of the cherries—you should have 6 mounds. In a small bowl combine the remaining 2 tablespoons of sugar with the nutmeg. Sprinkle on top of the batter. Bake for 25 or 30 minutes, or until the fruit is bubbling up in the middle of the pan and the dumplings are golden brown. The baking time can vary quite a bit, depending on the pan you use and how big the cherries are.

Sailor Duff Pudding

MAKES 8 SERVINGS

At the General Store in Horton Bay, where Hemingway bought fishing tackle and swapped yarns with the other fishermen, I happened on Kathryne Dilworth's cookbook, My Tomato Pudding and Other Favorite Recipes, *published in 1937. Dilworth's grandmother, Elizabeth, had a dining room in her house where she served meals to loggers and fishermen. She also prepared the wedding dinner for Hemingway and his first wife, Hadley.*

Her recipe for sailor duff interested me because these steamed puddings generally contain fruit, such as apples or plums. This delicately flavored and textured version has no fruit, perhaps because sailors had no access to fresh fruit. She steamed hers in an angel food "tin," but a regular steamed pudding mold is ideal. Serve with Very Special Hard Sauce, Crème Anglaise, or Cider Sauce (page 246).

        2 tablespoons (¼ stick) butter
        2 tablespoons dark brown sugar
        1 egg, beaten
      ½ cup light molasses
    1½ cups all-purpose flour
      ½ teaspoon baking soda
        1 teaspoon baking powder
      ⅛ teaspoon salt
      ½ cup boiling water

In a mixer bowl, cream the butter and brown sugar until fluffy. Add the egg and molasses. In a small bowl, mix the flour, baking soda, baking powder, and salt; add alternately with the boiling water in small amounts to the butter-sugar mixture. Mix thoroughly, then pour into a greased 6-cup pudding mold and steam over simmering water for 1½ hours. Unmold and serve immediately.

Each summer Boy and Girl Scouts from all over Michigan are chosen to serve one-week stints in the Governor's Honor Guard on Mackinac Island.

Caramelized Walnut Torte

——— ✳ ———

Another delightful offering from the Tapawingo Restaurant.

SWEET PASTRY

  12 tablespoons (1½ sticks) unsalted butter, softened
   2 cups all-purpose flour
      Pinch of salt
  ¼ cup granulated sugar
   1 egg yolk
  2 or 3 teaspoons heavy (whipping) cream

FILLING

   1 cup firmly packed brown sugar
  ⅓ cup (⅔ stick) unsalted butter
  3 tablespoons heavy (whipping) cream
  6 tablespoons dark corn syrup
2½ cups walnut halves, lightly toasted in 350° F. oven for 10 minutes

Combine the butter, flour, salt, and sugar in a food processor bowl. Process until all ingredients are evenly distributed. Add the egg yolk and cream, and mix until the dough comes together in the bowl. Transfer the dough to a very lightly floured surface and work into a flat round, about 1 inch thick. Wrap in plastic film and chill for 1 hour.

Preheat the oven to 400° F. On a lightly floured surface, roll the dough out to about a ³⁄₁₆-inch thickness, about 12 inches in diameter. Press into a 9- or 10-inch tart pan, trimming the excess. Line with parchment or foil and add pie weights or dried beans; bake for 15 minutes. Remove the weights, return the crust to the oven, and bake for another 5 minutes. Remove to a rack to cool.

Lower the oven temperature to 375° F. In a heavy saucepan over medium heat, combine the brown sugar, butter, cream, and corn syrup; bring to a boil and allow to boil for 1½ minutes. Transfer the walnuts to the pastry shell. Pour the hot syrup mixture over the nuts. Place the filled tart-shell on a cookie sheet and bake for 10 to 15 minutes, or until the caramel starts to bubble.

Remove from the oven and cool on a rack. While still warm, remove the outer ring. Serve the tart at room temperature with whipped cream or ice cream or drizzle with melted chocolate.

Bourbon Buttermilk Pie

——— ✳ ———

Heavy yellow buttermilk, flecked with bits of golden butter left over from churning, often found its way into cakes, muffins, breads, and pies. Buttermilk pie with a splash of bourbon stands on its own, though, as a very unique cream pie. No one is quite sure what it is, but everyone eats it with unmitigated pleasure.

     9-inch pastry shell (½ recipe Never-Fail Pie Crust, page 244)
  3 eggs
  ¾ cup sugar
  3 tablespoons all-purpose flour
1½ cups buttermilk
  1 teaspoon vanilla extract
  3 tablespoons bourbon
  3 tablespoons butter, melted (no substitutes)
     Grated nutmeg

Bake the well-pricked pie shell in a 400° F. oven for just 10 minutes. Reduce the oven temperature to 350° F. In a mixer bowl, beat the eggs and sugar until light and fluffy. Add the flour and beat again. With the beater running slowly, pour in the buttermilk. Add the vanilla, bourbon, and melted butter; blend. Pour the filling into the partially baked pie shell and dust the surface with nutmeg. Bake until the filling just sets, about 20 minutes, then turn off the oven and leave the pie in for 10 minutes longer. Remove the pie to a rack; it will continue to set as it cools. (Custard pies should not bake too long or the custard will curdle.)

English Toffee Cookies

———— ✱ ————

**MAKES APPROXIMATELY
120 COOKIES**

*These crisp cookies, with their frosting of milk choco-
late and pecans, really do have the taste and texture of
toffee. The recipe was originally from the* Detroit
Free Press *and is dated 1959. That newspaper, with
its excellent food pages, influenced and assisted Midwestern cooks for many years.*

 1 cup finely chopped pecans
 1½ teaspoons vegetable oil
 1⅛ teaspoons salt
 1 cup (2 sticks) butter, at room temperature
 1 cup brown sugar
 1 egg yolk, well beaten
 2 cups all-purpose flour
 1 teaspoon vanilla extract
 8 1½-ounce milk chocolate bars, broken in
    pieces

Preheat the oven to 350° F. Place the nuts in a
shallow pan or pie tin. Drizzle the vegetable oil
over the nuts and sprinkle with ⅛ teaspoon of the
salt. Mix well and bake for about 5 to 7 minutes,
watching the nuts carefully so they do not burn.
Remove from the oven and set aside.

Cream the butter, brown sugar, and remaining
teaspoon salt until fluffy, about 3 minutes. Add the
egg yolk and combine well. Blend in the flour and
vanilla. Transfer to an ungreased 12 x 17-inch pan
and spread the dough evenly with a rubber spatula.

Bake the cookie until deep golden brown, about
18 to 20 minutes on the lowest shelf of the oven.
Remove from the oven and immediately place the
chocolate bars on top; when they begin to melt
spread the chocolate over the hot cookie with a
spatula. Sprinkle the chopped pecans evenly over
the top and pat them down into the chocolate. Cut
at once into small rectangles, 1 x 1½ inches. To
store, pack in single layers divided by wax paper
and keep tightly covered or frozen. The cookies
will absorb moisture from the air and soften, so
do not leave them sitting out a long time before
serving.

Spiced Tomato Butter

———— ✱ ————

MAKES 6 PINTS

*Fruit butters are nearly a thing of the past; occasion-
ally you'll find them in specialty stores, but not often.
They are an old-fashioned preserve made with far less
sugar than jams or jellies. They do require long cooking as well as vigilant watching, since they scorch
easily. If you have a Flame Tamer, a pad on top of the
gas flame on your stove, that will help control the heat.
If you don't, cook the butter in your heaviest pan over
the lowest possible heat.*

*Butters are best served, I think, on hot little biscuits
when you are having roast meat, such as beef or pork.*

 8 large cooking apples, such as Jonathan or
    McIntosh, peeled, cored, and diced (about
    8 cups)
 8 large ripe tomatoes, cored, peeled, seeded,
    and diced (about 8 cups)
 2½ pounds brown sugar
 1 cup cider vinegar
 1 teaspoon ground cinnamon
 1 teaspoon ground allspice
 1 teaspoon ground ginger
 1 teaspoon ground cloves
 ½ teaspoon freshly ground pepper

In a large, deep, heavy kettle, place the apples and
tomatoes. Bring to a boil, lower the heat immediately, and cook until they are very soft. Press
through a sieve or food mill and return the puree
to the kettle. Add the remaining ingredients, bring
to a boil, lower the heat immediately to the lowest
possible point, and cook, uncovered, until the desired thickness is reached, about 25 to 35 minutes,
stirring constantly. (This is very imprecise, for the
cooking time depends on the amount of water in
the fruit and what kind of rainfall you have had in
your area.) When finished, the mixture should
round slightly in a spoon and have a gloss to it.
Pack while still hot in hot sterilized pint jars, leaving ½-inch headspace. Wipe the rims, seal, and
process the jars in a hot-water bath for 10 minutes.
Remove to a rack to cool and store in a dark place.

✳ M I N N E S O T A ✳

Here — she meditated — is the newest empire of the world: the Northern
Middlewest; a land of dairy herds and exquisite lakes, of new automobiles
and tar-paper shanties and silos like red towers, of clumsy speech and a
hope that is boundless. An empire that feeds a quarter of the world —
yet its work is merely begun. . . . And for all its fat richness, theirs is a
pioneer land.

She saw the prairie, flat in giant patches or rolling in long hummocks. It
spread out so, it went on so uncontrollably, she could never know it.

"It's a glorious country, a land to be big in," she crooned.

SINCLAIR LEWIS
Main Street, 1920

■ ■ ■

In the beginning, the first settlers described Minnesota as "an endless
sea of grass." Today its identity comes partly from its landscape and
partly from its history. The state divides itself into three regions—rural
Minnesota, the cities, and Up North. ✳ The farms help provide the
rest of the country with dairy products (Minnesota is second to Wisconsin in the production of cream, cheese, and butter), cattle, hogs, sugar
beets, barley, and turkey. The cities, dominated by Minneapolis and St.
Paul, are political centers; Minneapolis, affectionately called "Mill City,"

Breakfast Cheese Pie

✳

MAKES 12 SERVINGS

Related to cheese blintzes, this dish from Oshkosh makes a different and welcome brunch offering. It is cut in wedges like a pie, with a bottom layer resembling a delicate, faintly sweet crumbly cheese cake and a top layer that is cakelike and golden brown. Fresh fruit such as crushed strawberries, peaches, or blueberries is a good accompaniment, along with crisp bacon. Any leftovers can be frozen, then thawed and reheated in the microwave. The recipe can also be halved.

FILLING

   2 **pounds ricotta cheese**
   2 **eggs**
  ¼ **cup sugar**
  ¼ **teaspoon salt**
  ¼ **teaspoon fresh lemon juice**
  ½ **teaspoon grated lemon rind**
   8 **ounces cream cheese, softened**

BATTER

   1 **cup all-purpose flour**
  ½ **cup sugar**
   1 **tablespoon baking powder**
  ¼ **teaspoon salt**
   1 **cup (2 sticks) butter, melted**
   2 **eggs**
  ¼ **cup milk**
   1 **teaspoon vanilla extract**

In a large mixer bowl, combine all the filling ingredients and blend well. Set aside.

Preheat the oven to 300° F. In a large bowl, combine the flour, sugar, baking powder, and salt; mix well. Add the melted butter, eggs, milk, and vanilla and mix lightly but thoroughly by hand. Spoon half of the batter into 2 greased 9-inch pie pans. Top with the filling, spreading it out with a spoon, but don't mix it in. Drop the remaining batter on top of the filling by small spoonfuls, spreading it out gently to cover the filling as thoroughly as possible. (It will all come together during baking.) Bake for 1½ hours. Cut in wedges and serve with fresh fruit sauce and bacon.

BELOW: A small drove of Holsteins pose willingly for an ear of corn. OPPOSITE: Wagonloads of straw wait to be hauled into the barn for winter storage.

Smoked Salmon Cheesecake

from the 510 Restaurant

MAKES 10 TO 12 APPETIZER SERVINGS

The posh 510 Restaurant in Minneapolis is located directly across from the Walker Art Center and the Gutherie Theater. The dining room, dubbed "the Algonquin of Minneapolis," hosts literary dinners that feature a reception and a reading by an author, followed by a five-course meal.

Chef Scott Bergstrom has combined the smoked salmon from the Great Lakes with Minnesota cheeses to create a superb appetizer that he garnishes with caviar and fresh flowers. I think nasturtiums are especially handsome with this.

WALNUT CRUST

 2 cups French bread crumbs
 ½ cup chopped toasted walnuts
 ½ cup (1 stick) butter, melted
 ¼ cup shredded Gruyère cheese
 1 tablespoon chopped fresh dill

FILLING

 3 tablespoons butter
 1 medium onion, minced
 1¾ pounds cream cheese, at room temperature
 ⅓ cup half-and-half
 ½ cup shredded Gruyère cheese
 ½ teaspoon salt
 ¼ teaspoon freshly ground white pepper
 4 eggs
 ½ pound smoked salmon, finely chopped

 Caviar and fresh flowers, for garnish
 (optional)

In a medium bowl, combine the crust ingredients and blend thoroughly. Press into the bottom and 2 inches up the side of a well-buttered 9-inch springform pan. Place in the refrigerator while you prepare the filling.

Preheat the oven to 350° F. Melt the butter in a sauté pan. Add the onions and sweat them over medium-low heat until softened, about 3 to 5 minutes; do not allow them to color. In a mixer bowl, combine the cream cheese and half-and-half until smooth. Add the sautéed onion, Gruyère, salt, and pepper. Add the eggs, one at a time, combining briefly after each. Stir in the salmon. Transfer the cheese mixture to the chilled crust. Bake for 45 to 50 minutes or until the top is golden brown. Remove to a rack to cool, then cover and refrigerate. Serve in small wedges garnished with caviar and fresh flowers.

Real Fish Chowder with Cream and Potatoes

— ✳ —

MAKES 6 TO 8 SERVINGS

This is quite similar to a Finnish fish chowder called kalamolakka, *though the addition of white wine and spices makes that admittedly simple dish something very special. You will find cream-based soups such as this all over Minnesota, for the Finns as well as the Danes brought their affection for dairy dishes with them from Europe. Minnesotian Theophilus Haecker helped form the Minnesota Dairy Cooperative, and reminded his fellow farmer-members, "Treat the cow kindly, boys. Remember she's a lady."*

 2 pounds firm-textured, non-oily fish, such as walleye or whitefish, cut in large pieces
 2 6½-ounce cans minced clams, with liquid
 4 medium onions, chopped
 4 large baking potatoes, chopped
 ½ cup (1 stick) butter
 4 whole cloves
 1 large bay leaf
 1 large garlic clove, minced
 1 tablespoon minced fresh dill
 ½ cup dry white wine
 2 cups boiling water
 Salt and pepper to taste
 2 cups half-and-half
 Fried salt pork bits or bacon, for garnish

Preheat the oven to 375° F. In a heavy Dutch oven or iron pot, combine all the chowder ingredients but the half-and-half and garnish. Cover tightly and bake for 1 hour; do not stir. At the end of the hour, add the half-and-half and mix into the broth with a spoon, being careful not to break up the fish. Shut off the oven and return the covered pot to the oven for 5 to 10 minutes; it must not boil, or it will curdle. Ladle into bowls and sprinkle the salt pork or bacon bits on top.

Minnesota Wild Rice Soup

MAKES 4 TO 6 SERVINGS

At first taste it is hard to identify the subtle nutlike flavor of the wild rice in this satisfying soup. The carrot and onion give it color, and the mushrooms (use morels, if you can get them) play nicely off the firm texture of the rice.

2 tablespoons (¼ stick) butter
½ cup finely chopped onion
¼ cup finely chopped celery
¼ cup finely chopped carrot
1½ cups coarsely sliced fresh mushrooms (approximately ¼ pound), preferably morels
¼ cup all-purpose flour
¾ teaspoon salt
¼ teaspoon freshly ground white pepper
2 cups Beef Stock (page 239)
1 cup half-and-half
1 cup cooked wild rice
⅛ teaspoon bitters
1 tablespoon minced fresh chervil

In a deep saucepan, melt the butter over medium heat. Add the onion, celery, and carrot and sauté for 3 minutes, or until the onion is wilted. Lower the heat to medium-low, add the mushrooms, and cook 3 to 4 minutes longer.

Add the flour, salt, and pepper and cook until the mixture bubbles and begins to turn golden. Add the stock and half-and-half; cook and whisk until thick and smooth. Add the wild rice, bitters, and chervil and heat through.

Blackberry Soup
(Kissel)

MAKES 4 SERVINGS

Fruit soups were, and still are, very popular in Northern European countries. Those immigrating people— the Scandinavians, Germans, and Russians—prepared them in an astonishing number of combinations, many based on dried fruits and thickened with barley or tapioca.

Of all the fruit soups I tested, this one was the clear winner. It is a captivating Russian concoction using fresh or frozen blackberries and thickened with potato starch. Russian kissels are generally topped with cream and served as dessert, but you could certainly serve it as a first course, which is what I do.

2 cups blackberries, fresh or frozen
2¼ cups water
1 cinnamon stick
⅓ cup sugar
1 tablespoon fresh lemon juice
2 tablespoons potato starch (see Note)
Whipped cream or plain yogurt, for garnish

In a deep saucepan, bring the berries, 2 cups water, cinnamon stick, sugar, and lemon juice to a boil. Lower the heat, cover, and simmer for 10 minutes. Strain the mixture through a very fine sieve or muslin, discarding the pulp and cinnamon stick.

Return the strained juice to the saucepan and taste; add more sugar and lemon juice if necessary. In a measuring cup, dissolve the starch in the remaining ¼ cup water; add to the simmering juice, stirring until thickened. Cool and refrigerate. Serve in bowls with a dollop of whipped cream or yogurt.

NOTE: *Kissel* can be made from any red fruit —cherries, strawberries, raspberries, cranberries, and so on. The potato starch gives the thickened soup a transparent look; cornstarch can be substituted, but the mixture will be opaque.

✳ WILD RICE ✳

Prior to the nineteenth century "treaty era," Native Americans living in the Great Lakes area planned their lives around the seasonal harvests of the area's abundant resources. Fish, venison, and wild rice were the mainstays of their diet. Wild rice has always held religious significance for the Indians, and after the harvest, festivals were held to celebrate the cycle of the wild rice's growth.

Wild rice is traditionally harvested by two persons in a canoe, one poling the canoe through the wild rice paddies, the other using a "ricing stick" to bend the stalks over the canoe and knock off the ripe kernels. After harvesting, the rice is dried on sheets of birch bark, then parched over an outdoor fire to loosen the husk. The rice is then winnowed with long wooden pestles, and finally it is packaged for sale.

Today, Indian tribal governments have combined their wild rice expertise with the Great Lakes Indian Fish and Wildlife Commission, which represents eleven Chippewa tribes who have retained their treaty rights. The tribes and commission work together to manage and improve the wild rice resources, which have been depleted and misused during the last century.

Old-fashioned Midwestern Boiled Dinner

———— ✳ ————

Say what you will about the "new cuisine," there are times where one yearns for the familiar, uncontrived food of our childhood. The boiled dinner is one of those dishes that I always prepare right after New Year's, when I have had a surfeit of rich, elaborate food.

Practically every country has its interpretation of this country dish. The French call theirs pot-au-feu, *the Italians have* bollito misto, *and Jewish cooks substitute chicken and call it chicken in the pot.*

Some Midwestern cooks will make Puffy Dumplings (page 242) and cook them on top of the stove in some of the extra broth. It is not uncommon to pass bowls of fresh chopped onion and horseradish as an accompaniment to this meal.

MEAT AND BROTH

  2 pounds beef shank, cross-cut
  1 large onion, quartered
  1 medium carrot, quartered
  1 celery stalk, quartered
 ¼ green bell pepper, cut in 4 pieces
  1 large handful parsley sprigs
  6 whole cloves
  1 bay leaf
  1 teaspoon low-sodium beef bouillon granules
  1 teaspoon salt
 ¼ teaspoon freshly ground black pepper
  9 cups water

VEGETABLES

  4 small potatoes, halved
  4 small carrots, halved
  2 parsnips, peeled and cut in 2-inch chunks
  4 small wedges cabbage

    Minced parsley
    Chopped onion
    Prepared horseradish

Preheat the oven to 325° F. Place the beef in a deep roaster and add all the broth ingredients. Cover and bake for 2¼ hours.

Remove the carrot, celery, bay leaf, and other assorted large pieces of vegetable with a slotted spoon. Discard. Add the potatoes, carrots, and parsnips; bake, covered, for 30 minutes longer. Add the cabbage, pressing it down deep into the broth. Re-cover and bake 15 minutes longer, or until the vegetables are tender.

Ladle into large flat soup bowls and dip broth liberally over all. Top with the parsley and pass bowls of chopped onion and horseradish.

Chilled Beef Tongue

———— ✳ ————

What a treat it is to find thin-sliced tongue in a deli! With its delicate flavor and fine texture, tongue lends itself very well to sandwiches. It still is a cherished dish in the Midwest, and often appears with a selection of meats on buffet tables, especially in the summer.

Make this in advance, slice it, and keep it in the refrigerator, covered with its own cooking broth. If you have a pressure cooker, use it for this recipe—it really speeds the cooking process. Serve it with sweet hot mustard.

   1 large (up to 3 pounds) beef tongue
 3½ cups water
   1 tablespoon salt
   1 onion, quartered
   2 bay leaves
   6 peppercorns
   6 cloves

If using a pressure cooker, wash the beef tongue, then place it on the cooker rack with the remaining ingredients. Cover, bring to a boil, and allow the steam to flow from the pot. Put on the vent cock and cook for 45 minutes at the "cook" temperature. Let the steam return to the "down" position. Alternatively, cook the tongue and remaining ingredients in a deep pan for 3 hours, or until the meat is tender. Cool the meat and liquid separately.

When the tongue is cool enough to handle, slit the skin from thick end to tip on the underside and peel and pull away the skin. Skim the fat from the cooking liquid. Slice the tongue thinly. Pour the juice over the tongue slices and refrigerate until ready to serve.

Estonian Pork and Sauerkraut with Barley

MAKES 6 SERVINGS

Grains and vegetables flourished in Estonia; cabbage and barley were used in many ways there, as in all the Baltic states. This hearty dish was an ideal dinner during the cold Estonian winters and is no less welcome on a wintery Minnesota evening. The barley is an unexpected addition that gives the dish a bit of nubby texture that is very pleasant with the silky kraut.

This can also be prepared in a slow cooker, cooked on low for eight hours.

- 2 pounds sauerkraut
- 2 pounds boneless pork loin, whole or in large cubes
- ½ large apple, peeled, cored, and diced
- ½ cup regular pearled barley
- 1 tablespoon brown sugar, or more to taste
- 1 teaspoon salt
- ½ teaspoon coarsely ground black pepper

Place the sauerkraut in a large sieve, rinse, and drain well. Place the pork in the bottom of a 4- to 5-quart Dutch oven. Add the drained sauerkraut, apple, and barley. Add enough water to barely cover the kraut. Add the brown sugar, salt, and pepper and bring to a boil; reduce the heat and simmer, covered, until the pork is very tender, anywhere from 2½ to 4 hours. Add water as needed.

If the pork loin was left whole, cut it into bite-size cubes and return it to the pot with the kraut once the cooking is complete. Serve in soup plates with some of the broth.

Lemon Veal Tarragon Roast

MAKES 6 TO 8 SERVINGS

A veal roast makes a welcome change from the usual beef for a Sunday supper or special occasion. The lemony gravy does not overwhelm the delicate flavor of the meat.

- 1 (4-pound) veal shoulder roast
- 2 teaspoons grated lemon rind
- 1 teaspoon salt
- ¼ teaspoon coarsely ground black pepper
- 1 tablespoon finely minced fresh tarragon
- 1 small shallot, minced
- 1½ cups Chicken Stock (page 239)
- ¼ cup flour
- 1 tablespoon fresh lemon juice, or more to taste

Preheat the oven to 325° F. Place the rib roast in a shallow 9 x 13-inch roasting pan.

In a small bowl, combine the lemon rind, salt, pepper, tarragon, and shallot. With a sharp knife, make about 2 dozen slits 2½ inches deep in the top and sides of the roast. Insert some of the lemon rind mixture into each of the slits and rub any remaining mixture over the top of the roast.

Place the roast in the oven and cook for 2½ hours, or until a meat thermometer registers 170° F. Transfer the roast to a warm platter and let it stand for 8 to 10 minutes. Meanwhile, combine ½ cup of the stock and the flour in a small bowl and mix well. On the top of the stove, bring the pan juices and the remaining stock to a boil over medium-high heat. Whisk in the flour-stock mixture and lemon juice to taste. Simmer until the gravy is smooth and thickened, for about 4 or 5 minutes.

Slice the veal and serve with the lemon gravy.

Duck with Wild Rice Salad
à l'Orange

※

MAKES 8 TO 10
GENEROUS SERVINGS

This is the perfect buffet dish for entertaining—Indiana duck and Minnesota wild rice glossed with an orange–balsamic vinegar dressing, plus Missouri black walnuts added for good measure. In the spring, I serve this dish with marinated asparagus, and in the autumn, Brussels sprouts. It can be served either slightly warm or at room temperature. The recipe is an adaptation from The Nantucket Open-House Cookbook *by Sarah Leah Chase. Prepare the duck and stock one day in advance.*

1   6½-pound Pekin duck
    Salt and pepper
2   cups wild rice
2   quarts water
1   cup vegetable oil (not corn or olive)
4   medium carrots, cut in ¼-inch dice
1   large red onion, minced
3   cups duck stock or Chicken Stock
      (page 239)
¾   cup fresh orange juice
2   tablespoons Cointreau
1   tablespoon balsamic vinegar
½   teaspoon salt
½   teaspoon freshly ground pepper
4   tablespoons grated orange rind
1   cup golden raisins
1½ cups chopped black walnuts
8   scallions, both white and green parts, sliced
      on the diagonal

The day before serving, prepare the duck. Preheat the oven to 375° F. Remove the neck and giblets from the cavity and set aside for stock, if desired. Rinse the duck under cold water and dry with paper towels. Place on a rack, breast side up, in a shallow 8 x 13-inch roasting pan; sprinkle with salt and pepper. Roast approximately 1 hour and 45 minutes to 2 hours, or until a meat thermometer inserted in the thigh registers 180° F. Remove the duck from the oven and cool slightly. While it is still warm, remove all skin and discard; cut the

Ballooning is popular throughout the Midwest; from above, the landscape resembles a Monopoly board.

duck meat into long, narrow strips. Cover and refrigerate. Reserve 3 cups of stock.

Place the wild rice in a small bowl, add cold water to cover, and soak for 1 hour. In a large saucepan, bring the water to a boil; add the drained rice and boil for 5 minutes. Drain again and set aside. Preheat the oven to 375 ° F. Heat ¼ cup of the oil in a large skillet over medium-high heat. Add the carrots and onion and sauté, stirring frequently, for 10 minutes. Add the rice, stir to coat it with the oil, and cook several minutes longer. Transfer the rice mixture to a greased lasagne-type pan (a metal pan works better for this recipe), 13 x 11 inches, and pour in the stock. Cover the pan tightly with foil and bake until the liquid is absorbed and the rice is tender, about 45 minutes.

In a bowl, combine the orange juice, remaining ¾ cup vegetable oil, Cointreau, vinegar, salt, pepper, and orange rind. Pour over the hot rice. Add the reserved duck meat, raisins, and walnuts. Toss to combine, cover tightly, and allow to stand for 2 hours. Add the scallions. Serve the salad at room temperature.

Polish Pierogi

——— ✳ ———

After an unsuccessful revolution ravaged their home country, Polish immigrants flocked to America in large numbers. From Ellis Island, many migrated to the Midwest, settling in Milwaukee, Chicago, South Bend, Minneapolis, and St. Paul.

These people worked hard, raising large families on small incomes, so it is not surprising that Polish food was high in carbohydrates, frequently lightened by cabbage! One of their routine Friday night staples, still made today, is the pierogi, a poached filled dumpling, rather like a big oval ravioli, that is then sautéed. A variety of fillings are used: meat (though not on Fridays), cabbage, potatoes, prunes, cottage cheese—all savory and heartily good.

DOUGH

>   3 cups flour
>   ⅛ teaspoon baking powder
>   ⅛ teaspoon salt
>   4 tablespoons (½ stick) butter, softened
>   2 eggs
>   Milk
>   ½ cup vegetable oil
>   ½ cup (1 stick) butter

Sour cream, browned chopped onion, or maple syrup

To make the dough: In a large bowl, combine the flour, baking powder, and salt; cut in the softened butter with a pastry blender until coarse crumbs form. In a small bowl, beat the eggs slightly and transfer to a measuring cup. Add enough milk to make 1 cup. Pour over the crumbs and, by hand, stir until a stiff ball forms.

Transfer the dough to a lightly floured board and knead for about 3 minutes, or until the dough is smooth and elastic, adding a little more flour if

necessary. Cover the dough with plastic wrap and let it rest for 15 to 30 minutes.

When the dough has rested, divide it into 3 parts and roll out each portion as thin as a pie crust, about ⅛ inch thick. Using a 3-inch biscuit cutter, cut out circles of dough. Place 1 to 2 tablespoons of filling (this depends on how runny the filling is) slightly off center on each round. Moisten the edges with water, fold each round over to form a half-circle, and seal the edges with the tines of a fork. Be sure the seal is firm.

Cook the pierogis in a large stock pot, half full of boiling salted water, two at a time. After 2 to 3 minutes, they will float to the top; remove with a slotted spoon and drain on a cake rack set over a jelly roll pan. When cooled, remove the pierogis to greased wax paper in single layers—don't stack them, for they will stick. (The pierogis can be frozen at this point. Thaw the pierogis before sautéing them.)

To serve: In a large heavy skillet, combine ½ cup of butter and the vegetable oil over medium heat. When the butter is melted, sauté the pierogis on both sides, turning once, until golden brown and crisp, about 10 minutes. Remove and serve immediately, topping with sour cream, browned chopped onion, or maple syrup.

Cheese Filling with Sour Cream

>   1 pound farmer's cheese or very well drained
>   cottage cheese, large or small curd
>   2 egg yolks
>   1 tablespoon butter, softened
>   ¼ cup plus 2 tablespoons sugar
>   1 teaspoon vanilla extract
>   ½ teaspoon salt
>   ¼ cup golden raisins
>   1 cup sour cream

Place the cheese in a colander lined with cheesecloth and rinse under running water. Bring the ends of the cheesecloth together and wring out the excess water out of the cheese. Set aside.

In a large mixer bowl, beat the egg yolks for 3 minutes, or until they are pale yellow. Add the butter, cheese, 2 tablespoons of the sugar, vanilla, and salt; continue beating for 3 more minutes on low speed. Stir in the raisins. Spoon onto the pierogi dough and cook as directed above.

In a small bowl combine the sour cream and the remaining ¼ cup of sugar. Serve with the sautéed pierogis.

Potato and Cream Cheese Filling

MAKES 4 CUPS

    3   medium potatoes, peeled
    1   (8-ounce) package cream cheese, at room
        temperature
    ½   cup (1 stick) butter
    2   medium onions, finely chopped
    1   teaspoon sugar
    1   teaspoon salt
    ½   teaspoon freshly ground black pepper
    ¼   teaspoon grated nutmeg

Place the potatoes in a sauce pan with water to cover and bring to a boil; reduce the heat to moderate and cook until the potatoes are tender, about 15 to 20 minutes. Drain and mash. Place the hot mashed potatoes in a large mixer bowl and stir in the cream cheese until combined. Melt the butter in a large skillet over medium heat; add the onions and sauté for about 10 minutes, or until they are golden brown. Combine the onions, potatoes, and seasonings, and blend. Spoon onto the pierogi dough and cook according to the directions above. Additional browned onions may be served on top.

Barley with Mushrooms and Dill

— ✳ —

MAKES 6 SERVINGS

Barley actually belongs to the grass family and has more fiber than oats. Extremely versatile, it can be substituted for rice in many dishes. Raised for livestock as well, the nutty edible grain has long been a familiar ingredient in Russian and Northern European dishes. In the United States, Minnesota is the largest producer of barley.

I often make this for lunch. It is nutritious eating and the cooked mixture can be frozen.

    4   teaspoons vegetable oil
    1   medium onion, chopped
    1   medium carrot, finely chopped or shredded
    ½   small red bell pepper, chopped
    1   garlic clove, finely minced
    ½   pound mushrooms, coarsely sliced
    1   cup pearl barley
 1¾   cups Beef Stock (page 239)
    2   tablespoons minced parsley
    3   tablespoons minced fresh dill
    2   tablespoons fresh lemon juice
        Salt and pepper to taste

In a 10-inch sauté pan, heat the oil over medium heat. Add the onion, carrot, bell pepper, and garlic and sauté for 3 minutes. Add the mushrooms and sauté and toss for an additional 3 minutes. Add the barley and continue cooking until it is lightly browned, about 5 minutes. Add 1 cup of the stock, cover, and simmer over medium-low heat for 15 minutes. Add the remaining stock and continue simmering until the liquid is absorbed, about 10 minutes longer, stirring now and then. Stir in the parsley, dill, and lemon juice and check the seasonings. Serve hot.

Rutabaga Casserole
(*Lanttulaatikko*)

——— ✳ ———

MAKES 8 SERVINGS

This well-flavored casserole is a bit like a soufflé. It is an indispensable part of a Minnesota Finnish Christmas table, but most Scandinavians serve it year-round as well. Beloved in Northern European countries, rutabagas flourish in cool soil and have good keeping qualities. In late fall, some farmers packed the vegetable in their root cellars in barrels of sawdust to use all winter long.

Sometimes rutabagas go by the name of "Swedes" or "wax turnips," and the Scots call them "neeps." Call them what you will, the knobby rutabagas have played an important part in immigrant cookery.

2	rutabagas, approximately 2 pounds
¼	cup (½ stick) butter
2	tablespoons brown sugar
¾	teaspoon salt
½	teaspoon coarsely ground black pepper
½	teaspoon ground allspice
2	eggs, separated
2	slices brown bread, processed into fine crumbs

Cut the rutabagas in half (this is hard work, but stick with it) and peel the halves. Cut into 2 x 3-inch cubes and place in a deep saucepan with water to cover. Bring to a boil, reduce heat, and simmer, covered, for 30 to 40 minutes, or until the rutabagas are tender when pierced with a fork.

Drain very well and transfer to a mixer bowl with 2 tablespoons of the butter. Mash or whip with a small electric beater until smooth. Add the brown sugar, salt, pepper, and allspice. (This recipe can be prepared up to this point a day or two in advance and refrigerated.)

Preheat the oven to 350° F. Beat the egg whites until stiff peaks form; set aside. Beat the egg yolks for 3 minutes, or until light. Stir the egg yolks into the rutabaga mixture, then gently fold in the egg whites. Transfer to a greased 11 x 9-inch oval gratin dish. Melt the remaining 2 tablespoons of butter and combine with the bread crumbs. Sprinkle over the top of the rutabaga mixture. Bake for 1 hour, or until the top is a deep golden brown.

*OPPOSITE: **The countryside looks like green corduroy when photographed overhead from a balloon ride, a favorite Midwestern recreation.** BELOW: **Come autumn, piles of firewood for sale appear along the roadside.***

In those early years when the state was being settled, no self-respecting Minnesota farmhouse would be without a vegetable patch. Many Eastern European immigrants adhered to the precepts of "planting by the sign of the moon," and some gardeners still follow these guidelines, myself included.

Root vegetables, such as potatoes, carrots, and rutabagas, are planted in the dark of the moon, or when the moon is waning. This assures the gardener that the vegetables won't go to all "tops." Vegetables growing above ground, such as eggplant, squash, peas, and beans, are planted in the light, or waxing, of the moon to assure a heavy harvest.

Some other traditional planting tips that are still observed today: Blooming cherry trees signal the time to put out lettuce, onion sets, and radishes. When apple tree blooms are just past their prime, plant chard, sweet corn, and lima beans. The best time to plant corn is when new oak leaves are the size of a squirrel's ear. And six months from the date of the first thundershowers in the spring, you will have the first fall frost — and I must admit, I haven't seen that vary by more than a day or two.

My own rule of thumb for setting out tender spring plants is to wait until after the last full moon in May, when the chance of a killing frost is very remote — at least in Indiana, Ohio, Illinois, and Minnesota. Another sign is to listen for the spring peepers — a very pleasant chore. Legend has it that after these frogs have sung three times, there will be no more killing frosts.

Fresh Vegetable Stew
(Ghivetch)

✴

MAKES 6 TO 8 SERVINGS

It does my heart good to see the resurgence of interest in old ethnic recipes that are not only easy to prepare but good for us as well. Ghivetch is a nearly perfect vegetable dish, with a mélange of fresh ingredients simmered slowly in the oven with just a bit of broth and olive oil. And it is low in calories.

½ head cauliflower, separated into small
    flowerets
2 medium potatoes, peeled and diced
2 medium carrots, thinly sliced
½ medium eggplant, cut in small dice
1 16-ounce can Italian plum tomatoes,
    drained; or 4 fresh tomatoes, peeled,
    seeded, and diced
2 medium onions, thinly sliced
2 medium zucchini, thinly sliced
2 medium yellow squash, thinly sliced

½ cup fresh green peas
½ cup fresh cut green beans
1 green bell pepper, chopped
2 celery stalks, finely chopped
    Salt and pepper to taste
½ cup chopped fresh dill
½ cup chopped fresh parsley
3 bay leaves
1½ cups homemade Beef or Chicken Stock
    (pages 239)
⅓ cup olive oil

Preheat the oven to 350° F. In a large greased roaster or in a 4-quart casserole, arrange one-third of the vegetables in a single layer. Sprinkle with salt, pepper, dill, and parsley, and top with a bay leaf. Make 2 more layers with the remaining vegetables and seasonings.

In a small saucepan, heat the stock and olive oil. Pour the hot stock over the vegetables, cover the casserole tightly, and bake for 3 hours or until the vegetables are tender. Serve slightly warm or at room temperature.

Polish Sour Cream Beets with Horseradish

MAKES 6 SERVINGS

The unusual addition of horseradish and sour cream to beets gives them a piquant sweet-and-sour flavor. This vegetable dish is shocking pink and gorgeous on the dinner plate.

6 large fresh beets
4 tablespoons (½ stick) butter
2 medium onions, chopped
2 tablespoons all-purpose flour
2 tablespoons cider vinegar
⅓ cup hot water
1 teaspoon sugar
1 teaspoon salt
½ teaspoon freshly ground pepper
½ cup sour cream
2 tablespoons prepared horseradish

Preheat the oven to 400° F. Remove the leaves from the beets, leaving 1 inch of stem intact so the beets don't bleed during cooking. Wrap each beet in foil, place on a jelly-roll pan, and bake for 45 minutes to 1 hour, or until tender when pierced with a fork. Remove from the oven and cool for 30 minutes. Remove foil and peel away the skin, root, and stem. Dice the beets into ½-inch cubes.

In a large sauté pan, melt the butter over medium heat. Add the chopped onions, and sauté for 10 minutes. Slowly stir in flour and mix well. Add the vinegar, water, sugar, salt, and pepper. Bring to a boil, whisking, then add the beets; if the mixture appears too dry, add more water to almost cover the beets. Simmer over low heat for 10 minutes. Let cool slightly, about 10 to 15 minutes, then slowly stir in the sour cream and horseradish. Do not allow the mixture to boil, or it will curdle. Serve immediately.

Asian-American Slaw with Peanuts and Jalapeños

MAKES 8 SERVINGS

St. Paul has one of the largest settlements of Huang people in the United States, and Vietnamese are still arriving in vast numbers. It's not surprising that many Vietnamese groceries and restaurants have sprung up, or that their seasonings and recipes are finding their way into the food styles of Minnesota.

The salad is prepared with jalapeños, fresh ginger, peanut butter, and sesame oil, giving this familiar favorite a refreshing Asian flavor.

6 cups coarsely chopped green cabbage, about 1½ pounds
1 medium red bell pepper, chopped
1 medium onion, chopped
2 celery stalks, chopped
2 tablespoons chopped jalapeño peppers (2 to 3 small ones), all seeds and membranes removed
2 tablespoons minced fresh parsley
1½ teaspoons shredded fresh ginger
¼ cup chunky peanut butter
3 tablespoons soy sauce
2 tablespoons lime juice
1 tablespoon sugar
1 tablespoon dark sesame oil
1 teaspoon salt
½ cup coarsely chopped dry-roasted peanuts

In a large bowl, combine the cabbage, bell pepper, onion, celery, jalapeño, parsley, and ginger. In a small bowl, combine the remaining ingredients and toss with the cabbage mixture. Serve chilled or at room temperature.

OVERLEAF: At sunset, the cows amble in from the pasture and stop for a drink before going on to the barn.

Poticia

——— ✳ ———

MAKES 2 COFFEE CAKES

This jelly roll–style coffee cake, with its walnut-cinnamon filling, is a Yugoslavian favorite found in Minnesota bakeries and homemade on Slovenian tables. It could not be a Slovenian wedding without poticia (pronounced po-TEET-tsa) and cabbage rolls.

The rich yellow yeast dough is made with milk, eggs, and sugar. It requires three risings, so plan accordingly. It is an exceptional coffee cake.

CAKE

- 1 package active dry yeast
- ¼ cup warm water mixed with ¼ teaspoon granulated sugar
- ¾ cup milk
- ¼ cup granulated sugar
- ¾ cup (1½ sticks) butter, at room temperature
- 1 egg plus 2 egg yolks, lightly beaten
- 1 teaspoon salt
- 4¼ to 4½ cups all-purpose flour

WALNUT FILLING

- 1½ cups walnuts
- ½ cup heavy (whipping) cream
- 1 tablespoon butter, softened
- ½ cup dark brown sugar
  Grated rind of 1 lemon
- 1 egg, lightly beaten
- 2 teaspoons ground cinnamon

- 1 egg, lightly beaten
  Confectioners' sugar

In a small bowl, sprinkle the yeast over the warm sugared water. In a small pan, scald the milk and add the granulated sugar and ¼ cup of the butter. When cool, add the beaten egg, egg yolks, and salt to the milk.

Meanwhile, place 4¼ cups flour and the remaining ½ cup of the butter into a large food processor bowl or large mixing bowl. Process for 15 seconds or until well combined, then add the milk and egg mixture plus the yeast mixture. Process until the mixture forms a ball. If the dough is too sticky to form a ball, keep the processor on and add flour 1

tablespoon at a time until it comes together. Continue processing until the ball rotates around the bowl 25 times. If doing hand mixing or using the dough hook attachment on your mixer, mix or knead until a smooth dough is formed. If flour needs to be added, "less is more." Dough that is sticky is better than dry dough.

Let the dough rest 5 minutes, then turn it onto a floured surface and knead a few times. Place the dough in a lightly greased large bowl, turn once, and cover lightly with plastic wrap. Let rise in a warm spot (approximately 80° F.) until doubled, about 1 hour. Punch down thoroughly, oil the top, and let rise again until doubled, about 1 more hour.

Meanwhile, make the filling. Process the walnuts in a food processor until fine (or chop in a blender); transfer to a medium bowl. In a small saucepan, heat the cream to almost a boil. Add the hot cream to the nuts, along with the butter, brown sugar, lemon rind, egg, and cinnamon. Process or blend well.

After the dough has risen the second time, punch down and divide in half. Transfer to a floured surface and roll out each piece of dough into a rectangle about 14 x 24 inches and ⅛ inch thick (roll as thin as possible for a really fine poticia). Spread one rectangle with half the walnut filling, spreading it to within 1 inch of the edges. Starting from the long side of the rectangle, roll up the poticia firmly, jelly roll fashion. Repeat with the remaining dough and filling.

Transfer the rolls to a large greased baking sheet. Shape each into a coil or U shape, seam sides down. (The U shape is used for economy of space; a snail-like coil makes a more attractive gift.) Let the poticia rise again until doubled, about 45 minutes.

Preheat the oven to 350° F. Brush the tops of the poticia with the beaten egg and bake for 30 to 40 minutes, or until lightly browned. Remove to a rack to cool. Just before serving, sprinkle with confectioners' sugar. (If freezing, add confectioners' sugar after thawing.)

Velvet Mashed Potato Chocolate Cake

—— ✳ ——

MAKES 16 TO 20 SERVINGS

When I first scanned this old recipe, dated 1868, I was struck by the combination of ingredients and thought it would be either marvelous or dreadful. I am happy to report it is the former. It is extremely moist because of the mashed potatoes and raisins, and the texture is velvety smooth. The frosting, with its touch of citrus, is quite perfect with it.

CAKE

      2 medium potatoes
      2 cups all-purpose flour
    ½ teaspoon ground ginger
      1 teaspoon baking powder
      1 teaspoon baking soda
      1 teaspoon salt
      1 teaspoon ground cinnamon
    ¼ cup unsweetened cocoa powder
      1 cup (2 sticks) butter (no substitutes)
      2 cups granulated sugar
      4 eggs, separated
      1 teaspoon vanilla extract
      1 cup buttermilk
      1 cup raisins
      1 cup finely chopped pecans

FROSTING

    ½ cup (1 stick) butter (no substitutes)
    ¾ teaspoon grated orange rind
    ¼ teaspoon ground cinnamon
    ⅛ teaspoon salt
    ¼ cup unsweetened cocoa powder
    3½ cups (1 pound) confectioners' sugar
      1 tablespoon lemon juice
    ¼ cup milk

Peel the potatoes, cover with water, and boil until tender, about 25 minutes. Mash thoroughly; do not add milk or seasonings. Measure out 1 cup, cover to keep warm, and set aside. Preheat the oven to 300° F.

Sift together the flour, ginger, baking powder, baking soda, salt, cinnamon, and cocoa. In a large mixer bowl, cream the butter and granulated sugar for 3 minutes, then add the egg yolks and beat 1 minute longer. Stir the vanilla into the buttermilk, then add the flour mixture to the creamed mixture alternately with the buttermilk, beginning and ending with the flour mixture. With the beater running, add the 1 cup of potatoes, raisins, and nuts; combine lightly, not overbeating. Beat the egg whites until stiff peaks form, and by hand fold into the cake batter until just blended.

Pour the batter into a greased and floured 10-inch tube pan and bake for 1½ hours, or until the cake springs back when touched with your finger. Cool completely in the pan while you prepare the frosting.

In a large mixer bowl, cream the butter, orange rind, cinnamon, salt, and cocoa. Add the confectioners' sugar alternately with the lemon juice and milk until the mixture is creamy and smooth, beating well after each addition. Remove the cooled cake from the pan and spread the frosting on the top and sides of the cake. Cover tightly until ready to serve (see Note).

NOTE: If the weather is hot, refrigerate the cake so the frosting will not become overly soft. Bring to room temperature before serving.

Coconut Cream Pie

MAKES 8 TO 10 SERVINGS

Minnesota is second in the production of dairy products in the country (neighboring Wisconsin is first), and when you have large dairy herds, you find a plethora of dishes using milk, cream, butter, and cheese. This thick, rich cream pie shows off the Minnesota cook's skills with the riches from his or her home state. It will easily serve ten people, and the custard will never fail to set for you. Do use only whole milk.

1   7½-ounce can sweetened flaked coconut
1½ cups sugar
½   cup cornstarch
¼   teaspoon salt
1   cup cold whole milk
3   egg yolks
3   cups whole milk, scalded in large saucepan
4   tablespoons (½ stick) butter
2   teaspoons vanilla extract
      9-inch baked pastry shell (½ recipe Never-
      Fail Pie Crust, page 244)
      Whipped Cream Topping (page 247)

On a flat pan, in a 350° F. oven, toast ½ cup of the coconut for 5 minutes, stirring once. Set aside.

In a medium bowl, combine the sugar, cornstarch, and salt; gradually add the cold milk. In a small bowl, beat the egg yolks. Add them to the sugar-milk mixture and blend with spoon. Gradually add the hot milk. Transfer the custard to a large saucepan (use the same pan you scalded the milk in and save a dish) and cook over medium heat, stirring constantly with a wooden spoon or paddle. It may be necessary to use a whisk briefly at the end of the cooking period to smooth out all the little lumps, but don't use it earlier, for you don't want to create air bubbles in the custard.

When the custard bubbles up in the middle and thickens, remove from the heat and add the butter, vanilla, and untoasted coconut. Cool to lukewarm, then transfer to the pie shell. When the custard is completely cool, refrigerate. To serve, top with whipped cream topping and sprinkle with the toasted coconut.

Minnesota Wild Rice Pudding

MAKES 6 SERVINGS

The texture of this pudding is delightful—the custard is delicately firm and the wild rice is a tad chewy. Cooked wild rice freezes well and is nice to have on hand to use in dishes such as this. This is a most satisfying dessert as is, but you can serve it with Blueberry Slump Lemon Sauce (page 54) if you prefer.

2   cups half-and-half
4   eggs
½   cup sugar
½   teaspoon grated nutmeg
⅛   teaspoon salt
1½ teaspoons vanilla extract
¾   cup cooked wild rice
¼   cup golden raisins
      Grated nutmeg

Preheat the oven to 325° F. Scald the half-and-half —bubbles should form around the edges of the pan, but don't allow it to boil. In a mixer bowl, beat the eggs and sugar until frothy. Stir in the nutmeg, salt, vanilla, rice, and raisins, then gradually add the half-and-half.

Transfer the mixture to a greased 1-quart soufflé dish, and place inside a large metal baking pan. Fill the pan with hot water and bake for 55 minutes. Remove the soufflé dish from the hot water bath and cool completely, then refrigerate before serving.

The sun sets over one of the countless lakes that dot the Minnesota landscape.

✳ SINCLAIR LEWIS ✳

The publication of Sinclair Lewis's *Main Street* in 1920 caused an outcry in Minnesota; the author's satirical and often devastating glimpse of Gopher Prairie was based, all too recognizably, on his own hometown, Sauk Center.

Farther afield, however, the reactions to his book were considerably less negative; a million copies were sold and the book made him an international figure. Other books followed: *Babbitt,* considered an extension of *Main Street,* and *Arrowsmith,* for which he received (though declined to accept) a Pulitzer Prize. Other successes were *Elmer Gantry,* the tale of grasping evangelists, and *Dodsworth,* a poignant tale about a Midwestern American couple living abroad. There is much disguised (and not so disguised) biography in Lewis's work.

In 1930, Lewis won the Nobel Prize, which he did accept, and in later years, his attitude toward the small towns of his youth softened. In fact, the film version of *Elmer Gantry* had its gala premiere at the Main Street Theater in Sauk Center.

His boyhood home has been restored, and there is also a Sinclair Lewis Museum. Apparently the town has forgiven him.

Sinclair Lewis's Sinful Christmas Cookies

——— ✳ ———

MAKES 6 TO 7 DOZEN COOKIES

In his biography of Sinclair Lewis, Sinclair Lewis Home at Last, *John Koblas writes, "Lewis was extremely fond of cookies. He, in fact, concocted his own recipe, which he gave to Mrs. Schmitt of Mankato. From that time on, he always expected his favorite cookies when he arrived."*

In 1919, Lewis stayed with his friends, the Schmitt family in Mankato, which is south of Minneapolis, to do some writing. This is Lewis's recipe from the Koblas book, though the salt and almond extract are my additions. The cookies are very crisp and rather addictive—one keeps going back to the tin for another.

1 cup (2 sticks) margarine, at room temperature (don't use butter)
2 cups sugar
1¼ teaspoons almond extract
2 eggs
2¼ cups bread flour
2 tablespoons Dutch process cocoa
1 teaspoon salt
2 tablespoons bourbon
½ cup sliced almonds

Preheat the oven to 325° F. In a mixer bowl, beat the margarine and sugar until light, about 3 minutes. Add the almond extract and eggs, one at a time, beating well after each addition.

In a medium bowl, whisk together the flour, cocoa, and salt. Add to the butter mixture alternately with the bourbon, beginning and ending with the flour. Mix in the almonds by hand.

Drop by heaping teaspoons on greased cookie sheets and bake for 8 to 10 minutes, or until the cookies are just firm when the tops are touched with your finger; they should not brown around the edges. Allow to stand on the baking sheet a couple of minutes, then with a metal spatula, transfer to a wax paper–lined rack to cool. Store in an airtight container.

Walnut Frosties

To a Midwesterner layered cookies such as this one are collectively called bar cookies. Although brownies are popular all over, bar cookies such as these rich walnut treats seem especially favored in the Heartland states, where, with a covered dish, they are the essential ingredients for a potluck dinner.

COOKIE LAYER
    1   cup all-purpose flour
    2   tablespoons confectioners' sugar
    ½   cup (1 stick) butter

COCONUT WALNUT LAYER
    2   eggs
    1   teaspoon vanilla extract
    1   cup light brown sugar
    2   tablespoons all-purpose flour
    ½   teaspoon baking powder
    ⅛   teaspoon salt
    1   cup coarsely chopped English walnuts
    ½   cup flaked coconut

FROSTING LAYER
    1¼ cups confectioners' sugar
    2   tablespoons (¼ stick) butter, melted
    1½ teaspoons orange juice
    1½ teaspoons grated orange rind
        Pinch of salt

Preheat the oven to 350° F. In a bowl, combine all the ingredients for the cookie layer with a pastry blender (or pulse in a food processor). Pat into a buttered 12 x 7-inch flat glass baking dish. Bake until golden, about 10 minutes.

While the first layer is baking, prepare the filling. In a mixer bowl, beat the eggs and the vanilla until the eggs are pale yellow, about 2 minutes. In another bowl, combine the brown sugar, flour, baking powder, salt, walnuts, and coconut; add to the egg mixture and blend. Cool the baked first layer for 5 minutes, then pour the walnut-coconut mixture over the crust and bake for 25 minutes or until the top is golden and the center is done. Transfer to a wire rack and cool completely before frosting.

While the first two layers cool, combine all of the frosting ingredients in a small bowl until smooth. Spread over the top of the cooled cookie, allow to stand for 1 hour, then cut into squares. Store in layers separated by plastic wrap in an airtight container.

Almond Joy Cookies

A happy holiday custom around the Midwest is to have a cookie exchange, or Sweet Swap, as it is sometimes called. A hostess will ask approximately ten people to her house in early December, and everyone is to bring a platter of cookies; each guest brings a different kind and, after the swap, takes home a variety of treats for the holidays.

The recipe for Almond Joy Cookies came from a Minnesota church cookbook and would be perfect for a Sweet Swap. The cookie reminds one of a candy bar, hence its name, and it is quick to prepare.

    1   (14 ounce) can sweetened condensed milk
    2   ounces unsweetened chocolate
    ¼   teaspoon salt
    1   teaspoon vanilla extract
    3   cups shredded coconut
    45 whole salted almonds

Preheat the oven to 350° F. In the top of a double boiler, combine the condensed milk, chocolate, and salt. Cook over rapidly boiling water, stirring often, for 5 to 7 minutes, or until the mixture thickens. Remove from the heat and stir in the vanilla and coconut.

Form cookies by dropping teaspoons of the mixture on a well-greased baking sheet, 1 inch apart. Top each with a whole almond. Bake on the middle shelf of the oven for 10 to 12 minutes, watching the cookies carefully after 8 or 9 minutes, as the bottom can get too brown. Immediately remove cookies from the pan with a metal spatula and cool on a wax-paper-covered rack.

NOTE: These freeze very well.

The rivers of Missouri are often very beautiful. . . . Giant sycamores hang over their banks and in the summer when the current moves slowly these are duplicated in the stream below. . . . Missouri's summer moon is big and white and cuts out vivid clear edges. . . . There is over these summer night waters and on the shadowed lands that border them an ineffable peace, an immense quiet, which puts all ambitious effort in its futile place and makes of a simple drift of sense and feeling the ultimate and proper end of life.

THOMAS HART BENTON
An Artist in America, 1937

■ ■ ■

In St. Louis, Eero Saarinen's soaring arch, a shining stainless-steel rainbow, marks the "Gateway to the West." It is also the symbol of St. Louis's role during the frontier period, when it was a stopover for explorers and settlers before they fanned out to settle the rest of America. ✳ The top of the arch sways gently, giving itself to the winds. Stretching away below is a panoramic view of St. Louis, a sprawling city founded by a Frenchman as a fur trading center. ✳ Lewis and Clark first extolled the riches of Missouri and the Mississippi River valley lands; eastern pioneers weren't far behind them. Southerners, too,

lured by the fertile rolling hills and bottom-land, came from Virginia, Tennessee, and Kentucky with their families and slaves to raise corn, cotton, and tobacco. They settled in the central part of the state; there were so many of them that the area was nicknamed "Little Dixie." They never lost their taste for sorghum molasses, bourbon pies, chess pies, cornbread, pecans, and sweet potatoes; the Southern influence is obvious on Missouri's bountiful tables.

Transportation has always played a vital part in Missouri's history; St. Joseph was the eastern terminal of the Pony Express. Look-ing for relay riders to carry mail, an 1860 ad was quite specific: "Wanted: Young Skinny Wiry Fellows, Not Over 18. Must Be Expert Riders Willing To Risk Death Daily. Or-phans Preferred. Wages $25 a Week."

Daniel Boone, the intrepid frontiersman from Kentucky, led a group of pioneer fam-ilies in dugout canoes up the Ohio River. They finished the trek into the wilderness on horses and finally came by foot to central Missouri. This was truly "the Boonies."

Hopeful immigrants—the Irish, Bohe-mians, French, and Scots—arrived overland by wagon or on the river by packets, barges, and steamboats. Mark Twain, the bard of Missouri, loved the riverboats. He wrote, "A steamboat is as beautiful as a wedding cake, but without the complications." Steamboat cooking reflected the food of the South. In the dining rooms, for those who could afford it, platters of chicken, fried salt pork, ham,

and catfish lined the tables, plus dishes made from the fruits and vegetables bought from farmers along the river.

Another important culinary influence ap-peared on the scene in the 1830s, when a wave of educated, liberal, and hardworking Germans settled in St. Louis. As always, they started wineries, breweries, and packing houses, willing to work hard to establish a good life for themselves. And from their number they provided clergymen, scholars, musicians, and artisans to help civilize Mis-souri's frontier life. They hated the institu-tion of slavery and influenced Missouri's course when the Civil War began in 1861.

St. Louis flourished; with its location at the confluence of the Mississippi and Mis-souri rivers, the city was a Southern-belle sort of town with an Eastern look to it. Today the city has moved into the future by restoring its past, including the riverfront with its warehouse district and the Union Railroad Station. Buzzing with activity and crammed full of inviting new shops and res-taurants, it is as lively today as it was a hundred years ago.

Across the state on the western border is Kansas City, and it is as Western as St. Louis is Eastern; there is an expansiveness here. Railroads were the backbone of the town, bringing in cattle, pigs, sheep, and wheat; it is still an agribusiness capital. Today it is a metropolis, a sophisticated place with a flourishing arts community, wide streets, and green meadow parks dotted with Henry

Moores. And, of course, there is Kansas City barbecue, an enthusiasm of the whole area, as important as baseball or ballet.

Hannibal, a typical river town, is very much like it was during Mark Twain's youth; barefoot boys still fish along the banks of the river and dream of exploring caves and running away from home. From Cardiff Hill, you can look out over the fabled Mississippi, magnificent in its grandeur and power, rolling on as it has since time began. *

CORNMEAL MOLASSES PANCAKES * CURRIED WALNUTS * FIRE AND ICE SOUP * COLD CREAM OF PEAR SOUP * LENTIL SOUP * SMOKED BRISKET, KANSAS CITY STYLE * CHICKEN FRIED STEAK * VEAL HAM LOAF WITH SOUR CREAM SAUCE * MIDWESTERN FRIED CHICKEN * MISSISSIPPI CATFISH * FRIED OKRA * BAKED ONIONS WITH OLIVE OIL * GINGERED SWEET POTATOES WITH CRISPY WALNUT CRUST * STUFFED PICKLED PEPPERS * CREAMY COLE SLAW * WILTED COUNTRY SALAD WITH BACON DRESSING * SPINACH SALAD WITH FRESH STRAWBERRIES * SAGE CORNBREAD MADELEINES * BLACK WALNUT BREAD * CORNMEAL PIE * RHUBARB CHESS PIE * GROUND CHERRY PIE * WALNUT BOURBON PIE * BLACKBERRY JAM CAKE WITH SHERRY SAUCE * SCHAUM TORTE * CIDER CAKE WITH DARK CARAMEL NUT FROSTING * DOUBLE PECAN COOKIES

Cornmeal Molasses Pancakes

——— ✳ ———

When people from Virginia and Kentucky came to Missouri to work the rich farmland, one of the recipes they brought with them was for these pancakes, which they ate topped with more molasses and with ham and red-eye gravy.

The pancakes are soft and delicate, with just a hint of the molasses flavor. They resemble an ethereal corn-bread in the shape of a puffy flat cake. Serve them Missouri style, with maple syrup and crisp bacon.

    1   egg, beaten
 1¼   cups buttermilk
    1   tablespoon plus 1 teaspoon dark molasses
   ¼   cup (½ stick) butter, melted
    1   cup unbleached all-purpose flour
   ½   teaspoon salt
   ½   teaspoon baking soda
    2   teaspoons baking powder
   ½   cup yellow cornmeal, preferably stone-
         ground

In a large bowl, combine the egg, buttermilk, molasses, and melted butter. Add the flour, salt, baking soda, and baking powder. Add the cornmeal last, stirring just until combined; the batter will be slightly lumpy. Drop by tablespoonfuls on a hot, greased griddle until bubbles form around the outer edges. Turn and brown on the other side. Serve with butter and sorghum molasses, or maple syrup.

A merry-go-round at a local county fair waits for young riders.

Curried Walnuts

Missourians have a love affair with nuts, possibly because their soil lends itself so well to the raising of them. I was given a jar of these curried nuts as a bread-and-butter gift one time by a dinner guest, and the recipe was tied to the container with a ribbon. The nuts are a bit sweet but not too sweet, and are intriguingly spiced. Serve them with cocktails; they are just right for that. Make them in triple batches and freeze them so you will always have a supply on hand.

1	pound walnut halves
½	cup sugar
2½	tablespoons corn oil
½	teaspoon salt
¼	teaspoon freshly ground pepper
¼	teaspoon cayenne pepper
1¼	teaspoons ground cumin
½	teaspoon ground ginger
½	teaspoon ground coriander
½	teaspoon chili powder
¼	teaspoon ground cloves
¼	teaspoon ground cardamom

Preheat the oven to 325° F. Blanch the walnuts in boiling water for 1 minute and drain well in a colander. While the nuts are still warm, transfer them to a bowl and add the sugar and oil; combine and let stand for 15 minutes.

Arrange the nuts in a single layer on a jelly roll pan and bake for 25 minutes, stirring about every 8 minutes. In a small bowl, combine the remaining ingredients. When the nuts are brown and crispy, remove them from the oven and sprinkle the seasonings over the still-warm nuts. Toss until well coated, then spread the nuts out in a single layer to cool completely. Store in an airtight container.

Fire and Ice Soup

My husband and I were invited to a country house for a summer buffet. The house sat on a hill overlooking meadows dotted with wildflowers—daisies, bouncing-bets, wild sunflowers—a beautiful sight. Our hostess began the meal with this innovative soup, which was the very essence of that August evening.

½	cup chopped onion
1	large garlic clove, chopped
1	3-ounce can peeled green chilies, drained (not pickled)
1	to 2 fresh jalapeño chilies, minced very finely by hand
2	pounds ripe tomatoes, or 1 35-ounce can Italian-style tomatoes, undrained
2	tablespoons olive oil
3	tablespoons all-purpose flour
3	cups Chicken Stock (page 239)
4	teaspoons sugar, or more to taste
1	teaspoon ground cumin
1	teaspoon salt
½	teaspoon ground coriander
½	teaspoon freshly ground pepper
½	cup sour cream
	Chopped fresh parsley or crumbled corn chips, for garnish

In a food processor bowl, chop the onion and garlic together. Add the canned and fresh chilies and combine. (If you like highly seasoned food, use 2 jalapeños; if not, use 1.)

Peel, quarter, and process the tomatoes—you need 1 quart of pulp. In a deep saucepan, heat the olive oil over moderate heat. Add the onion mixture and sauté for 3 minutes or until the onions are soft. Add the flour to the onion mixture and cook 1 minute longer, stirring constantly. Add the tomatoes and stock all at once. Bring to a boil, stirring smooth with a whisk. Add the sugar, cumin, salt, coriander, and pepper. Reduce heat and simmer uncovered for 15 minutes. Cool, then transfer the tomato mixture to a food processor. Add the sour cream and blend. Refrigerate until well chilled. Serve in glass cups or soup bowls and garnish as desired.

NOTE: The fresh tomato pulp can be frozen, as well as the jalapeños, which sometimes are hard to find in the winter. To freeze jalapeños, split them, remove the seeds, then wrap each in a small piece of plastic wrap and freeze in plastic containers. A box of these will add zip to your cuisine all winter long.

Cold Cream of Pear Soup
——— ✳ ———
MAKES 6 SMALL SERVINGS

Canned pears, pickled pears, pear chutney, and pear preserves were popular at the turn of the century, when every house had a pear tree in the backyard along with at least two apple trees. Cold fruit soups were very common among the early German settlers, and so was the combination of milk and anise, served as a milk punch. This is a marvelously subtle soup; the anise is almost undetectable, but it does make the soup special.

- 1 teaspoon plus ⅛ teaspoon anise seed
- 5 whole cloves
- 2½ cups half-and-half
- 1 28-ounce can pears in syrup, undrained
  Sliced fresh pear and mint leaves, for garnish

In a medium saucepan, combine the anise seed, cloves, and half-and-half. Bring barely to a boil; bubbles should just be forming around the edges of the pan. Remove from the heat and let the mixture stand, covered, for 1 hour.

In a food processor or blender, puree the pears with their syrup. When the half-and-half mixture is completely cool, strain it through cheesecloth or a fine sieve into the pureed pears; blend and chill. To serve, pour the soup into colored or tinted bowls, and garnish with 2 or 3 very thin slices of fresh pear, arranged in a fan shape, and a mint leaf.

Lentil Soup
——— ✳ ———
MAKES 16 SERVINGS

On a cold night, this hearty winter soup is most welcome. Serve it with corn muffins and a fruit dessert such as Apple Cheese Crisp (page 230) and ask in a few friends—it's good enough to share, and it yields a generous amount. The extra can be frozen.

- 4 slices bacon, chopped
- 2 cups dried lentils
- 4 quarts homemade Beef Stock (page 239)
- 1 meaty ham bone or 1 cup lean leftover ham, cut up
- 2 celery stalks, chopped
- 1 large onion, chopped
- 4 medium potatoes, peeled and grated
- 1 16-ounce can whole tomatoes
- 2 teaspoons salt
- 1 teaspoon freshly ground pepper
- ½ teaspoon dried thyme
- 2 bay leaves

In a small skillet, sauté the bacon until crisp; drain on paper towels. Rinse the lentils and transfer to a large kettle; add the stock, bacon, and remaining ingredients, cover, and bring to a boil. Skim off the foam, lower the heat, and simmer, partially covered, for 1 hour or until the lentils are tender. Discard the bay leaves. If using a ham bone, lift out and cut off the meat, then return the meat to the soup.

THE BASIC METHOD FOR ✷ K.C. BARBECUE

Kansas City barbecue is a combination of long, slow cooking and smoking, not grilling. The sauce is added either at the very end of the cooking period or served on the side. A dry rub, a mixture of spices and sugar, is always applied to the meat before cooking.

The barbecue unit itself is important — your open grill won't work for this style of cooking. Ideally the unit should have a vented cover and adjustable fire pans or grids. Start the charcoal briquets well in advance of the time you want to start cooking, placing them in a pile to one side of the grill. When they are white with ash on the outside, place chunks of hickory (or any other preferred wood) on top to give the meat that wonderful smoky flavor. Place the meat fat side up on the grill, on the side away from the fire. Close the lid, leaving the vents barely open. Do not open the lid except to add more briquets or wood. The temperature should register around 200° to 250° F. at meat level (you will need a thermometer for this).

A book you might find helpful about barbecuing is *The All-American Barbecue Book,* by Rich Davis and Shifra Stein.

Smoked Brisket, Kansas City Style

— ✻ —

MAKES 12 SERVINGS

A dry rub is a very important step in making authentic Kansas City barbecue. The mopping sauce should be served with the meat, not brushed on it during cooking. This brisket can be served with a knife and fork, but most folks eat it in a sandwich, slathered with the barbecue sauce and with cole slaw on the side.

The rub recipe is from Dr. Rich Davis, who serves first-rate barbecue at his restaurant, the K.C. Masterpiece Barbecue and Grill.

The rub and sauce can be made a week in advance. Store the rub in a small covered container, and the sauce in the refrigerator.

RUB

- ½ cup sugar
- ½ cup ground black pepper
- ½ cup paprika
- ¼ cup chili powder
- ¼ cup salt
- 2 tablespoons garlic powder

Whole untrimmed beef brisket, about 7 pounds (order special)

SAUCE

- 2 tablespoons vegetable oil
- ½ cup chopped onion
- 4 garlic cloves, finely minced
- 2 cups catsup
- ¼ cup molasses
- ¼ cup Worcestershire sauce
- 2 teaspoons prepared horseradish
- 1 bay leaf
- 1 teaspoon chili powder
- 1 teaspoon ground cumin
- ½ teaspoon coarsely ground black pepper
- ½ teaspoon dried basil
- ½ teaspoon dried thyme
- ¼ teaspoon dried rosemary

Prepare a covered grill (see Basic Method, page 156). In a small bowl, combine the sugar, pepper, paprika, chili powder, salt, and garlic powder.

Thoroughly rub the brisket all over with the rub mixture. Cook the meat slowly over indirect heat at about 200° F. for 3 to 4 hours. The internal temperature should be 165° F.

Remove the meat from the grill and wrap tightly in foil, return it to the grill and continue cooking, still at 180 to 200° F. for an additional 3 hours or until tender.

To make the sauce, heat the oil in a medium saucepan. Add the onion and garlic and sauté until the onion is transparent, about 3 to 4 minutes. Add the remaining ingredients and simmer, uncovered, over low heat until the mixture is slightly thickened, about 10 minutes.

To serve, remove the meat from the grill and allow it to stand 10 minutes. Remove the foil and slice very thin. Serve with the warm barbecue sauce.

Hand-forged metal tools create abstract shapes when leaned against a shed.

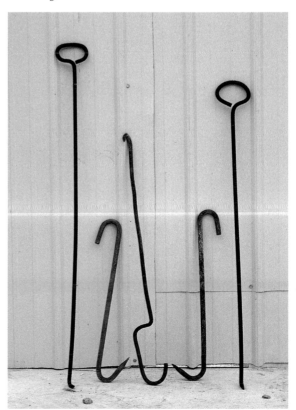

Chicken Fried Steak

This dish has many versions around the country, but generally the meat is round steak, pounded well to break down the tough fibers, then dredged in flour and fried like chicken. In some local butcher shops, you can buy the meat already pounded out, and it is called cubed steak. This is a very easy recipe. Serve it with mashed potatoes, of course.

- 1½ pounds beef round steak, cut in 6 slices
- ½ cup all-purpose flour
- ½ teaspoon salt
- ½ teaspoon ground pepper
- ¾ teaspoon Midwestern Spice Blend (page 243)
- 3 tablespoons vegetable oil, or a bit more
- 1 cup Beef Stock (page 239) or water, approximately
- ¼ cup chopped onion
  Parsley, for garnish

Pound the round steak slices to ¼-inch thickness with a meat mallet (mine is very old, made of metal, with sharp little teeth—a very handy tool, but you could use your rolling pin). Preheat an electric frying pan (or skillet) to 325–350° F.

On a large piece of wax paper, combine the flour, salt, pepper, and spice blend and dredge the meat in the mixture. Add the oil to the skillet and heat.

Sear the steak on both sides, turning with tongs; it will take about 10 minutes. Add the stock or water and onion, cover tightly, lower heat, and simmer until the meat is very tender, about 30 to 45 minutes. Check periodically and add more liquid if necessary—the flour will absorb quite a bit of it. Garnish with parsley.

Veal Ham Loaf with Sour Cream Sauce

Hermann, Missouri, is home to many German families, the descendents of a group of German immigrants who were disgruntled by the English influence in Philadelphia and relocated en masse to Hermann, in part because it resembled the Rhine River Valley. Just over two hundred people arrived in the spring of 1838, and within a year they had built a tidy town of brick and frame buildings. Today, more than a hundred of those buildings are listed on the National Register and the entire town is a National Historic Site.

This sprightly veal loaf from a Hermann church cookbook is enlivened with horseradish and a sour cream and mushroom sauce.

VEAL LOAF
- 2½ pounds ground veal
- ½ pound ground ham
- ½ teaspoon salt
- ½ teaspoon freshly ground pepper
- ¼ cup catsup
- ¼ cup prepared horseradish
- 1 cup cracker crumbs
- ½ green bell pepper, diced
- 1 medium onion, diced
- 1 egg, beaten
- 1 cup chopped fresh mushrooms

SOUR CREAM SAUCE
- ½ cup chopped fresh mushrooms
- 1 tablespoon butter
- 1 tablespoon all-purpose flour
- 2 tablespoons minced fresh parsley
- 1 cup sour cream
- ½ teaspoon sweet paprika
- ½ teaspoon salt
- ¼ teaspoon freshly ground pepper

Preheat the oven to 350° F. In a large bowl, combine the loaf ingredients and mix thoroughly, using your hands if necessary. Form the mixture into a loaf and place in a 9 x 13-inch pan. Bake uncovered for 1 hour. Remove from the oven, drain off the drippings (reserving 2 tablespoons for sauce), and allow to sit for 10 minutes before slicing.

While the loaf rests, sauté the ½ cup mushrooms in the reserved drippings in a small saucepan over medium-high heat until cooked, about 3 to 5 minutes. In a small bowl, rub the butter and flour together to make a smooth paste. Add the butter-flour mixture to the mushrooms and cook and stir until the sauce bubbles up in the center of the pan, about 3 minutes. Add the rest of the ingredients, lower the heat, and cook for about 5 minutes, or until the mixture is heated through and thickened, but not boiling. Ladle a few tablespoons of sauce over each slice of loaf, passing the rest separately in a sauceboat.

Midwestern Fried Chicken

✶

MAKES 4 SERVINGS

Fried chicken in the Midwest—how shall I describe it? It is not french fried, nor is it sautéed and finished off in a cooking liquid. Midwestern fried chicken is pan fried and always has a crust, half crunchy, half tender.

For preparing chicken, some cooks still swear by cast-iron skillets, but I have graduated to an electric fry pan; being able to control the temperature during the long frying period is a boon, I think.

The golden brown crispy crust of this recipe is well seasoned, with just a hint of basil and thyme. Chilling the chicken first in ice and water (an old professional barbecuer's trick), keeps the chicken moist and juicy.

In the summer, fried chicken is served with Creamy Potato Salad (page 83), but in the cooler months the cook might fix gravy from the pan drippings and serve it over mashed potatoes or Hot Biscuits (page 4).

1 3-pound frying chicken, cut into 8 serving pieces
1 egg
⅔ cup water
1¼ cups vegetable oil
¾ cup all-purpose flour
2 teaspoons salt
2 teaspoons freshly ground black pepper
½ teaspoon cayenne pepper
½ teaspoon garlic powder
½ teaspoon onion powder
½ teaspoon dried basil
¼ teaspoon dried thyme
2 cups milk

Wash the chicken and place in a large glass bowl with lots of ice. Add water to cover and allow to stand for 1 hour. Drain and pat dry.

In a small bowl, beat the egg, water, and ¼ cup of the vegetable oil with a rotary beater or whisk. In a paper sack, combine the flour with the rest of the dry ingredients. Set aside 2 tablespoons of the flour mixture for the gravy. Heat the remaining cup of oil in a 12-inch skillet or an electric fry pan set to 350° F.

Dip each piece of chicken in the egg mixture and then shake 2 or 3 pieces at a time in the flour mixture. Fry the chicken, uncovered, for 7 minutes on one side; using tongs, turn over and cook 7 minutes more. Lower the heat to 300° F., cover, and cook 10 minutes longer. Remove with tongs to a heated platter lined with paper towels.

To make the gravy, drain off all but 2 tablespoons of the pan drippings in the skillet. Stir in the reserved flour and cook, whisking, over medium-low heat until the mixture bubbles up and thickens, about 2 to 3 minutes. Add the milk all at once and continue whisking and cooking until the mixture thickens. Lower the heat and simmer for 10 minutes. Transfer to a gravy boat. Serve chicken immediately or cool to room temperature and serve within an hour or two.

Mississippi Catfish

✱
MAKES 6 TO 8 SERVINGS

The Mississippi River winds up through the Midwest, and above it, little towns perch on the rocky bluffs. The river shore is an ideal place for throwing out a line and bringing in one of the river's famous and succulent catfish. Catfish farms are also common, and some connoisseurs prefer the farm product to the river variety, insisting the river water can give the fish a musky taste.

Dip the filleted catfish into this spicy batter and sauté them until golden brown. Serve with Tartar Sauce (page 240).

Every visitor to Hannibal makes a pilgrimage to Tom Sawyer's Fence. OPPOSITE: *Even a frothy mug of root beer advertising a local eatery makes reference to Hannibal's favorite son, and a statue pays tribute to Twain's memorable characters.*

1½ cups yellow cornmeal
1 teaspoon garlic powder
1 teaspoon celery salt
½ teaspoon cayenne pepper
½ teaspoon freshly ground black pepper
¼ teaspoon grated nutmeg
3 eggs
1½ cups milk
1 teaspoon fresh lemon juice
   Dash of Worcestershire sauce
12 catfish fillets, each about 6 ounces
   Butter and vegetable oil

In a pie pan, combine the cornmeal and seasonings. In a shallow bowl, beat the eggs, milk, lemon juice, and Worcestershire.

Pat the fillets dry with paper toweling. Dip each fillet first in the egg mixture, then in the cornmeal mixture, coating well. In a heavy skillet, heat about 2 tablespoons butter and 2 tablespoons of oil until hot. Sauté the fish on both sides, but don't crowd the skillet. Repeat until all the fish is fried, adding more oil and butter as you go.

TOM SAWYER'S FENCE
HERE STOOD THE BOARD
FENCE WHICH TOM SAWYER
PERSUADED HIS GANG TO
PAY HIM FOR THE PRIVILEGE
OF WHITEWASHING. TOM
SAT BY AND SAW THAT IT
WAS WELL DONE.

Fried Okra

—— ✳ ——

MAKES 6 SERVINGS

Among all the dishes we associate with the South, okra is one of the first that springs to mind. It came to the United States from the Congo regions of Africa, via the West Indies.

Okra dipped in cornmeal and fried is considered a sublime dish by folks who've been raised close to the Southern states. Nathalie Dupree, author of New Southern Cooking, *writes, "Southern cooking is primarily home cooking, not chef's art." Certainly that doesn't make it any less delectable for most of us. In this recipe of hers, she suggests that fried okra should be served immediately after it is prepared.*

    2 pounds okra
    ½ cup yellow cornmeal
    ½ cup all-purpose flour
    2 teaspoons salt
    2 cups peanut oil
       Salt
       Freshly ground pepper

Wash and drain the okra. Cut off the caps on the stem ends and cut the okra into ¼-inch pieces. In a bowl combine the cornmeal, flour, and salt; add half the okra and toss. Spread out on a flat surface to dry for a few minutes, then toss in the cornmeal and flour again. Repeat with remaining okra.

Meanwhile, pour in enough oil to reach halfway up the side of a cast-iron skillet or frying pan and heat. Test to be sure the oil is hot enough by adding a piece of okra; it should sizzle. Add the okra in batches, leaving enough room in the pan to turn the okra without layering it. Brown lightly on both sides. Resist the temptation to turn the okra too soon—if you stir too much, the cornmeal will fall to the bottom of the pan and burn. When browned and crisp on both sides, in about 3 to 4 minutes, transfer the okra to paper towels. If there is a great deal of burnt coating in the pan, pour out the oil and wipe the bottom of the pan clean. Pour the oil back into the pan and repeat with the remaining okra. Season with salt and pepper.

Like all the Midwestern states, Missouri has a history filled with strong, resourceful and independent women. Laura Ingalls Wilder wrote nine of her books at her farm in Mansfield, including the beloved *Little House on the Prairie.* Hannibal native Margaret Tobin Brown was nicknamed the "Unsinkable Molly Brown" after surviving the sinking of the *Titanic.* Wearing buckskins and spurs, Martha Canary, alias Calamity Jane, rode as a U.S. Army scout during the 1872 Sioux Indian conflict and was famous for her vocabulary as well as her shooting skills. Nor should we forget Carry Nation, the passionate and determined hatchet-wielding prohibitionist. Her monument in the Belton cemetery bears the understated inscription: "She hath done what she could."

Baked Onions with Olive Oil

———— ✳ ————

MAKES 1 SERVING

The longer I cook, the more I appreciate that the simplest things are best. These onions are a case in point. Quick to prepare, they are a bit sweet but with a touch of tartness from the lemon juice. They are nice to look at too, and can also be used as a garnish. The recipe is for a single onion, which will serve one person as a vegetable, or two as a garnish. You can prepare any number you want by using these proportions.

    1   medium onion, peeled and halved
    ½   teaspoon olive oil or butter
    ½   teaspoon brown sugar
        Salt, pepper, and paprika to taste
    ¼   teaspoon lemon juice
        Minced fresh parsley or chervil, for garnish

Preheat the oven to 350° F. Place the onion halves, cut side up, in a greased flat baking dish. Top with the olive oil or butter and the brown sugar, salt, pepper, and paprika, and bake for 1 hour, or until the onion is tender in the center and deep golden brown. Remove from the oven and drizzle the lemon juice over the onion halves.

Gingered Sweet Potatoes with Crispy Walnut Crust

———— ✳ ————

MAKES 8 TO 10 SERVINGS

This recipe came from a Springfield church cookbook, and the crystallized ginger and pralinelike topping show the town's links with Southern cookery. Use a mixture of half English walnuts and half black walnuts; black walnuts are so distinctively flavored that a whole cup of them overwhelms the delicacy of the dish.

    3   large sweet potatoes
    1   cup granulated sugar
    2   eggs, lightly beaten
    10   tablespoons (1¼ sticks) butter
    1½   teaspoons grated orange rind
    ½   teaspoon ground ginger
    ¼   teaspoon salt
    ¼   teaspoon freshly ground pepper
    1   tablespoon finely minced crystallized ginger
    ¼   cup all-purpose flour
    ½   cup English walnuts
    ½   cup black walnuts
    ¾   cup dark brown sugar

Bake the potatoes at 425° F. for 1 hour, then turn the heat down to 350° F. (see Note). Scoop out the potato flesh and place in the bowl of a food processor; puree until smooth. In a large mixer bowl, combine the sweet potato puree, granulated sugar, eggs, 4 tablespoons of the butter, orange rind, ground ginger, salt, pepper, and crystallized ginger. Blend well and spread in a greased 13 x 9-inch flat baking dish.

In a small bowl, combine the flour, nuts, remaining 6 tablespoons of butter and the brown sugar. Sprinkle over the potato mixture and bake for 1 hour, or until the top is browned and puffs slightly.

NOTE: If using a glass dish, reduce baking temperature to 325° F.

Stuffed Pickled Peppers
———— * ————

MAKES ABOUT 6 QUARTS

During the Victorian era, pickled peppers were one of the fancier relishes found on dinner tables, though they had been on the food scene long before that. They are attractive—whole green or red bell peppers (the red ones are prettier, I think) stuffed with spiced cabbage slaw—and one of them provides a generous amount of relish, to be sure. Many cooks cut them in half before serving them on a platter. They were made in crocks in those early days, and the instructions of one recipe in my files begins "Clean 50 peppers . . ."

This is a more manageable recipe and it's a good sweet-and-sour meat accompaniment, nicely spiced. The peppers must soak overnight in a salt brine before you stuff them. Because they are processed, you must peel off the outer skin before serving. Be sure the peppers will fit into wide-mouthed canning jars.

12	medium green or red bell peppers
1	cup pickling salt (don't use iodized)
6 to 7	cups shredded green cabbage
2¼	cups sugar, or more as needed to taste
2	tablespoons mustard seed
1	tablespoon celery seed
1	teaspoon ground pepper
½	teaspoon salt
18	cinnamon sticks
24	whole cloves
6	cups cider vinegar
3	cups water

On the day before canning, cut the top from stem end of each pepper, reserving the end. Remove the seeds and membranes and put peppers and stem ends in a large bowl; then add the pickling salt and enough water to cover the peppers. Cover and let stand overnight in a cool place; they don't need to be refrigerated.

Drain the peppers, rinse, and drain again, turning the peppers upside down on paper towels. In a large mixing bowl, combine the cabbage, remaining salt, ¾ cup of the sugar, the mustard seed, celery seed, and ground pepper; mix well. Squeeze the water out of the mixture with your hands and press very firmly into the pepper shells. Replace the tops of the peppers and fasten with toothpicks. (Some cooks used to sew these shut with coarse thread, but I wouldn't go that far!) Pack into hot wide-mouthed quart jars, leaving ¼-inch headspace. You will get 2 peppers into each quart jar. Add 3 cinnamon sticks and 4 cloves to each jar.

In a large saucepan, combine the vinegar, water, and remaining 1½ cups sugar and bring to a boil; taste and adjust sweetening. Pour the hot liquid over the peppers, leaving a ½-inch headspace. Remove air bubbles by running a knife down the inside of the jar (don't poke the peppers). Adjust the caps. Process for 15 minutes in a hot-water bath. Remove to a rack to cool, then store in a cool place for 2 weeks before using.

OVERLEAF: "The Gateway to the West," silhouetted against a St. Louis sunset.

Creamy Cole Slaw

——— ✲ ———

MAKES 5 TO 6 SERVINGS

In Missouri, as it is nearly everywhere in the Midwest, cole slaw is mostly creamy style. It is generally made with sweetened mayonnaise, but there is a school of slaw makers who still prepare a boiled dressing, the early forerunner of commercial bottled salad dressings like Miracle Whip. It is a tradition worth reviving. Laced with dry mustard, boiled dressing is good on potato salad; thinned with additional cream, it can also be served with roast pork, ham, or fish.

BOILED DRESSING

  2 eggs
  3 tablespoons sugar
1½ tablespoons all-purpose flour
1¼ teaspoons salt
 ½ teaspoon dry mustard
 ¼ cup cider vinegar
 ¼ cup water
  1 tablespoon butter or olive oil
  3 tablespoons light cream or milk

COLE SLAW

  6 cups shredded green cabbage (about 1¾ pounds)
  1 large carrot, shredded (about ¾ cup)
  1 celery stalk, finely chopped (about ½ cup)
  1 small onion, finely chopped (about ¼ cup)
 ½ green bell pepper, finely chopped (about ½ cup)
 ¼ cup minced fresh parsley
1½ teaspoons celery seed
  1 teaspoon mustard seed
 ½ teaspoon coarsely ground pepper

In a small saucepan, beat the eggs thoroughly; add the sugar, flour, salt, and mustard. Combine the vinegar and water and beat into the egg mixture, then add the butter or olive oil, and cook over low heat, stirring constantly, until thick, about 5 to 8 minutes. The mixture will become very lumpy; not to worry—just beat it until it is smooth. When very thick, remove from the heat and add the cream or milk. Cool. (This can be made a day in advance and refrigerated.)

In a large bowl, combine the vegetables and seasonings. Add the cooled dressing and toss lightly to combine.

NOTE: If you prefer not to make the boiled dressing, you can substitute the following: 1 cup commercial mayonnaise, ½ cup sugar, and ¼ cup cider vinegar; combine, pour over the slaw ingredients, and toss.

Wilted Country Salad with Bacon Dressing

——— ✲ ———

MAKES 4 TO 6 SERVINGS

Old-fashioned? You bet. Country restaurants still serve this salad, and of course it can easily be made at home. Use firm loose-head lettuce such as Bibb and curly endive (chicory) for this dish. Serve it in a wooden bowl to be authentic. By adding hard-cooked eggs, the traditional garnish, you practically have a whole meal.

  2 cups torn Bibb lettuce
  2 cups torn spinach leaves
  2 cups torn curly endive (chicory) leaves
  6 slices bacon, diced
  2 eggs, beaten
 ½ cup distilled white vinegar
 ½ cup sugar
 ½ cup water
  2 hard-cooked eggs, peeled, sliced, and coarsely crumbled

Wash and dry the salad greens and place in a large wooden bowl. Cover with a tea towel and refrigerate until needed.

In a medium skillet, sauté the bacon until crisp and golden brown; do not drain. In a small bowl, whisk together the beaten eggs, vinegar, sugar, and water; add to the bacon and drippings, reduce temperature, and cook, stirring continually, until thickened. Pour the hot mixture over the greens and cover with a skillet lid until the greens are a bit wilted, about 3 minutes. Toss lightly. Top with the crumbled hard-cooked egg.

Spinach Salad with Fresh Strawberries

from the Fedora Café and Bar

—✳—

MAKES 6 SERVINGS

As in all Midwestern states, strawberries are much-loved in Missouri. Though the favorite way to eat the berries is on shortcake or in jam, they do appear in unexpected places, such as in this spinach salad. They hold their own with the crisp green spinach, and the cooked poppy-seed dressing is just right for it. The recipe is from the Fedora Café and Bar in St. Louis.

POPPY SEED DRESSING

- 1 cup sugar
- 1½ teaspoons dry mustard
- 1½ teaspoons coarse salt
- ½ cup cider vinegar
- 1 cup plus 3 tablespoons vegetable oil
- 1½ teaspoons poppy seeds

SALAD

- ¼ cup pecans
- ⅛ teaspoon ground cinnamon
- 1 pound fresh spinach, well washed, with tough stems removed
- 1 red onion, peeled
- 24 fresh strawberries, quartered
- Additional poppy seeds, for garnish

In the top of a double boiler, combine the sugar, mustard, salt, and vinegar. Cook over hot water until the sugar is dissolved, then transfer to a blender. With the motor running, slowly add the oil to thicken. Add the poppy seeds and blend. Refrigerate until needed.

Arrange the pecans on a baking sheet and sprinkle with the cinnamon. Bake for approximately 5 minutes, or until toasted and fragrant. Cool.

Tear the spinach into bite-size pieces and arrange on 6 chilled plates. Slice the onion paper thin, separate into rings, and scatter over the spinach. Divide the strawberries equally among the salads and top with the toasted pecans. Drizzle dressing over all and sprinkle with additional poppy seeds if desired.

Sage Cornbread Madeleines

—✳—

MAKES 30 MADELEINES

French madeleine cookie tins are so attractive that it is nice to use them for things other than cookies. In Missouri, where cornbread is one of the classic hot breads, bakers are always looking for new ways to present it. These sage-flavored cornbreads are a novel adaptation of an old favorite and a perfect addition to the roll basket as an accompaniment to soups and salads.

- 1¼ cups yellow cornmeal
- ½ cup all-purpose flour
- 2 tablespoons sugar
- 1 tablespoon baking powder
- 1¼ teaspoons powdered sage
- 1 teaspoon salt
- ¼ teaspoon ground white pepper
- 2 eggs
- 3 tablespoons corn oil
- ¾ cup buttermilk, at room temperature

In a large mixing bowl, whisk together the cornmeal, flour, sugar, baking powder, sage, salt, and white pepper. In a small bowl, beat the eggs lightly, then blend in the the oil and buttermilk.

Make a well in the dry ingredients and pour in the egg mixture. Blend by hand until well combined, then allow the mixture to stand for 10 minutes. Preheat the oven to 375° F.

Grease the madeleine molds and place 1 tablespoon of batter in each mold. Bake for 9 to 11 minutes, or until the cornmeal madeleine is puffed and shrinks away from the side of the pan. Tip out onto a paper-lined rack and allow to cool.

NOTE: The madeleines can be made in advance, frozen, and then reheated before serving.

Black Walnut Bread

MAKES 2 LOAVES

With black walnuts being one of the state's important crops, it is to be expected that Missourans would have devised many wonderful ways to showcase them. Bernard Clayton, the guru of bread bakers and author of the best-selling The Complete Book of Breads, *adapted this one from a Missouri semiquin-centennial cookbook. The combination of onions and black walnuts gives this bread an almost smoky taste. It is an unforgettable bread that is delicious toasted. The aroma of the nuts and onion baking in the loaves will arouse appetites, but fend everyone off until the bread has cooled.*

1 package active dry yeast
2 teaspoons salt
5 to 6 cups bread flour, approximately
2 cups hot milk (120–130° F.)
½ cup (1 stick) butter, at room temperature
¾ cup minced onion
1 cup chopped black walnuts
   Cornmeal
1 egg, beaten with 1 tablespoon milk

In a large mixing bowl blend the yeast, salt, and 2 cups of the flour. Pour in the hot milk and stir to make a light batter. Add the butter. Stir vigorously with a wooden spoon—or with a mixer's flat beater attachment—until the butter has been absorbed into the batter. Add the remaining flour, ½ cup at a time, stirring all the while with a wooden spoon until the dough forms a mass that can be lifted from the bowl and placed on a floured work surface. (The dough may be left in the mixer bowl if the kneading is to be done with the dough hook.)

If kneading by hand, knead the dough with a strong push-turn-fold motion for 8 minutes, breaking the kneading rhythm occasionally by lifting the dough and sending it crashing down onto the work surface to aid in the formation of gluten. If using a mixer, knead with the mixer dough hook for 8 minutes. If the dough is sticky, sprinkle liberally with flour. As it is kneaded it will become smooth and elastic.

Drop the kneaded dough into a greased bowl, cover with plastic wrap, and set aside at room temperature to double in volume, about 1½ hours.

While the dough is rising, combine the onion and walnuts in a small bowl and sprinkle with a little flour to keep the bits separate.

Place the dough on a floured work surface and knead for a moment or so to collapse the dough. Push the dough into a flat shape. Spread half the onion-nut mixture over the surface of the dough, and turn in the edges over the middle of the dough to completely cover the onion and nut pieces. Knead and work the dough until the onion and nuts disappear. Flatten the dough again and spread the balance of the mixture over it. Knead and work the dough until the pieces are distributed evenly throughout the dough.

Cover the dough with a towel or plastic wrap and let rest for 10 to 15 minutes to relax the dough.

Grease a baking sheet and sprinkle with cornmeal, or use a nonstick baking sheet. Cut the dough into 2 equal pieces. Shape each into a ball and place on the baking sheet. (Or these can be baked in 2 greased 9 x 5 x 3-inch loaf pans.) Press to flatten slightly, and cut a design on the top with a sharp knife.

Cover the loaves with plastic wrap or a towel and let rise for about 1 hour and 15 minutes, or until the dough has nearly doubled in volume.

Preheat the oven to 375° F. 15 to 20 minutes before baking.

Remove the covering from the dough and brush with the egg glaze. Bake until the crust is a golden brown and the loaf sounds hard and hollow when it is turned over and thumped with a forefinger, about 30 to 40 minutes. Allow the bread to cool before serving.

*TOP: **Black walnuts in the September sunshine, still in their green husks, resemble exotic fruit.** BOTTOM: **Sunlight refracting off the spray of these giant irrigation systems creates a rainbow effect.***

Cornmeal Pie

*

The popularity of Southern chess-type pies crosses all state boundaries, though most of them are found in the southern Midwestern states, instead of the northern ones. It's no wonder this particular recipe traveled so far. It has just a little bit of cornmeal in it, hence its name. The texture is a tad grainy, unexpected, and altogether nice.

Dough for 9-inch pastry shell (½ recipe Never-Fail Pie Crust, page 244)
1   cup brown sugar minus 2 tablespoons
1   cup granulated sugar minus 2 tablespoons
2   tablespoons all-purpose flour
1   tablespoon yellow cornmeal
¼   teaspoon salt
2   eggs
¼   cup (½ stick) butter, melted
½   cup evaporated milk
1   teaspoon vanilla extract
¾   cup chopped hickory or other nuts
¼   cup shredded coconut

Preheat the oven to 350° F. Roll out the dough on a floured surface and fit into a 9-inch pie pan. In a large bowl, combine the sugars, flour, cornmeal, and salt; set aside. In a mixer bowl, combine the eggs, butter, milk, and vanilla until just mixed—don't let too many bubbles form. Combine with the sugar mixture and blend until smooth. Pour into the pastry shell and sprinkle the top with the nuts and coconut. Bake for 35 minutes, or until lightly puffed and golden brown. Remove to a rack to cool.

Rhubarb Chess Pie

*

A chess pie is a dessert that traveled north and westward; still, you are more apt to find them in states like Missouri and Ohio, which are closer to the Mason-Dixon line. The origin of the name is cloudy, but a plausible story is that because the pie is so sweet, it was always stored in a tall wooden cabinet with pierced-tin doors to keep out of the way of children and insects. These cabinets were sometimes called pie chests. "Keep away from the pie chess', you kids." I hear it plainly, don't you?

2   cups rhubarb, cut in ½-inch cubes
    8-inch pastry shell (½ recipe Never-Fail Pie Crust, page 244)
1¼ cups sugar
4   tablespoons (½ stick) butter, softened
3   eggs
1   tablespoon cider vinegar
1   teaspoon vanilla extract
    Red food coloring (optional)
    Ground cinnamon

Preheat the oven to 350° F. Place the rhubarb in the pie shell. In a medium bowl, combine the sugar and butter. In a small bowl, beat the eggs slightly, then add the vinegar and vanilla. Add to the sugar mixture and mix well. Tint with a bit of red food coloring, if desired. Pour over the rhubarb and sprinkle cinnamon liberally over the top. Bake for 50 to 60 minutes or until the pie is golden—it will puff slightly. Cool and serve with a dip of ice cream on the top.

Ground Cherry Pie

I have had several long-distance phone calls requesting this old recipe, so it is obviously time to record it.

Ground cherries grow wild on low bushy plants along uncut country roadsides and in uncultivated fields. They are especially prolific in the Mississippi Valley.

The fruit goes by several regional names: husk tomatoes, chew cherries, strawberry tomatoes, or winter cherries. The ground cherry plant is the first cousin to the ornamental Japanese lantern, which it resembles. The firm fruit, which is nestled in a husk, is about the size of a cherry and looks like a green tomato, though the color varies from green to yellow to red. To me, it also resembles a tiny Mexican tomatilla.

Its flavor has been likened to tomatoes and strawberries, and the fruit is most commonly used in pie, though I have also eaten it in chili sauce and jam. I see ground cherries occasionally at farmer's markets around the country.

Pastry for a 2-crust 9-inch pie (½ recipe
   Never-Fail Pie Crust, page 244)
3 tablespoons quick-cooking tapioca
½ cup granulated sugar
½ cup brown sugar
¾ teaspoon almond extract
½ teaspoon grated nutmeg
   Dash of salt
2½ cups husked ground cherries
2 tablespoons (¼ stick) butter

Line a 9-inch pie pan with pastry and set aside. Preheat the oven to 400° F. In a medium bowl, combine the tapioca, sugars, almond extract, nutmeg, and salt. Sprinkle half the mixture in the bottom of the pastry shell and top with the cherries. Sprinkle the remainder of the sugar mixture over the cherries and dot with the butter. Top with a lattice-designed or other decorative top crust.

Bake for 10 minutes, then lower the heat to 350° F. and bake about 45 to 50 minutes longer, or until the crust is deep golden and the juices in the pie are bubbling up in the center. Cool before cutting.

Walnut Bourbon Pie

Black walnut trees flourish in Missouri, the nuts planted by squirrels, a casual but effective gardening technique. Black walnuts have a well-deserved reputation for being tough to crack—a hammer and a strong arm are necessary. Their flavor is richer and tangier than English walnuts, so they add real personality to any dish.

This pie has Southern roots, and the chocolate and bourbon are a terrific combination.

2 ounces (2 squares) unsweetened chocolate
1 cup sugar
1 cup light corn syrup
3 tablespoons bourbon
4 tablespoons (½ stick) butter
1 teaspoon vanilla extract
   Pinch of salt
3 eggs, lightly beaten
1½ cups black walnut halves and pieces
   10-inch pastry shell (¾ recipe Never-Fail
      Pie Crust, page 244)
   Whipped cream or ice cream (optional)

Preheat the oven to 375° F. In a medium saucepan melt the chocolate, sugar, corn syrup, bourbon, butter, vanilla, and salt over low heat. Let the mixture cool, then stir in the eggs. Place the nuts in the pie shell and pour the chocolate mixture over them. Bake for 15 minutes, then reduce the heat to 325° F. and bake 30 to 40 minutes longer; the filling will still be a bit shaky, but deep golden brown. Cool to room temperature. Serve plain or with whipped cream or ice cream, if desired.

Blackberry Jam Cake with Sherry Sauce

—— ✱ ——

MAKES 6 TO 8 SERVINGS

The Germans settling in Hermann brought with them their love and knowledge of wine. Between 1850 and 1900 they developed a successful wine industry, making the state the nation's second largest producer of wine and third largest supplier of wine in the world. Then came Prohibition. That was the end of the wine for a while—for everyone. The pragmatic citizens turned the wine cellars into caves for growing mushrooms. Today, the industry has come full circle, and wineries are once again operating in Hermann.

Wine was a common flavoring in those early years, and this sherry sauce is a very old recipe. Serve it warm over the cake for a most original and indulgent dessert.

CAKE
- ½ cup (1 stick) butter, softened
- ⅔ cup sugar
- ⅔ cup blackberry jam
- ½ teaspoon grated nutmeg
- ½ teaspoon baking soda
- 1 tablespoon cold water
- 2 tablespoons sour cream or milk
- 2 eggs, beaten
- 1 cup all-purpose flour
- ⅔ cup raisins mixed with 1 tablespoon flour

SHERRY SAUCE
- 1 egg
- 1 cup sugar
- ½ cup (1 stick) butter
- Pinch of salt
- ¼ teaspoon vanilla extract
- ½ cup sweet sherry

Preheat the oven to 350° F. In a large bowl, beat the butter until creamy with a wooden spoon. Add the sugar and continue beating until light and fluffy. Beat in the jam and nutmeg. In a small bowl, dissolve the baking soda in cold water. Add the sour cream and eggs and mix completely. Stir this into the jam mixture. Add the flour and beat until thoroughly mixed. Lightly stir in the raisins. Pour the mixture into a buttered 9-inch square pan and bake for 35 to 40 minutes, or until golden and the top springs back when touched with your finger. Cool on a rack.

While the cake bakes, cream the egg, sugar, butter, and salt for the sauce in a small saucepan. Over low heat, stir and cook the mixture until thick, about 5 minutes. Add the vanilla and sherry and continue cooking for about 3 minutes more. If the sauce appears too thick, add more sherry.

*LEFT: **Ripening grapes with taffeta-like leaves flourish in Missouri.** RIGHT: **A whimsical piece of folk art enhances a country garden.***

Schaum Torte

German in background, this voluptuous dessert is very similar to a large meringue, or to Australia's Pavlova. This torte is usually served with fresh strawberries, peaches, or raspberries, or just with sweetened whipped cream. You will find it most attractive and quick to prepare. The meringue has a thin crisp layer on top, and inside it is very soft, but it holds its shape when cut. It can be refrigerated; the top crust remains crisp. The meringue will "weep" a tiny bit, but that is the nature of meringues and the fruit sauce will cover it.

6 egg whites, at room temperature
1 teaspoon vanilla extract
1 teaspoon cider vinegar
¼ teaspoon salt
2 cups superfine sugar (see Note)
   Lightly sweetened fresh fruit (strawberries, raspberries, etc.)

Preheat the oven to 225° F. Place the egg whites, vanilla, vinegar, and salt in a large mixer bowl; beat first on medium speed, then increase the speed to high. As soft peaks form, gradually add the sugar and continue beating until the whites become very thick and glossy and stiff peaks form.

Transfer to a greased and floured 9-inch springform pan and, with a spatula, smooth the top. Bake for 1 hour. The torte will double in size during baking, but will fall as it cools—this is perfectly all right. When completely cool, remove the springform ring, cut the torte into wedges, and serve with your choice of fresh fruits.

NOTE: Superfine sugar is sometimes called bar sugar. It dissolves instantly and is ideal for desserts using egg whites. It has a tendency to absorb moisture and form little lumps; nothing serious—just whiz them out in your food processor, then proceed with the recipe.

Cider Cake with Dark Caramel Nut Frosting

Both Red and Golden Delicious apples were developed by Stark Brothers Nursery, founded in Missouri in 1816, and the original pioneer log cabin of the first James Stark remains on the nursery grounds. By grafting scions (cuttings) that he had brought with him from Kentucky onto wild crabapple trees, James Stark grew the first cultivated fruit west of the Mississippi. Stark Brothers is now the largest nursery in the world (see Source List).

Cider was an important commodity for the settlers, and they used it in many ways, including in this cake. It is a nice plump cake with a delicate texture and decided cider flavor. The frosting is a bit like chewy homemade caramels with nuts.

CAKE

1 cup (2 sticks) butter, at room temperature
2 cups granulated sugar
3 eggs, separated
3½ cups all-purpose flour
1 teaspoon baking soda
1 teaspoon baking powder
½ teaspoon salt
½ teaspoon ground cloves
½ teaspoon ground cinnamon
1 cup cider

CARAMEL FROSTING

1 cup dark brown sugar
⅓ cup light cream or milk
½ cup (1 stick) butter
½ cup chopped pecans
1 teaspoon vanilla extract
   Pinch of salt

In Missouri, native wild pecans are harvested from natural groves of trees. One of the largest groves is close to the town of Nevada, halfway between Joplin and Kansas City.

Missouri wild nuts have a shorter growing season than cultivated Southern pecans. They have a higher oil content as well, and tend to be more plump and moist.

To harvest the nuts, workers clamp mechanical shakers around the tree trunks. Hydraulic power from a nearby tractor sends a tremendous vibration up the tree, and off fall the nuts. They can be picked up by hand, but the large growers have machines that sweep the pecans off the ground. Still, half the nuts in Missouri—and there are 5,640 acres of trees—are harvested by hand. These are sold mainly at local fruit stands and produce markets (see Source List).

Cracked nuts, sold in bags, are a favorite Missouri TV snack and are eaten as casually as the rest of the country munches popcorn.

Preheat the oven to 350° F. In a large mixer bowl, cream the butter and sugar for 3 minutes. In a small bowl, beat the egg yolks thoroughly, and add to the butter mixture. Sift together the flour, baking soda, baking powder, salt, cloves, and cinnamon. Add this to the butter mixture alternately with the cider, beginning and ending with the flour.

In a large mixer bowl, beat the egg whites until stiff and fold into the batter with a rubber spatula. Pour the batter into a greased 9 x 13-inch pan and bake for 30 minutes, or until cake just shrinks away from the sides of the pan and the top springs back when touched with your finger.

While the cake is baking, prepare the frosting. In a small saucepan, combine the brown sugar, cream, and butter. Bring the mixture to a boil over medium heat and cook for 5 minutes, whisking all the time. Lower the heat if necessary. Stir in the nuts and vanilla and keep warm.

As soon as the cake is removed from the oven, pour the warm caramel over the top. Let the cake cool in the pan before cutting into squares and serving.

Double Pecan Cookies

✳

MAKES 3 DOZEN COOKIES

These elegant little cookies, a Missouri specialty, are a bit crisp, quite thin, and have an intense pecan flavor.

- ½ pound pecans
- 1 cup brown sugar, well packed
- ⅛ teaspoon salt
- 1 egg white
- 1 teaspoon vanilla extract
- Few drops of pecan extract (optional)
- 36 pecan halves

Preheat the oven to 350° F. Place half the pecans in a food processor bowl and pulse until finely ground; transfer the ground nuts to a medium mixing bowl. Repeat with the remaining pecans. Add the brown sugar, salt, egg white, and extracts. Stir well. Form the dough into large marble-size balls and place on a large greased baking sheet. Don't crowd them—12 to a sheet is plenty. Press a pecan half into each one. Bake for about 8 or 9 minutes, or until cookies are a deep golden brown. Let the cookies stand on the sheet for 3 minutes, then transfer with a spatula to a wire rack to cool.

And then far away, a mile or more on the opposite side of the valley, I saw a small house with an enormous cupolaed barn. It was already twilight and the lower valley was the ice-blue color of a shadowed winter landscape at dusk and the black, bare trees on the ridge tops were tinted with the last pink light of the winter sunset. There were already lozenges of light in the windows of the distant house. . . . I thought, "This is the place."

On that late winter afternoon, one had a curious sense of being sheltered from the winter winds, from the snow, from the buffetings and storms of the outside world.

LOUIS BROMFIELD
"Pleasant Valley," 1939

■ ■ ■

Ohio is the gateway to the Midwest. The political, economic, and social patterns as well as the influence of ethnic food styles on Midwestern country foods appeared first in Ohio. It was a bellwether region; what happened in this state was repeated in the rest of the Midwest as the other states were settled. ✸ Rolling fields, small towns, sprawling industrial cities, and Ohio's practical, canny people set the tone for America's further advance. The state's motto, "With God, All Things Are Possible," has always been taken seriously by the earnest

Buckeyes, and summed up the settlers' attitudes about the development of their state.

From the beginning, Ohio was both urban and rural, and has remained that way to this day. Cleveland, Cincinnati, Toledo, Youngstown, Akron, and Dayton all provided work for the European immigrant communities of Hungarians, Polish, and Italians who streamed into Ohio looking for a new and better life. Because of them, we find ravishingly good recipes for sauerkraut, tomatoes, and pork, plus fine beers and wines.

The countryside was settled primarily by New Englanders who came to live and till the soil in northern Ohio. Their Puritan work ethic is still very much alive.

Virginians and Kentuckians arrived in southern Ohio, with their affection for corn and molasses coming right along with them. Amish and Mennonites made central Ohio their home, and many Germans settled in the cities to work in the flour mills, meatpacking plants, distilleries, breweries, and later iron foundries. In terms of cookery, the German beer halls and restaurants kept their cuisine boisterously alive. Industrious and influential, these German folk shared Jefferson's belief that a moderate and reflective pace of life on bountiful land was the foundation of freedom and democracy.

By 1860, Ohio's rural population pushed its production of grain, pork, and dairy products to the top in the nation, and champagne made from Catawba grapes was shipped "back east." With Lake Erie on the north, and the Ohio River on the south, all Ohio needed was an interlocking system of canals and railroads to link its farmers with the outside world. And when that happened —and it did—Ohio never looked back.

In the cities, the ethnic food ways remain in small neighborhoods where the social life still revolves around the church and family. Out in the countryside, the farmers raise lamb, turkeys, chicken, corn, wheat, oats, and tomatoes, and they come together in hearty country dishes with primarily German overtones, Midwestern to the core. But the proof is in the pudding, and the pudding is very good. ✶

COUNTRY SAUSAGE WITH APPLE RINGS ∗
ELDERBERRY BLOSSOM FRITTERS ∗ APPLE
BUTTERNUT SOUP ∗ CINCINNATI CHILI ∗ PEPPERED
LAMB STEAKS WITH ROASTED GARLIC SAUCE ∗
GERMAN MEAT LOAF ∗ SMOKED PORK LOIN CHOPS
WITH MAPLE BOURBON GLAZE ∗ GRILLED CHICKEN
WITH BASIL AND GARLIC ∗ OHIO CHICKEN POT PIE
∗ CURRIED CHICKEN SALAD LOAF ∗ GRILLED FRESH
WALLEYE WITH GARDEN TOMATOES ∗ FRIED FISH
WITH BEER BATTER COATING ∗ BRUSSELS SPROUTS
IN CREAM ∗ BROCCOLI WITH BUTTERED CRUMBS ∗
BAKED SWEET SAUERKRAUT WITH TOMATOES AND
BACON ∗ SAUTÉED POTATOES AND ZUCCHINI ∗
LOUIS BROMFIELD'S TOMATO JUICE ∗ HOME EC
CLUB MACARONI SALAD WITH SWEET PICKLE ∗ COLE
SLAW WITH APPLE AND HONEY DRESSING ∗ GERMAN
POTATO SALAD ∗ BLUEBERRY MUFFINS ∗ STICKY
CARAMEL BUNS ∗ RHUBARB TRIFLE ∗ DRIED CHERRY
UPSIDE-DOWN CAKE ∗ SAUERKRAUT CHOCOLATE CAKE
∗ PUMPKIN MOUSSE ∗ RAISIN CRUMB PIE ∗ BLACK
RASPBERRY SILK PIE ∗ PEANUT BUTTER PIE ∗
BUCKEYES ∗ PEACH-ONION CHUTNEY WITH RAISINS

Country Sausage with Apple Rings

MAKES 4 SERVINGS

In Ohio, the farm country is lush and idyllic. Here in the gentle rolling hills, orchards flower in May and the sorghum fields turn to rusty red plumes in the fall. Cattle herds roam the pastures just as the buffalo did before the Revolutionary War.

The farm people who work this land are hearty eaters, and big breakfasts start their active days. Sausage patties served with apple rings is a popular country dish, especially when coupled with creamy scrambled eggs.

- 1 pound well-seasoned loose pork sausage
- 3 medium Jonathan or Golden Delicious apples
- 1 teaspoon ground cinnamon
- 1 tablespoon brown sugar

Shape the sausage into 8 patties a bit larger than the diameter of the apples. Place in a heavy skillet and sauté over low heat until well done but not crisp, about 10 to 15 minutes. While the sausage is cooking, core the unpared apples and cut into ¼-inch-thick slices. Transfer the cooked sausage to a heated platter and set aside, or place on an oven-proof platter and keep warm in the oven at 170° F. Drain all but 1 tablespoon of drippings from the skillet, reserving the extra drippings.

Place as many apple rings as will fit comfortably into the skillet. Sprinkle lightly with cinnamon and brown sugar. Cover and cook over medium-low heat until tender, turning once, taking care not to break up the slices. Remove the cover and continue to cook until the slices have a rich glaze. Drain and place on the warm serving platter with the sausages while you cook the remaining apple slices, adding more drippings as needed.

This antique dinner bell still calls the family to meals.

Elderberry Blossom Fritters

MAKES 30 FRITTERS, OR
8 TO 10 SERVINGS

Elderberry bushes, heavy with delicate white flowers, bloom along the roadsides in mid-July, and their scent perfumes the countryside. The blossom clusters, or panicles, should be picked with dew on, cut into manageable clusters, then frittered.

This is an exceptionally good fritter batter, delicate and cakelike, that can be used for other fruits such as bananas. Part of the batter is made two hours in advance of frying, so plan accordingly. Fritters in the Midwest generally are served as a side dish at breakfast or brunch, or as a meat accompaniment at lunch or dinner. For breakfast, serve them with maple syrup, blueberry syrup, or thinned cherry preserves.

- 2 eggs, separated
- 2 tablespoons sugar
- 1½ cups milk
- 1 teaspoon vanilla extract
- ¼ teaspoon grated nutmeg
- ¼ teaspoon salt
- ⅛ teaspoon almond extract
- 2 cups all-purpose flour
- 8 panicles of elderberry blossoms
  Vegetable oil, for deep frying
  Confectioners' sugar

In a mixer bowl, beat the egg yolks and sugar until light. Add the milk, vanilla, nutmeg, salt, and almond extract and blend. Beat in the flour; it will look like thick gravy at this point. Cover and refrigerate for 2 hours.

Just before using, beat the egg whites until stiff but not dry and fold into the flour mixture. In an electric skillet, heat 2 inches of oil to 360° F. With scissors, cut the elderberry panicles into smaller pieces or divisions, each about 2 x 3 inches.

With tongs, dip the well-dried blossoms into the batter and then into the hot fat. Fry for 2 minutes, then turn and fry a minute longer on the second side. Remove with a slotted spoon and drain on paper towels. Keep the fritters warm in a 200° F. oven while the others are being prepared. Serve hot, dusted with confectioners' sugar.

Apple Butternut Soup

MAKES 4 TO 5 SERVINGS

Autumn in the Midwest is a beautiful time. From Ohio to Minnesota, the woods are aflame, and in country lanes, green knobby hedgeapples lie among golden pools of fallen leaves. The vegetable garden is nearly finished, but still to come are the cabbages, kale, and winter squash. Butternut squash with its mellow yellow flesh, always yields a fine soup. But add apples, cider, cream, and spices, and you have something quite special.

- ¼ cup peanut oil
- 2-pound butternut squash, peeled, seeded, and cut into 2-inch pieces
- 2 Northern Spy or McIntosh apples, peeled, cored, and cut into 2-inch pieces
- 1 large onion, peeled and coarsely chopped
- ¾ teaspoon curry powder
- ¾ teaspoon mace
- ½ teaspoon ground cardamom
- 1 cup apple cider
- 1 quart Chicken Stock, preferably homemade (page 239)
- ½ cup half-and-half
- ½ teaspoon salt
- ¼ teaspoon white pepper
- ¼ cup finely minced scallions, both green and white parts

Heat the oil in a large stockpot over medium-low heat. Add the squash, apples, and onion, and stir to coat with oil. Sauté, stirring occasionally, for 15 minutes, or until the onion is transparent. Stir in the curry, mace, and cardamom and continue cooking until the onion begins to brown, about 10 minutes longer.

Add the cider and bring the mixture to a boil. Reduce heat and cook for 3 minutes. Add the stock, lower the heat to medium-low, and simmer the mixture, partly covered, for another 35 minutes, or until the squash is very tender.

Transfer the mixture to a food processor bowl and process until the soup is smooth. Return the soup to the stockpot and cook, uncovered, over medium-low heat, until reduced by about one-fourth. Stir occasionally.

Stir in the half-and-half, salt, and pepper and bring again to a simmer. Pour into warmed bowls and sprinkle the scallions over the top.

Cincinnati Chili

MAKES 8 GENEROUS SERVINGS

The chili in Cincinnati is like chili nowhere else. The original recipe was developed by cooks in the Greek-owned chili parlors and was served over hot spaghetti with an assortment of toppings—a sort of do-it-yourself chili. Admittedly unorthodox, decidedly delicious, it is also a lot of fun for a buffet dinner. Serve this with Sour Cream Corn Muffins (page 85) and beer.

CHILI
- 4 cups water
- 2 8-ounce cans tomato sauce
- 1 5-ounce can tomato paste
- 2 cups chopped onions
- 1 cup chopped celery
- 2 tablespoons chili powder
- 2 tablespoons fresh lemon juice
- 1 tablespoon sugar
- 2 bay leaves
- 4 garlic cloves, finely minced
- 2 teaspoons ground cinnamon
- 1 teaspoon salt
- 1 teaspoon black pepper
- 1 teaspoon freshly ground cumin
- ½ teaspoon ground allspice
- ¼ teaspoon ground cloves
- 1 pound lean ground beef
- 1 pound lean ground pork
- 1 pound thin spaghetti, broken in half, cooked, and tossed with 3 tablespoons olive oil

TOPPINGS
- 2 cups hot kidney beans
- 2 cups chopped onions
- 2 cups grated cheddar cheese

In a deep kettle, combine all the chili ingredients except the meats and spaghetti. Cover and bring to a boil. Crumble in the meat gradually and return the mixture to a boil. Reduce the heat and simmer for 1 to 2 hours, uncovered, until the chili is as thick as you like. Discard the bay leaves. Serve in large flat soup bowls, ladled over hot spaghetti; top with the beans, onions, and shredded cheese—in that order, if you want to do it the Cincinnati way.

Peppered Lamb Steaks with Roasted Garlic Sauce

———— ✷ ————

MAKES 4 SERVINGS

This recipe came to me from Stephen Schmidt, author of Master Recipes, *who now lives in Manhattan but spent a lot of time in the Midwest and remembers the food with fondness. He taught a series of classes on Midwestern cookery at the Lazarus Cooking School in Cincinnati, and this recipe was created especially for the school.*

I think lamb steaks are a fine change from filet mignon. Start marinating them a few hours before dinner, then finish up the sauce just before serving.

Using wine and brandies in cookery was not uncommon in early Midwestern cookery, and there are all sorts of coy references to its usage in early cookbooks, written by and for "genteel" ladies.

4   leg of lamb steaks, ¾-inch thick (6 to 8 ounces each)
1   teaspoon white peppercorns
1   teaspoon black peppercorns
1   teaspoon green peppercorns
1   large garlic head
2   tablespoons plus 2 teaspoons olive oil
    Salt
½   cup cognac
½   cup Beef Stock (page 239)
3   to 4 tablespoons unsalted butter
    Fresh lemon juice
2   tablespoons minced fresh parsley

Trim the fat from the lamb and pat dry with paper towels. Coarsely crush all the peppercorns—this can be done in a spice grinder or by placing the peppercorns in a plastic bag and pounding them with a rolling pin—and rub them evenly over both sides of the steaks. Wrap the meat in plastic and refrigerate for 1 to 4 hours.

Preheat the oven to 350° F. Separate the garlic cloves but do not peel. Turn into a baking dish and toss with 2 teaspoons of the olive oil until coated. Bake for 10 to 15 minutes, stirring once, or until very soft. When cool enough to handle, peel by pressing the root end of each clove between your thumb and the blade of a paring knife and gently tugging. The skin peels away easily, without damaging the clove.

Heat 1 tablespoon of the oil in a 10-inch skillet. Salt the lamb steaks and in batches sauté 2 to 3 minutes per side over moderately high heat for medium-rare. Continue until all steaks are cooked, placing finished steaks in a warm oven and adding more oil to the skillet if needed. Pour all the fat out of the skillet and add the cognac, stock, and 4 of the garlic cloves, mashing the garlic well with a fork. Boil over high heat until the liquid is reduced to about ¼ cup. Add the remaining garlic. Remove the pan from the heat and drop in the butter, swirling the pan until the butter is incorporated into the sauce. Taste and adjust seasoning with lemon juice. Pour the sauce over the lamb steaks, sprinkle with parsley, and serve at once on heated plates.

German Meat Loaf

MAKES 8 SERVINGS

With Ohio having such a high percentage of citizens with a German heritage, you can expect all sorts of good dishes made with sauerkraut. This meat loaf is seasoned with both kraut and rye bread crumbs—an inspired combination. Serve the moist and sassy meat loaf with mashed potatoes and a glass of beer. Meat loaf has never been so good!

2   cups soft unseeded rye bread crumbs
1   16-ounce can sauerkraut, drained
2   eggs, lightly beaten
½   cup milk
½   cup chopped onion
1   teaspoon caraway seed
½   teaspoon ground pepper
2   tablespoons catsup or chili sauce
2   pounds lean ground beef

Preheat the oven to 350° F. In a large bowl combine all the ingredients except the meat and mix well. Add the ground beef and mix thoroughly. Pat into a thick, flat loaf approximately 10 inches long and 8 inches wide and place on a rack in a greased or foil-lined 9 x 13-inch pan. Bake for 1¼ hours, or until nicely browned. Let stand 10 minutes before slicing.

Smoked Pork Loin Chops with Maple Bourbon Glaze

★

MAKES 4 SERVINGS

Rated as one of the best restaurants in the nation, the Phoenix in Cincinnati is located in an impeccably restored 1893 structure. The elegant dining rooms with their stained-glass windows are among the most luxurious in town.

The menu's emphasis is on American regional cuisine, and this recipe is similar to one of their dishes that I most favor. It combines Ohio's smoked pork chops and maple syrup, neighboring Kentucky's bourbon, and Missouri's pecans in a most satisfactory way. Serve it with wild rice seasoned with additional sage.

2   teaspoons vegetable oil
4   6-ounce smoked center-cut pork loin chops
½   cup bourbon
1   tablespoon chopped fresh sage
½   cup maple syrup
2   cups Chicken Stock (page 239)
2   cups half-and-half
½   cup chopped toasted pecans
¼   teaspoon salt
¼   teaspoon ground white pepper

In a large heavy sauté pan, heat the oil. Sauté the chops slowly on both sides until golden brown and cooked through, about 15 minutes total. Transfer to a heat-proof platter, cover, and place in a 140° F. oven while preparing the sauce.

In the same saucepan, combine the bourbon, sage, maple syrup, and stock. Simmer over medium-low heat until the sauce is reduced by half, about 7 minutes. Add the cream and reduce again by half, about 10 minutes longer. Add the remaining ingredients, stir to combine, and pour over the chops. Serve immediately.

*LEFT: **Sauerkraut pizza is one of the zesty offerings at the Waynesville Sauerkraut Festival.** RIGHT: **Cincinnati has been nicknamed Porkopolis; in the Flying Pigs sculpture at Bicentennial Commons on the banks of the Ohio River, pigs perch atop replicas of riverboat stacks.***

Grilled Chicken with Basil and Garlic

★

MAKES 6 SERVINGS

I was first served this chicken at a dinner party close to Louis Bromfield's Malabar Farm. The cook had picked the basil leaves from his own herb garden, which he then slipped under the skin of the chicken, along with fresh garlic. After marinating the chicken overnight, he grilled it and poured a creamy garlic sauce over the top.

We ate our meal on his patio, and as the purplish-blue Ohio twilight deepened, the fireflies appeared, winking in unison among the sweet nicotiana.

2 garlic cloves, thinly sliced
½ cup large fresh basil leaves
4 large whole chicken breasts, boned and
    halved, skin left on

MARINADE
¼ cup white wine or Chicken Stock
    (page 239)
¼ cup fresh lemon juice
½ teaspoon salt
¼ teaspoon freshly ground pepper
1 garlic clove, finely minced

SAUCE
1 large head garlic
1 cup Chicken Stock (page 239)
2 tablespoons chopped fresh basil
2 tablespoons heavy (whipping) cream

    Basil leaves, for garnish

Slide some of the sliced garlic and basil leaves under the skin of each chicken breast half. In a small bowl, combine the marinade ingredients and whisk until blended. Arrange the chicken breasts in a 3-quart flat glass dish and pour the marinade over them. Cover and refrigerate overnight.

To make the sauce, separate the garlic into cloves; it is not necessary to peel them. Place the garlic cloves in a small saucepan with the stock and simmer, covered, for 30 minutes. Cool slightly. Pour into the bowl of a food processor fitted with the steel blade (or a blender) and puree. Pour through a fine strainer and return to the saucepan. Add the chopped basil and the cream and set aside until the chicken is ready to serve.

Fire up a grill or preheat the broiler. Cook the chicken 3 inches from the heat, about 7 to 10 minutes on each side. Transfer to a warm serving platter. Reheat the garlic sauce and pour over the chicken. Garnish with additional basil leaves.

Ohio Chicken Pot Pie

★

MAKES 10 TO 12 SERVINGS

Chicken pot pies in the Midwest tend to be meaty, with just a few vegetables for color, and served with a gravy on top. They are substantial, heartwarming dishes, so it's no wonder they're making a comeback.

3 pounds chicken pieces, white and dark meat
1 large carrot, quartered
1 bay leaf
½ cup (1 stick) butter
¼ cup chopped celery
¼ cup chopped onion
7 tablespoons all-purpose flour
1 teaspoon poultry seasoning
2 cups milk
½ teaspoon salt, or to taste
½ teaspoon freshly ground pepper, or to taste
¼ cup chopped parsley
    Pastry for 2-crust pie (1 recipe Never-Fail
      Pie Crust, page 244)
1 tablespoon fresh lemon juice

In a deep kettle, cover the chicken with water (or chicken broth). Add the carrot and bay leaf, bring to a boil, then reduce heat and simmer until very tender, about 30 minutes. When the chicken is cool enough to handle, discard the skin and bones and bay leaf and cut the meat into bite-size pieces—you should have 3½ to 4 cups of chicken. Chop 2 of the carrot pieces very finely and combine with the chicken in a greased 9 x 13-inch flat pan. Cover with plastic wrap and refrigerate. Chill the broth until the fat rises and can be discarded.

Preheat oven to 375° F. In a large saucepan, melt ¼ cup of the butter over medium heat; add the celery and the onion and cook until tender, but not brown, about 4 to 5 minutes. Stir in 3 tablespoons of the flour and the poultry seasoning and cook and stir until the mixture bubbles up in the middle of the pan. Add 1 cup of the milk and 1 cup of the broth and whisk and cook over medium heat until the mixture thickens; season with ¼ teaspoon of the salt, ¼ teaspoon pepper, and the parsley.

Pour the sauce over the chicken and set aside. Roll out the pastry to fit the top of the dish, crimping the edges to the top of the dish; slash the top so the steam can escape. Bake for 45 minutes, or until the top is golden brown and bubbling up in the center.

While the pot pie bakes, make the gravy. In a medium saucepan, melt the remaining ¼ cup butter and add the remaining 4 tablespoons flour and ¼ teaspoon salt and pepper. Cook and stir until the mixtures bubbles in the pan, about 2 minutes; do not allow it to brown. Whisk in 1 cup of the broth, the remaining 1 cup of milk, and the lemon juice and cook and whisk the gravy over medium heat until thickened, about 3 minutes. Serve with the baked pot pie.

Curried Chicken Salad Loaf

——— ★ ———

MAKES 10 GENEROUS SERVINGS

Ladies still entertain at lunch in the Midwest—and chicken salad, in some form, is a popular entrée. You'll find this salad loaf is pleasingly seasoned and nicely different. Serve it with Tomato Bread (page 50).

6 whole chicken breasts
2½ cups Chicken Stock (page 239)
2 teaspoons low-sodium chicken bouillon granules
1 envelope unflavored gelatin
1½ cups toasted English walnuts
1 celery stalk
½ small onion
½ cup mayonnaise
¼ cup sour cream
¼ cup finely minced fresh red bell pepper or canned red pimiento
1 tablespoon curry powder
1 tablespoon sweet mustard
1 tablespoon sweet pickle juice
½ teaspoon powdered ginger
¼ teaspoon ground white pepper
Lettuce leaves
Additional mayonnaise, seasoned (see Note)

Place the chicken in a shallow sauté pan with the chicken stock. Bring to a boil, then immediately reduce to a slow simmer and cook gently for 20 to 25 minutes, or until the chicken is cooked through. While the chicken is still warm, remove the skin and bones and discard. Boil the chicken stock over high heat until reduced to 1½ cups, about 15 minutes. Add the bouillon powder. Stir the gelatin with a bit of cold water, add to the hot stock, and heat until it is dissolved. Set aside. Chop the chicken coarsely in the food processor or by hand—some large pieces are good for texture. Transfer to a large bowl and add the nuts. Chop the celery and onion together in the food processor; add to the chicken and combine.

Add the mayonnaise, sour cream, red pepper, curry powder, mustard, pickle juice, ginger, white pepper, and reduced stock, and blend well. Coat a 9 x 5-inch loaf pan with vegetable spray and pour in the chicken mixture. Cover and chill overnight. To serve, unmold and cut into thick slices. Serve on lettuce leaves.

NOTE: Season some additional mayonnaise with a bit of parsley, chives, and capers, and serve alongside.

Grilled Fresh Walleye with Garden Tomatoes

from the Peasant Stock

———— ✶ ————

MAKES 4 SERVINGS

The Midwest is dotted with good restaurants pridefully serving outstanding regional food without fanfare from the national media.

At the Peasant Stock in Dayton, the house is always full, and the menu regularly features Ohio's own fine foods, like fresh Lake Erie fish, impeccably prepared. Try this recipe when you want to use the grill; the charcoal and wood flavors complement the herbaceous tomato mixture.

    1 large fresh tomato
    2 tablespoons olive oil
    1 teaspoon chopped fresh dill
       Salt and pepper to taste
    2 pounds Walleye fillets, cleaned and scaled

Prepare the grill or range-top char unit. Chop the tomato into ¼-inch chunks. Toss with 1 tablespoon of the olive oil, the dill, and the salt and pepper. Let sit at room temperature for 15 minutes.

Lightly brush the fillets with the remaining oil and place on the grill, skin side up. Cook approximately 3 minutes, then turn. Cook another 2 to 3 minutes and remove to a heated plate. (Cooking times will vary according to fillet size; the flesh should be snow white.) Top with the tomato mixture and serve.

Longfellow called Cincinnati "Queen City of the West," but to lots of folk, Cincinnati means beer. The Oldenberg Brewery, OPPOSITE, makes beer the old German way, with no preservatives, sugar, corn, or rice. It's pure barley, hops, yeast, and fresh Ohio water.

Fried Fish with Beer Batter Coating

———— ✶ ————

MAKES 4 SERVINGS

All over the Midwest, Friday night is "Fish Fry Night." It is an all-you-can-eat event held in church basements, American Legion halls, high school auditoriums, and country taverns. In the spring, the fish might be smelt, tiny silvery fish that are scooped out of the rivers with nets as the fish are on their spawning runs. More commonly, though, the fish will be perch or whitefish. The platters are kept full of the crispy golden-brown deep-fried fish, and the traditional accompaniment is Creamy Cole Slaw (page 166).

BATTER
    ½ cup beer
    ½ cup water
    ½ teaspoon salt
    ½ teaspoon freshly ground pepper
    ⅛ teaspoon grated nutmeg
    1 teaspoon minced garlic
    ¾ cup all-purpose flour
    ¼ cup cornstarch
       Dash of hot red pepper sauce

       Peanut oil, for frying
    8 whitefish fillets or 16 perch fillets (See Note)
       Tartar Sauce (page 240)

In a shallow bowl, combine the batter ingredients and beat well with a rotary beater or whisk. Fill a deep electric fry pan with the peanut oil to about ¼ to ½ inch deep. Heat the oil to 375° F. Pat the fish fillets dry and coat thoroughly with batter. Drop the fish into the hot oil with tongs, and cook until golden brown, approximately 10 to 15 minutes, depending on thickness of fish. Serve with tartar sauce.

NOTE: The fish will cook more evenly if the fillets are not too thick.

Brussels Sprouts in Cream

MAKES 4 TO 5 SERVINGS

Who says Brussels sprouts are boring? This is a very spiffy vegetable dish, an adaptation of an English recipe brought to Ohio by New Englanders. I found it in an old Congregationalist cookbook. The sprouts are served sliced instead of whole, which gives the dish a different texture and look on the plate. Try it with ham.

The tiny little cabbages are a fall vegetable that grow on a tall single stiff stalk. A row of them in the garden actually looks a bit militant. They are one of the last crops to be harvested before winter and a touch of frost improves the sprouts' delicate flavor.

> 2 cups heavy (whipping) cream
> 1½ pounds Brussels sprouts
> 1½ teaspoons finely minced fresh ginger
> 1 teaspoon finely minced garlic
> ½ teaspoon freshly grated nutmeg
> ¼ teaspoon salt
> ⅛ teaspoon white pepper

In a heavy sauté pan, heat the cream over medium-low heat. Bring to a boil and simmer at a slow boil until the cream is reduced by one-third and is thick and yellow.

Meanwhile, rinse and trim the sprouts. Cut each into 6 slices about ⅛ inch thick. When the cream is reduced, add the seasonings, then add the sprouts and gently turn them to coat with the cream. Cook the sprouts, turning frequently, for about 5 to 6 minutes, watching them carefully so they do not scorch. They should be cooked through but still crisp. Serve immediately; this does not reheat well.

Broccoli with Buttered Crumbs

MAKES 4 SERVINGS

This vegetable, which looks like a bouquet of tight green flowers, is easy to grow and can be found in Ohio farmer's markets all summer long. Store the stalks in a bowl of water in the refrigerator, the top covered with a big plastic bag; the broccoli will stay very fresh for several days.

The secret to good broccoli dishes is not overcooking; the broccoli should still be a bit crunchy and bright green when served. Topping it with crumbs is an old farm custom with German antecedents.

> 2 tablespoons (¼ stick) butter
> 1 cup fresh brown bread crumbs (the kind with nuts is ideal)
> 2 tablespoons chopped fresh parsley
> 2 tablespoons chopped fresh chives
> 1 teaspoon minced fresh rosemary, or ½ teaspoon dried
> ½ teaspoon grated lemon rind
> Salt and pepper
> 1½ pounds broccoli
> 2 teaspoons melted butter
> 1 tablespoon fresh lemon juice

In a heavy skillet over low heat, melt the butter. Add the bread crumbs and sauté, stirring constantly, until they are golden brown. Transfer to a small bowl and stir in the parsley, chives, rosemary, lemon rind, and salt and pepper to taste. Set aside.

Cut the broccoli tops off and separate into flowerets. Cut off the top 3 inches of the stems, peel, and cut into ½-inch pieces. Bring 2½ quarts of hot water to a boil, add the broccoli (the water should cover it liberally), and cook it over high heat, uncovered until it is barely tender, about 3 to 5 minutes.

Remove immediately, drain, and place in a serving bowl. Drizzle the melted butter and lemon juice over the top and sprinkle the bread crumb mixture over all.

Baked Sweet Sauerkraut with Tomatoes and Bacon

———★———

MAKES 4 TO 6 SERVINGS

The Ohio Sauerkraut Festival is held in Waynesville (population 2,000) the second week of October and attracts thousands of people. Remember, this state was settled by Germans; they flock to sample the food and buy crafts at the festival's five hundred booths. It is sort of like a krauty Mardi Gras.

This old, old recipe is a real treasure. The few ingredients—all listed in the title—would have been in any Ohio kitchen at the turn of the century. The dish is baked quite a long time, until the top caramelizes, the liquid cooks away, and the kraut is nearly transparent.

If you consider sauerkraut as sort of the staff of life (and many do), you might be interested in a Waynesville cookbook, One Nation Under Sauerkraut, *by Dennis E. Dalton (see Source List). It includes recipes for sauerkraut cookies, sauerkraut candy, sauerkraut ice cream . . . I'm serious!*

- 1 14-ounce can tomatoes, coarsely chopped, undrained
- 1 16-ounce can sauerkraut, undrained
- 1 cup sugar
- 6 slices raw bacon, cut in ½-inch pieces
- ½ teaspoon freshly ground pepper

Preheat the oven to 325° F. Grease a flat (see Note) 2-quart glass baking dish. Place all the ingredients in the dish and combine thoroughly. (You may have to use your hands to distribute the bacon evenly.) Bake, uncovered, for 2 hours and 15 minutes, or until the top begins to brown deeply and most of the liquid has cooked away.

NOTE: It is important to use a flat dish so the liquid evaporates as it cooks.

Sautéed Potatoes and Zucchini

from the Peasant Stock

———★———

MAKES 6 SERVINGS

The Peasant Stock's interior is warm and inviting, with provincial country ambience, fresh hanging plants, and a pleasant glassed-in garden room. This recipe started out as a breakfast dish, but ended up being quite a bit more sophisticated and is served as an entrée accompaniment at lunch and dinner.

- 3 to 4 tablespoons olive oil
- ½ pound cooked potatoes, sliced, with skin on
- 1 small onion, finely diced
- ½ teaspoon minced garlic
- ¼ pound zucchini, sliced
  Salt and pepper

Heat the oil in a large skillet. Over medium-low heat, sauté the potatoes until golden, about 15 minutes, turning occasionally. Add the onion and garlic and continue sautéing for 3 to 4 minutes, or until the onion is softened. Add the zucchini and continue cooking just until the zucchini begins to soften; the slices should still be a bit firm. Add salt and pepper to taste, and serve.

☆ MALABAR FARM ☆

The name of the place is almost too fanciful for a country spot in Ohio. Pulitzer Prize–winning author Louis Bromfield created his farm out of rocky, worn-out land and named it Malabar, after the hill overlooking the harbor of Bombay and the southwest coast of India.

Many of Bromfield's novels were brought to the screen; one of the most famous was based on his popular book, *The Rains Came* (1937). The money he earned from his writings was plowed back into the Ohio land, as he became increasingly involved with agricultural issues and soil conservation.

Through his efforts, Malabar became a well-known experimental and research farm. As its fields flourished, the visitors came, both humble dirt farmers and the famous, whom the gregarious author met in New York, Hollywood, and Paris. The comfortably elegant thirty-two-room mansion hummed with many parties and meetings; Humphrey Bogart and Lauren Bacall were married at Malabar in 1945.

Through his writings and lectures, Bromfield struggled to show how traditional rural values could be reconciled with the modern industrialized agriculture that emerged after World War II. He was far ahead of his time — indeed prophetic. His five books about his life at Malabar are the most lasting of his literary achievements.

Bromfield's land is now operated as the Malabar Farm State Park, open to the public.

Louis Bromfield's Tomato Juice

——— ☆ ———

MAKES 4 OR 5 QUARTS

In all of Bromfield's writings about Malabar Farm, his enthusiasm for his gardens is obvious. Much of his produce was made into a drink named "Doctor Bromfield's Special Vegetable Compound and Celery Tonic," served as a juice, as a hot soup in winter, and as a jellied tomato consommé in the summer.

1 peck tomatoes (approximately 17 pounds)
1 bunch celery
8 garlic cloves
4 medium onions
4 bay leaves
4 medium carrots
2 green or red bell peppers
1 large bunch fresh spinach
1 large bunch fresh parsley
2 tablespoons mustard seed
2 tablespoons sugar
2 tablespoons salt
½ teaspoon cayenne pepper

Wash, core, and chop the tomatoes very coarsely. Clean and coarsely chop the rest of the vegetables. Divide all the vegetables and remaining ingredients between 2 large, deep kettles.

Cover and bring to a boil, lower the heat, and simmer for about 45 minutes, or until the vegetables are completely softened. Let stand until just cool enough to handle, but still very hot. Force the mixture through a sieve or food mill then return the juice to the kettles and reheat if necessary.

Pour the hot juice into hot pint or quart jars, leaving ½ inch of headspace. Seal and process in a hot-water bath for 40 minutes for pints and 45 minutes for quarts. Start counting the time from when the water returns to a full rolling boil after the jars have been immersed. Remove the jars to a towel-covered rack to cool; store in a dark place.

Home Ec Club Macaroni Salad with Sweet Pickle

— ★ —

MAKES 6 SERVINGS

Extension Service Homemakers Associations, created in 1914 to teach homemaking skills primarily to rural women, are still going strong across the Midwest, and are supervised by graduate home economists. These associations, like the 4-H Clubs for young people, are part of the Land Grant College Extension Service Program, which was created under President Lincoln.

At the Home Ec Club monthly meetings, carry-in dinners are sometimes part of the entertainment (What am I saying? The meals are *the entertainment!) and the women bring an assortment of mouth-watering dishes, including macaroni salads. This version is unusually creamy and colorful, with bits of tomato, red bell pepper, snipped dill, and lots of sweet pickle.*

- 1 tablespoon vegetable oil
- ½ pound dried shell or elbow macaroni
- 1 tablespoon milk
- 1 large tomato, peeled, seeded, and coarsely chopped
- 4 sweet pickles, coarsely chopped, and ½ tablespoon sweet pickle juice
- 6 scallions, finely chopped, tops included
- 1 small red bell pepper, finely chopped
- ¼ cup chopped fresh parsley
- ¼ cup chopped fresh dill
- ¾ cup mayonnaise, or a bit more
- ¼ cup sour cream
- 1½ teaspoons celery seed
- ½ teaspoon coarsely ground black pepper
- 1 teaspoon salt

In a large saucepan, bring 2 quarts of water to a boil; add the oil, then the macaroni. Boil over medium heat for 14 to 16 minutes or until the macaroni is just tender. Drain, rinse under cold water, and drain again. Transfer to a large bowl, add the milk, and toss.

Add the tomato, pickles, scallions, bell pepper, parsley, and dill; combine. In a medium bowl, whisk together the mayonnaise, sour cream, celery seed, pickle juice, black pepper, and salt. Pour over the macaroni and mix well. Cover and refrigerate.

Students in Carol Plew's Home Ec class try their hands at cakes, pies, and yeast breads.

Cole Slaw with Apple and Honey Dressing

✶

MAKES 6 SERVINGS

In all the fruit orchards scattered about the Midwest you will find beehives, for the bees are necessary for the trees' cross-pollination. The happy by-product is honey, which is spread on biscuits and other hot breads, and used frequently as a sugar substitute, as in this updated old favorite, cole slaw.

Cabbage, combined with apple, pecans, and sunflower seeds, then glossed with honey and lemon juice, is a nice change from the typical salad with mayonnaise dressing.

- 1 head green cabbage (about 1 pound), shredded (use a 4 mm food processor blade)
- 2 carrots, grated
- 1 large green-skinned apple, unpeeled, cored, and diced
- ½ cup toasted Missouri pecans
- ½ cup toasted sunflower seeds
- ½ cup minced parsley

DRESSING
- 3 tablespoons honey
- ¼ cup fresh lemon juice
- 2 tablespoons vegetable oil
- ½ teaspoon celery salt
- ½ teaspoon salt
- ½ teaspoon coarsely ground black pepper

In a large bowl, toss together the shredded cabbage, carrots, apple, nuts, seeds, and parsley. In a small bowl, whisk together all the dressing ingredients. Pour the dressing over the cabbage mixture and combine lightly. Refrigerate for at least 30 minutes before serving.

German Potato Salad

✶

MAKES 12 TO 15 SERVINGS

You will find many versions of German potato salad across the country; this one is more delicate in flavor than most and can be made a day or two in advance, then reheated in the oven before serving. Serve it with an Indiana honey-baked ham (see Source List).

- 14 medium red potatoes
- 2 pounds bacon
- ¾ cup cider vinegar
- ½ cup sugar
- ½ cup water
- 1 large onion, chopped
- 1 teaspoon celery seed
- 1 teaspoon dried marjoram, or 1 tablespoon fresh
- ½ teaspoon salt
- ½ teaspoon coarsely ground black pepper
- ¼ cup chopped fresh parsley or chervil, for garnish

In a large deep saucepan, cook the potatoes with their skins on until tender, about 25 minutes. With scissors, cut the bacon into small pieces. Place the pieces in a large skillet and sauté the bacon over medium heat until crisp, about 5 to 6 minutes. Remove the bacon with a slotted spoon to paper towels to drain. Reserve the bacon fat.

Pour off all but ¾ cup of the bacon fat, and add the vinegar, sugar, and water; bring to a boil.

Peel the potatoes and slice paper-thin into a greased shallow 3-quart casserole or bowl. Add the bacon, onion, and seasonings, except the parsley. Pour the hot liquid over all and toss gently until the potatoes are covered. Cool, cover with foil, and refrigerate overnight.

Remove the potatoes from the refrigerator and allow to come to room temperature, about 2 hours. Preheat the oven to 300° F. Bake, covered, for 35 to 45 minutes, or until the mixture is heated through. Sprinkle the top with the parsley or chervil and serve warm.

The Inn at Honey Run is located in Holmes County, which is the center of the country's largest Amish population. It is one of the most scenic parts of Ohio, and the inn, a contemporary structure of stone and glass, is hidden away in deep woods.

The decor is a mix of Shaker furniture and Amish quilts, and the dining room overlooks a wooded ravine that is dotted with many bird-feeders among the wildflowers and ferns.

The restaurant is open to the public and the food is like the decor — both contemporary and Amish — and the kitchen does have Amish cooks. Ideally located for sightseeing in Amish country, the inn is also close to Kingwood Gardens in Mansfield, Louis Bromfield's Malabar Farm, and Roscoe Village, a restored canal-era town.

Blueberry Muffins

from the Inn at Honey Run

——— ✳ ———

MAKES 18 MUFFINS

Though not an Amish recipe, this is the most popular bread served at the Inn at Honey Run. These are just the thing to have for breakfast after enjoying a bird walk about the wildflower-filled woods surrounding the inn.

Do not overmix the muffins; they will have "tunnels" in them.

2⅓ cups all-purpose flour
1¼ cups sugar
1½ teaspoons baking powder
¾ teaspoon baking soda
½ teaspoon salt
¼ teaspoon grated nutmeg
⅛ teaspoon ground cloves
2 tablespoons grated orange rind
2 eggs
½ cup vegetable oil
1¼ cups buttermilk
1 cup blueberries, fresh or frozen (see Note)

Preheat the oven to 400° F. Line 18 muffin cups with paper liners. In a large bowl, combine the flour, sugar, baking powder, baking soda, salt, and spices. Stir the orange rind into the dry mixture. In a small bowl, combine the eggs, oil, and buttermilk with a rotary beater or whisk; gently stir in the blueberries.

Add the egg mixture all at once to the flour mixture, stirring just until the dry ingredients are moistened (about 15 full stirs around the bowl); the batter will be thin. Fill the muffin cups three-fourths full and bake 18 to 20 minutes or until the tops are lightly browned. If serving immediately, remove the muffins from the pans and cool slightly on wire racks, or keep warm by leaving in muffin pans, slightly tipped to allow steam to escape.

NOTE: If using frozen blueberries, do not defrost before adding to the muffin batter. Chopped fresh cranberries can be substituted for the blueberries.

Sticky Caramel Buns

★

MAKES 4 DOZEN SMALL BUNS

The Midwestern Amish women are famous for their yeast breads. This recipe is from an Ohio Amish lady who made wonderful noodles and angel food cakes that she sold to only a few special customers. Occasionally Rebecca would make a recipe or two of these irresistible sticky buns (we would call them nut rolls). If she liked you, she might ask you to sit down for a cup of coffee and a bun. And if she really liked you, she would sell you some. The rolls are quite small, which I find perfect for entertaining.

BUNS

4½ to 5½ cups all-purpose flour
½ cup granulated sugar
2 packages active dry yeast
2 teaspoons salt
¾ cup milk
½ cup water
½ cup (1 stick) butter
1 egg, at room temperature, beaten

CARAMEL TOPPING

1½ cups brown sugar
¾ cup light corn syrup
¾ cup softened butter
1 cup chopped nuts

⅓ cup butter, melted
½ cup brown sugar

*OPPOSITE: **An appreciative tot munches a sticky bun on a walk through the park.***

In a large mixer bowl, combine 1½ cups of the flour, the granulated sugar, yeast, and salt. In a small pan, combine the milk, water, and butter. Heat slowly until warm.

Gradually add the butter mixture to the dry ingredients and beat until smooth. Add the egg and enough flour (about 3 cups) to make a thick batter. Beat again until smooth. Turn out onto a well-floured board and knead in the remaining flour, or until an elastic dough forms; you may not need all of the flour.

Place the dough in a well-greased bowl and butter the top. Cover and let rise until doubled in bulk, approximately 1 hour.

Meanwhile, in a mixer bowl, combine the brown sugar, corn syrup, and softened butter until well blended. Grease three 9-inch cake pans. Divide the caramel topping among the pans and spread to cover pan bottoms (about ½ inch thick), and sprinkle with the nuts.

Punch down the dough and divide into 3 parts. On a floured surface, roll each piece into a 20 x 8-inch rectangle. Brush each with 2 tablespoons of the melted butter, and sprinkle each with about 3 tablespoons of the brown sugar. Roll up firmly, jelly roll fashion, starting from the long side. Pinch the ends together and cut into 1-inch slices. Place the slices cut side down in the prepared pans. Cover, and let rise until doubled in bulk, about 45 minutes.

Preheat the oven to 350° F. Bake the rolls for 20 to 25 minutes, or until golden brown. Cool for 5 minutes in the pans, then invert onto wax paper to cool.

Rhubarb Trifle

———★———

MAKES 16 SERVINGS

There are many interpretations of trifle, and I am hopelessly in love with all of them. This version with rhubarb is a nice surprise because the flavor is unexpected. I have tried sprinkling the cake first with sherry, but there is already so much moisture in the rhubarb that it makes the dish entirely too soggy, so skip the tipsy part—it is quite delicious without it. The cake can be made ahead and frozen, the rhubarb and custard made a day in advance, and the whole thing combined on the day it is to be served.

RHUBARB SAUCE

> 5 to 6 cups chopped rhubarb (about 2½ to 3 pounds)
>
> 2 tablespoons water
>
> 2 cups sugar
>
> 2 tablespoons cornstarch mixed with ¼ cup water
>
> Red food coloring (optional)

CUSTARD

> 6 egg yolks
>
> 1 cup sugar
>
> 3 tablespoons cornstarch
>
> Pinch of salt
>
> 3 cups milk
>
> 1 tablespoon butter
>
> 2 teaspoons vanilla extract
>
> **Easy Country Sponge Cake (page 244)**
>
> **Whipped Cream Topping (page 247)**
>
> ¾ cup chopped macadamia nuts

Combine the rhubarb, 1 or 2 tablespoons of water, and sugar in a large saucepan. Bring to a boil, lower heat to medium, and cook, uncovered, until the rhubarb is completely softened, about 8 to 10 minutes. Add the cornstarch and water mixture to the rhubarb and cook until thickened, about 5 minutes. Add food coloring, if extra color is desired. Cool completely and refrigerate.

To make the custard, place the egg yolks in a heavy saucepan and whisk them briefly. Combine the sugar, cornstarch, and salt in a small bowl and whisk into the eggs. Blend in the milk and cook over medium-low heat until the mixture thickens, about 5 to 7 minutes. Stir it constantly and watch it carefully so it doesn't scorch. Remove from heat.

Stir in the butter and the vanilla. Top with a round of wax paper laid directly on the hot custard to prevent a skin from forming. Cool completely and refrigerate.

To assemble, slice the sponge cake horizontally into 3 layers. Cut each layer into 8 wedges, like pie, then cut each pie-shaped piece into approximately 9 pieces. Place one of the cut-up layers in the bottom of a deep round bowl, and top with one-third of the custard, then one-third of the rhubarb. Repeat 2 more times. Cover with the Whipped Cream Topping, then sprinkle the macadamia nuts on top of the whipped cream. Refrigerate at least 6 hours.

Dried Cherry Upside-Down Cake

———★———

MAKES 6 TO 8 SERVINGS

Upside-down cake—just the words conjure up images of mothers in bibbed aprons preparing home-cooked meals at white enameled stoves with pots of African violets sitting on the window sill above the sink.

This exceptionally good recipe is an updated version of that old favorite, using dried cherries, pecans, and a touch of rum. The recipe is from Stephen Schmidt.

> 2 cups dried tart cherries (see Source List)
>
> ¼ cup dark Jamaican rum
>
> 1 cup (2 sticks) butter, at room temperature
>
> ¾ cup firmly packed dark brown sugar
>
> 1 cup walnut or pecan halves
>
> ¼ teaspoon ground cinnamon
>
> ¼ teaspoon salt
>
> 1 cup confectioners' sugar
>
> 2 egg yolks
>
> 1 whole egg
>
> ¾ teaspoon vanilla extract
>
> ¾ cup unsifted cake flour
>
> Unsweetened whipped cream

Cover the cherries with 2 cups of very hot tap water and let stand 45 minutes. Drain, pressing gently; the cherries should seem plump and moist but not sodden. Return the cherries to their soaking bowl, add the rum, and stir. Let stand for 30 to 60 minutes, stirring several times.

Melt 1 stick of the butter in a 9-inch cast-iron skillet. Remove from the heat and stir in the brown sugar. Sprinkle the cherries and their liquid on top, making a fairly even layer, then distribute the nuts over the cherries, pressing them down lightly. Sprinkle with cinnamon and set aside.

Preheat the oven to 325° F. With an electric mixer, beat the remaining ½ cup of butter and salt for 3 minutes at high speed. Add the confectioners' sugar gradually and beat 3 minutes longer. Add the egg yolks one at a time and beat for 2 full minutes longer after the last has gone in. Add the whole egg and vanilla and beat only until the mixture looks smooth and creamy. Sprinkle or sift the flour on top and fold it in gently.

Spread the cake batter evenly over the cherries and bake for 30 to 40 minutes, or until the top is browned and a cake tester inserted in the center of the cake comes out clean. Let the cake stand for 3 minutes after removing from the oven, then run a knife around the sides and invert onto a serving platter. Serve warm or at room temperature, with whipped cream on the side.

Sauerkraut Chocolate Cake

———— ★ ————

MAKES 12 TO 16 SERVINGS

Yes, you read correctly—sauerkraut cake. This recipe is very old and very wonderful. It probably came into being because some frugal housewife had some extra kraut to use up and tossed it in a cake she was stirring up at the time. The kraut creates a very moist cake, though you will not be able to taste it. If you refrigerate it, be sure to bring it to room temperature before serving.

1	16-ounce can sauerkraut, rinsed and well drained
⅔	cup margarine
1½	cups sugar
3	eggs
2	teaspoons vanilla extract
½	cup unsweetened cocoa powder
1	teaspoon baking powder
1	teaspoon salt
1	teaspoon baking soda
2¼	cups all-purpose flour
1	cup cold water
	Quick Chocolate Frosting (page 245)

Squeeze all excess moisture from the kraut with your hands. Chop it finely with a knife or pulse 4 or 5 times in a food processor bowl; set aside. Preheat the oven to 350° F.

In a large mixer bowl, beat the margarine and sugar until fluffy, about 3 minutes. Add the eggs one at a time, mixing well after each addition. Add the vanilla, cocoa, baking powder, salt, and baking soda; blend. Add the flour alternately with the water, beginning and ending with the flour. Fold in the sauerkraut. Pour into a greased 13 x 9-inch pan and bake for 30 minutes or until the center of the cake springs back when you touch it with your finger. Cool and frost with chocolate frosting.

Pumpkin Mousse

———★———

MAKES 8 TO 12 SERVINGS

In Ohio, pumpkin appears in pies, cakes, cookies, and breads, and is eaten with pleasure all year long. This pale creamy mousse with its touch of marmalade gives plain pumpkin pie a lot of competition!

- 2 packets unflavored gelatin
- ½ cup light rum
- 1 (1 pound) can unsweetened pumpkin puree
- ½ cup granulated sugar
- ½ cup brown sugar
- ½ cup orange marmalade
- 2 egg yolks
- ½ teaspoon grated nutmeg
- ¼ teaspoon ground allspice
- ¼ teaspoon ground mace
- 1 teaspoon ground cinnamon
- 2 teaspoons vanilla extract
- ½ teaspoon salt
- 2 cups heavy (whipping) cream

In a small saucepan, sprinkle the gelatin over the rum and bring to a boil over low heat, stirring until the gelatin dissolves. In a large mixer bowl, combine the pumpkin puree, sugars, marmalade, egg yolks, nutmeg, allspice, mace, cinnamon, vanilla, and salt, and mix thoroughly. Whisk the hot gelatin mixture into the pumpkin mixture.

In a separate bowl, whip the cream until stiff peaks form. Carefully but thoroughly fold it into the pumpkin mixture. Pour into a large glass serving bowl and refrigerate until firm, about 6 hours, or overnight.

OPPOSITE: The Circleville Ohio Pumpkin Show gives an award for the biggest pumpkin grown within a 17-mile radius. This one weighed in at nearly 400 pounds. Its size gives it a distinct personality.

Raisin Crumb Pie

———★———

MAKES 6 TO 8 SERVINGS

Raisins were a precious commodity in the pioneer days and were used sparingly to make scanty supplies last longer. This pie has just a few raisins in its filling and a spicy crumb topping to add a contrasting texture. It is an excellent interpretation of raisin pie, and a scoop of vanilla ice cream on top makes it even better.

PIE
- Shallow 9-inch pastry shell (½ recipe Never-Fail Pie Crust, page 244)
- ½ cup dark raisins
- 2¼ cups water
- 1 cup brown sugar
- 1 tablespoon fresh lemon juice
- ½ teaspoon salt
- 2 tablespoons cornstarch
- 2 tablespoons (¼ stick) butter

TOPPING
- 1 cup all-purpose flour
- 1 cup brown sugar
- 1 teaspoon ground ginger
- 1 teaspoon ground cinnamon
- ½ teaspoon baking soda
- ¼ cup (½ stick) butter, softened

Preheat the oven to 375° F. Prick the crust with a fork and prebake it for just about 5 minutes; it should not yet be coloring.

In a 2-quart saucepan, combine the raisins, 2 cups water, brown sugar, lemon juice, and salt. Bring to a boil over medium-high heat, stirring occasionally.

In a small bowl, combine the cornstarch with the remaining ¼ cup of water; whisk it into the raisin mixture and continue cooking and stirring until mixture is thick and bubbly, about 2 minutes. Stir in the butter and let the mixture cool. Pour the cooled filling into the crust; set aside.

In a small bowl or food processor, combine the flour, brown sugar, ginger, cinnamon, baking soda, and softened butter until crumbly. Sprinkle the crumb topping over the raisin pie. Bake for about 25 to 30 minutes or until the top is golden brown. Cool and refrigerate.

Black Raspberry Silk Pie

MAKES 8 SERVINGS

The small berries of the Midwest give the pie baker and jam maker happy opportunities all summer long. First come the strawberries, then the raspberries (both black and red), followed by blueberries, currants, gooseberries, blackberries, elderberries, and in some states, whortleberries and ground cherries.

Certainly one of the most elegant of pies is this Black Raspberry Silk Pie, divinely smooth with an intense fruit flavor.

One thing to remember about custard pies like this is not to overbake them. They will turn tough and grainy.

2 cups fresh black raspberries or blackberries, or 1 12-ounce bag frozen berries, thawed
3 eggs, at room temperature
1½ cups heavy (whipping) cream, at room temperature
¾ cup sugar
1 teaspoon vanilla extract
 Pinch of salt
 9-inch baked pastry shell (½ recipe Never-Fail Pie Crust, page 244)
 Fresh berries and fresh mint leaves, for garnish

Preheat the oven to 425° F. In a blender or food processor, puree the berries, then strain through a fine-mesh sieve to remove the seeds. In a medium bowl, lightly beat the eggs. Stir in the cream, sugar, vanilla, salt, and berry puree; mix until thoroughly blended. Pour the filling into the pie shell and bake for 10 minutes. Lower the heat to 325° F. and continue baking for 35 minutes longer, or until the filling jiggles slightly in the center (but does not ripple in waves). Transfer the pie to a wire rack and let it cool completely.

Cover the pie loosely with foil and refrigerate for at least 1 hour before serving. Garnish the top with a few berries.

NOTE: You want just a little wobbliness left in the center of the pie when it comes out of the oven. As it cools, it will firm up.

Peanut Butter Pie

from the Inn at Honey Run

MAKES 6 TO 8 SERVINGS

Cream pies like these are served at Amish weddings, but always at the noon meal; since the Amish have no electricity or refrigeration, there is no way to keep them cool all day. Fruit pies are reserved for the evening wedding meal.

This is a favorite pie among the Amish, and is served in all of their Midwestern communities. Vanilla custard is layered in a pie shell with sweetened peanut butter crumbs and then topped with whipped cream.

Hot Butterscotch Velvet Sauce (page 246) can be drizzled over the top of this pie just before serving, if you are so inclined.

⅓ cup smooth peanut butter
¾ cup confectioners' sugar
3 cups milk
¼ cup cornstarch
½ cup granulated sugar
¼ teaspoon salt
3 egg yolks
2 tablespoons (¼ stick) butter
1 teaspoon vanilla extract
 9-inch baked pastry shell (½ recipe Never-Fail Pie Crust, page 244)
 Whipped Cream Topping (page 247)

In a small bowl, combine the peanut butter and confectioners' sugar until crumbly; set aside. In a medium saucepan, combine the milk, cornstarch, granulated sugar, and salt. Stir in the egg yolks. Cook over medium heat, stirring constantly until mixture thickens and comes to a boil; boil for 1 minute then remove from the heat. Stir in the butter and vanilla. Place plastic wrap on the surface of the cream filling and set aside to cool.

Spread ⅔ cup of the peanut butter crumbs in the baked and cooled pie shell, covering the bottom and sides of the shell. Pour the cream filling over the crumbs and chill thoroughly. Spread on the whipped topping and sprinkle with the remaining peanut butter crumbs. Refrigerate until serving.

Buckeyes

---·★·---

MAKES 3 DOZEN BUCKEYES

In the fall, along quiet small-town streets, children gather after school to pick up buckeyes, those glossy round treasures that fall off the buckeye trees after a frost. If Ohio were to declare a state candy, this recipe would be it. These taste like peanut butter candy bars and are out of this world. Some cooks like to leave a bit of the peanut butter ball exposed when dipping it in the chocolate so it more closely resembles a real buckeye.

- 4 cups crunchy or smooth peanut butter
- 1 cup (2 sticks) butter, at room temperature
- 6 cups confectioners' sugar
- 2 tablespoons vanilla extract
- 1 12-ounce bag semisweet chocolate morsels
- ½ cup shaved paraffin

In a large mixer bowl, beat the peanut butter, butter, confectioners' sugar, and vanilla together. Cover and chill until firm, or overnight. Roll into small buckeye-size balls, about 1 inch in diameter, and place on shallow, wax paper–lined pans. Chill until firm.

In the top of a double boiler, melt the chocolate morsels and paraffin. With a candy dipper or toothpick, dip the balls into the chocolate and drain on a cake rack. When firm, refrigerate until serving time.

Peach-Onion Chutney with Raisins

---·★·---

MAKES ABOUT 12 TO 14 HALF-PINT JARS

Chutney is a nice condiment to have on hand to serve with meat dishes that could use a little picking up—a bit of zip, if you please. Serve it in a cut-glass bowl and dip it out onto your plate next to roast beef, pork, or turkey. A jar of this makes a nice little gift, too.

- 5 cups pitted, peeled, and chopped peaches
- 2 medium onions, thinly sliced
- 2 cups brown sugar
- 1¾ cups cider vinegar
- 1½ cups raisins
- 1 lemon, seeded and finely chopped in a food processor
- 2 tablespoons mustard seed
- 1 tablespoon ground ginger
- 1½ teaspoons salt
- ½ teaspoon hot red pepper flakes
- ¼ teaspoon ground allspice

In a large, heavy stockpot, combine all of the ingredients and bring to a boil. Reduce the heat to low and simmer, uncovered, for about 1 hour. As the mixture thickens, stir frequently to prevent sticking. Pour hot into hot jars, leaving ¼-inch headspace. Adjust caps and process for 10 minutes in a hot-water bath.

As I looked back upon my life on that woodland farm, it all seems very colorful and sweet. I am re-living the days when the warm sun, falling on radiant slopes of grass, lit the meadow phlox and tall tiger lilies into flaming torches of color. I think of blackberry thickets and odorous grapevines and cherry trees and delicious nuts which grew in profusion. We loved every day for the color it brought, each season for the wealth of its experience, and we welcomed the thought of spending all our years in this beautiful home where the wood and the prairie of our song did actually meet and mingle.

HAMLIN GARLAND
A Son of the Middle Border, 1914

■ ■ ■

Wisconsin is dazzlingly green, silky, and luxurious looking, especially in midsummer. Morning mists blanket the gentle valleys but rise in smoky veils and disappear as soon as the sun's hurrah pierces the east with crimson. Instinctively, one is glad to be here and exults in the generosity of the land. ★ Its cuisine is a dance of color. In four distinct areas—the prairie in the southeast; the hills of the southwest; the central plain; and the marshes, lakes, and majestic forests in the north—variety is its keynote. ★ Settlers from other parts of America and immigrants from abroad came to farm, to mine lead and zinc, to work in the river cities and lake ports, and to take jobs in the urbanizing industrial southeast. For nearly all of them, Wisconsin immediately felt like home. To the Cornish miners, Wisconsin was reminiscent of England; the Scandinavians found the winters similar to what they had known in Europe; the Germans thought this was another Rhineland; and the French thought the land looked like Alsace.

So they lumbered, mined, quarried, tanned, fished, milled, canned, brewed, and built a farm-implement industry. They created a culture that emphasized family, church, local events, hard work, individual responsibility, order, and decorum. Their self-image was progressive, and their state motto unified them and summed it all up: "Forward."

Following the precedent set by their Yankee and northern European forefathers, Wisconsin farmers excelled in making their favorite limburger, cheddar, and mozzarella cheeses, and Colby cheese was developed here. Thirty-five percent of the cheese consumed in the United States today is from Wisconsin. Sour cream, ice cream, and yogurt are important to the economy as well.

But let's not forget the pastry and breads. Kringle, a thin, fruit-filled breakfast ring that's unique to Racine, is a Danish dream, and while it's almost impossible to duplicate this crispy breakfast treat at home, it mails wonderful well (see Source List). And here we find Cornish pasties again.

The farms and orchards are lush with produce and fruit. One-third of the nation's cranberries grow in the northwest part of the state, and we also find cherries, snap beans, peas, beets, cabbage, sweet corn, lima beans, cucumbers, carrots, and potatoes.

Add duck, another one of Wisconsin's staples, and turkey, and a dozen kinds of freshwater fish . . . and you have a zesty, lively cuisine, a hearty blend of flavorful possibilities that dance and sway across Wisconsin's hills and lakes and fields and forests ahead of one's best efforts to capture all of these in a market basket. ✶

FRANK LLOYD WRIGHT'S STEEL-CUT OATMEAL *
SWEDISH PANCAKES * TURKEY LIVER PÂTÉ * CREAM
OF SUGAR SNAP PEA SOUP * CORN CHOWDER *
CHEDDAR CHEESE, SAUSAGE, AND BEER SOUP *
SWEDISH MEAT BALLS * FLEMISH BEEF AND BEER *
BOOYAH * BRAISED DUCK WITH FRUITED RICE *
DOOR COUNTY FISH BOIL * GRILLED BRATWURST *
HUNGARIAN CABBAGE ROLLS * BROILED BABY
ZUCCHINI WITH BACON AND CHEESE * ESCALLOPED
TOMATOES * BUTTERNUT SQUASH WITH WHITE
BEANS TALIESIN * CREAMY CHEESE POTATOES *
LIMAS AND PEAS BAKED WITH HERBS * VEGETABLE
JAM * WELSH SAFFRON BREAD * SWEDISH LIMPA
BREAD * CRANBERRY MOUSSE WITH RASPBERRY
SAUCE * DOOR COUNTY MONTMORENCY CHERRY PIE
* APPLE CHEESE CRISP * BLACK FOREST TORTE *
PRUNE-BLACK WALNUT CAKE * RICH CUSTARD
PEACH ICE CREAM * CRANBERRY SALSA * FRUIT
CHILI SAUCE * APPLE CIDER MARMALADE

Frank Lloyd Wright's Steel-Cut Oatmeal

———✳———

MAKES 2 SERVINGS

Wright, a Wisconsin native, preferred all of his foods simply prepared and insisted on steel-cut oatmeal every morning. This is his recipe, quite unchanged. Serve it with milk or cream, brown sugar, and if you are feeling expansive, a dab of butter, too.

This dish can also be made with regular oatmeal, but the steel-cutting of the oats creates sharp-edged pieces, which gives the cooked porridge a chewier texture. Steel-cut oatmeal, sometimes called Irish or Scottish oats, is available at health-food stores or specialty-food shops.

2⅓ **cups water**
⅜ **teaspoon salt**
⅓ **cup steel-cut (Irish) oats**
   Salt to taste

In the top of a double boiler, bring the water and salt to a boil over direct heat. Add the oats and simmer over direct heat for 5 minutes. Cover pan tightly with foil, then cover with the lid. Place the double boiler over boiling water, place an asbestos pad over very low heat, and cook very slowly overnight. In the morning, stir and add water if too thick, or cook down if necessary.

Swedish Pancakes

———✳———

MAKES 5 DOZEN VERY THIN 3-INCH PANCAKES

Al Johnson's Swedish Restaurant is in Sister Bay, at the northern tip of Door County. The structure, hand-carved and built in Norway, was disassembled and sent to the town, where it was reassembled by a crew of Norwegian workers. The roof is grassy sod, and in the summer, goats—yes, live goats—keep it neatly trimmed. Being greeted by an overhead munching goat is admittedly a drawing card, but this would still be the place to eat the very best Swedish food in Door County, even if there were no goats on the roof.

Thin Swedish pancakes with lingonberry preserves (see Source List) can be ordered at every meal, and while the chefs there do not give out their recipe, this one comes satisfyingly close. You can substitute other tart red fruit preserves for the lingonberries.

4 **eggs**
2 **tablespoons (¼ stick) butter, melted**
2 **cups milk**
1½ **cups all-purpose flour**
½ **teaspoon salt**
1½ **teaspoons ground cinnamon**
2 **tablespoons sugar**

In a large mixing bowl, beat the eggs thoroughly. Add the rest of the ingredients in the order given and beat until smooth. Heat a griddle to medium hot (360° F.) and lightly grease it with butter.

Spoon about 1 tablespoon batter onto the griddle for each cake. Cook until lightly browned on the bottom, about 2 to 3 minutes. Loosen the edges with a spatula, turn, and lightly brown on the second side. The cakes will be a bit irregular in shape and lacy thin.

Transfer the cakes to a heated plate and arrange in a circle, slightly overlapping. Set a small bowl of lingonberry preserves in the center.

The resident roof grazer takes an afternoon rest in the sunshine.

Turkey Liver Pâté

Turkey farming is a big industry in Wisconsin, and cooks there have devised many interesting ways to use America's native bird. Turkey liver pâté is every bit as good as chicken liver pâté, and frequently turkey livers are more economical. Nicely seasoned with herbs and wine, this pâté can also be frozen.

½ cup (1 stick) butter or rendered chicken fat
½ cup olive oil
2 very large onions, chopped
2 pounds turkey livers, rinsed, trimmed of membranes, and quartered
1 bay leaf
¼ teaspoon dried oregano
½ teaspoon dried basil
1 teaspoon salt
¼ teaspoon freshly ground pepper
1 tablespoon Worcestershire sauce
3 shakes hot red pepper sauce
2 tablespoons dry sherry
2 tablespoons dry white wine
1½ tablespoons Dijon mustard
Grated hard-cooked egg and minced fresh parsley, for garnish

Heat the butter and olive oil in an 11-inch sauté pan; add the onions and sauté until golden, about 8 to 10 minutes. Rinse and drain the livers and add to the skillet with the bay leaf. Cook over medium-low heat until the livers are no longer pink in the center, but not brown, about 10 minutes. Add the oregano, basil, salt, pepper, Worcestershire sauce, and red pepper sauce, and cook 3 minutes longer.

Stir in the sherry, white wine, and mustard, and allow the mixture to cool slightly. Remove the bay leaf. Transfer to a food processor bowl in 2 batches and process until well pureed and smooth. Chill. Heap in a bowl and garnish with grated eggs and a sprinkle of parsley.

Cream of Sugar Snap Pea Soup

Every host or hostess should have a repertoire of green soups, for they are such a good and colorful way to start a meal. Pureed sugar snap peas seasoned with cumin and fresh coriander create an aristocratic and hauntingly flavored soup.

This can be served either hot or cold. For a knockout contrast, serve it with croutons made from Tomato Bread (page 50). The recipe is from a small Door County cookbook, The Down to Earth Vegetable Cookbook, *by Circle Arts.*

3 small shallots, minced
2 tablespoons (¼ stick) butter, or vegetable oil
½ pound sugar snap peas, or 1½ cups shelled fresh peas or ½ pound snow peas, strings removed
2½ cups vegetable stock or Chicken Stock (page 239)
2 tablespoons fresh lemon juice
¼ teaspoon ground cumin
½ cup heavy (whipping) cream
1 tablespoon minced fresh coriander
Dash of hot red pepper sauce
Salt and pepper

Sauté the shallots in the butter until softened, about 5 to 7 minutes. Add the peas and stir-fry until just tender, 2 to 3 minutes. Stir in the stock, lemon juice, and cumin and simmer 10 to 15 minutes. Let stand 10 minutes, then puree the mixture in a food processor or blender. Stir in the cream, coriander, and red pepper sauce. Add salt and pepper to taste. Heat through, but do not bring to a boil. Serve hot.

Corn Chowder

from L'Etoile

———— ✱ ————

*"I come from a large family dedicated to food,"
said Odessa Piper, seated in her Madison restaurant,
L'Etoile. Her education about food continued as she
farmed and studied the principles of sustainable agriculture on small farms in New England and Wisconsin. She opened L'Etoile just about the same time
Madison's Farmer's Market was being established just
across the street on Capitol Square. The restaurant's
menus are designed to showcase regional ingredients as
they come into season at the market.*

- 4 ears of corn, husked and silked
- 3 tablespoons vegetable oil
- ½ green bell pepper, diced
- ½ red bell pepper, diced
- 1 jalapeño pepper, seeded and minced
- 1 celery stalk, diced
- ⅓ cup diced onion
- 2 teaspoons minced garlic
- ½ cup dry white wine
- ¼ cup fresh lime juice
- 3 cups heavy (whipping) cream
- 1 tablespoon chopped fresh cilantro, plus extra
     for garnish
  Salt and pepper to taste

Fill a 4-quart pot with about 1½ inches of water;
bring to a boil. Add the corn and cook just until
the ears turn deep yellow, about 5 minutes. Remove the corn from the water with tongs and cool.

Using a sharp knife, remove the kernels from
the cobs; set aside. Return the cobs to the pot and
simmer for 15 minutes. Discard the cobs and reduce the liquid over high heat by one-half. Strain
and set aside.

In a stockpot, heat the oil over medium heat.
Add the peppers, celery, onion, and garlic and
sauté until tender, about 10 minutes. Add the wine,
lime juice, reserved corn, reserved corn liquid, and
cream. Simmer, uncovered, until reduced to desired consistency. Just before serving, stir in the
chopped cilantro. Season with salt and pepper to
taste, and garnish with additional cilantro.

Cheddar Cheese, Sausage, and Beer Soup

from Quivey's Grove

———— ✱ ————

*When I think of Wisconsin foods, cheese and beer
immediately come to mind. Quivey's Grove, an attractive restaurant housed in an 1855 fieldstone mansion,
combines those two indigenous foods to create a savory
soup that is rich, hearty, and satisfyingly thick.*

- 2 quarts water
- 1 pound smoked ham pieces
- 1 small onion, finely chopped
- ½ teaspoon freshly ground black pepper
- 1 cup (2 sticks) margarine
- 1½ cups all-purpose flour
- 2 cups milk, or more if necessary
- ¾ cup beer
- 12 ounces sharp cheddar cheese, grated
- 12 ounces cooked bulk sausage, chopped
- ¼ cup chopped fresh parsley
- ¼ teaspoon hot red pepper sauce (optional)

In a large pot, combine the water, ham, onion, and
black pepper. Bring to a boil, then reduce heat and
simmer, uncovered, for 1 hour. Strain, skim the fat
from the surface, and return the stock to pot,
keeping it warm. Reserve the ham.

In another heavy saucepan, prepare a roux by
melting the margarine until bubbly, then whisking
in the flour, cooking and stirring for 5 minutes
over medium-low heat. Do not let this mixture
stick or get too brown. Slowly add the hot stock
and milk, stirring until thick and smooth and
melted. Add the beer, blending until smooth.
Sprinkle in the cheese gradually, whisking the
mixture to blend. Add the chopped sausage to the
soup along with the reserved ham, parsley, and red
pepper sauce if desired. Serve immediately or keep
warm over very low heat or in a double boiler.

ABOVE: *Wikstrom's Delicatessen in Chicago is a food source for homesick Scandinavians all over the Midwest.* OPPOSITE: *On the square surrounding Madison's Capital Building, an open-air market is set up every Saturday.*

Swedish Meat Balls

————— ✱ —————

MAKES 6 TO 8 SERVINGS

Since the Swedish are the second largest ethnic population in Wisconsin, you find lots of recipes for Swedish meat balls in this state. The Swedes make theirs differently from the Norwegians: Swedish meat balls generally are a bit smaller, their texture smoother (mashed potatoes are an important ingredient), and the seasonings include allspice, nutmeg, and cloves. You will always find them on a smorgasbord, and they are also a hearty main dish served with buttered noodles. This recipe can be made in advance and frozen.

MEATBALLS

  2 eggs
  ½ cup mashed potatoes
  2 cups fine dry bread crumbs
  3 tablespoons minced onion
  1 teaspoon salt
  ½ teaspoon brown sugar
  ½ teaspoon freshly ground pepper
  ¾ teaspoon ground allspice
  ¾ teaspoon grated nutmeg
  ¼ teaspoon ground cloves
  ¼ teaspoon powdered ginger
  1 pound ground round
  ½ pound lean ground pork
  3 tablespoons butter or more

SAUCE

  2 tablespoons all-purpose flour
  ¼ teaspoon salt
  ¼ teaspoon grated nutmeg
    Dash of hot red pepper sauce
  1 cup Beef Stock (page 239)
  1 cup half-and-half

Beat one of the eggs in a large bowl. Add the mashed potatoes, ½ cup of the bread crumbs, the onion, and all the seasonings; combine well. Place the meats in a food processor bowl and pulse a few times or until the meat looks smooth. Transfer to the mixing bowl with the potatoes and seasonings and combine lightly with your hands.

Shape into balls about 1 inch in diameter. In a small bowl, beat the remaining egg and pour into a pie pan. Pour the remaining bread crumbs into another pie pan. Roll the balls first in the egg, then lightly in the crumbs.

In a 10-inch skillet, melt the butter over medium heat; add the meat balls and brown on all sides, about 8 to 10 minutes, turning them with tongs. Drain on paper towels while preparing the sauce.

To the drippings in the skillet, add the flour and seasonings. Heat and stir until the mixture bubbles, then add the stock and half-and-half. Whisk until smooth—the sauce will be a bit thin. Return the meat balls to the skillet, and simmer for 10 minutes; the gravy will thicken as they cook.

Flemish Beef and Beer

— ✶ —

MAKES 6 SERVINGS

More beer is drunk in Wisconsin than in any other state in the Union. I don't know what conclusion we can draw from this except to recognize that these people know how to make beer that is irresistibly good. Since 1840, more than three hundred breweries have opened (and, sadly, closed) in Wisconsin. Today, there are three major breweries left—Miller, Helleman, and Pabst—and they are all flourishing.

Flemish Beef and Beer is an ideal company dish: it holds its heat in a casserole on the buffet; it can be eaten with just a fork; and it can be prepared at a reasonable cost—an attribute not to be overlooked. The traditional accompaniment is boiled potatoes and, of course, a glass of beer.

½ cup vegetable oil
1 large onion, thinly sliced
1 garlic clove, minced
2 pounds round steak
2 to 3 tablespoons all-purpose flour
1 teaspoon salt
¼ teaspoon freshly ground pepper
2 parsley sprigs, chopped
½ teaspoon grated nutmeg
½ teaspoon dried thyme
1 bay leaf, crumbled
1 12-ounce can of beer
1 tablespoon brown sugar

Preheat the oven to 325° F. Heat half the oil in an 11-inch sauté pan. Add the onion and garlic and sauté over medium heat until transparent, about 5 to 7 minutes. Transfer the sautéed vegetables to a small bowl with a slotted spoon. Trim any fat from the meat and cut the meat into cubes. Dredge the meat in the flour mixed with the salt and pepper. Add the remaining oil to the pan (you may need a bit more) and brown the meat well on all sides.

Place the meat on the bottom of an 11 x 7-inch glass baking dish and spread the sautéed vegetables over the top. Sprinkle with the parsley, nutmeg, thyme, and bay leaf. Pour in the beer and sprinkle brown sugar over all. Cover and bake for 2½ to 3 hours or until the meat is tender.

Booyah

— ✶ —

MAKES 6 GENEROUS SERVINGS

Among the ethnic groups that settled around the area of Green Bay was a community of Belgians. When they first arrived in Wisconsin more than a century ago, they found turtles, good for eating, along the swampy shore of the bay. Using the turtle meat, they devised a hearty soup they called Booyah.

The swamps and turtles are long gone, but booyah lives on, now made with chicken. Booyah dinners are community affairs, sponsored by local churches or fire departments as fund-raisers.

If you prefer, you can cook the chicken and stock the day before. What really makes this dish different from chicken soup is that the pieces are always very large chunks.

3 pounds meaty chicken pieces
1 large onion, quartered
2 bay leaves
1 large carrot, peeled and cut in 1-inch chunks
1 large potato, peeled and cut in 1-inch chunks
2 celery stalks, cut in 1-inch chunks
1 teaspoon low-sodium chicken bouillon granules
½ teaspoon salt
¼ teaspoon freshly ground pepper
1 cup (3 ounces) medium-wide noodles
⅓ cup fresh or frozen green peas
    Minced fresh chervil or chives, for garnish

Place the chicken pieces, onion, and bay leaves in a large stockpot and add enough water to cover by 3 inches. Bring to a boil over high heat, then lower the heat, and simmer, covered, for 30 minutes, or until the chicken is tender when pierced with a fork. With tongs, remove the chicken to a pan to cool slightly. While still warm, strip the meat from the bones in large pieces, discarding the skin and fat. You should have approximately 3½ to 4 cups of chicken. At this point, you can refrigerate both the stock and the chicken. Skim the congealed fat off the top of the chicken stock before proceeding. If you do not refrigerate the stock, place a double thickness of paper toweling on top of the stock to soak up the excess fat.

Add the carrot, potato, celery, and seasonings to the stock and bring to a boil. Lower the heat and simmer the vegetables, covered, for 20 minutes. Add the noodles and cook for 5 minutes. Add the peas and the reserved chicken and cook 5 minutes longer, or until the noodles are tender and the chicken is just heated through.

Transfer to a large heated soup tureen and serve at the table in large soup plates. Garnish with fresh chervil or chives.

Braised Duck with Fruited Rice

———— ✶ ————

MAKES 4 SERVINGS

Wisconsin raises ducks commercially by the thousands, and the folks in the Badger State prepare duck dishes as frequently as the rest of us do chicken. You will enjoy this braised duck with its touch of apricot, cinnamon, and cumin, and it is prepared with rice, all in one large skillet. You can buy just the duck legs and thighs at your meat market, which makes serving duck ever so much easier.

    1 teaspoon peanut oil
    4 duck legs and thighs
    1 medium onion, chopped
 3½ cups duck stock or Chicken Stock
       (page 239)
    2 tablespoons balsamic vinegar
 1½ teaspoons salt
    1 cup long-grain rice
    1 cup dried apricot halves
    1 cup golden raisins
    2 teaspoons sugar
    1 teaspoon ground cinnamon
    1 teaspoon ground cumin
  ¼ teaspoon freshly ground pepper
       Chopped fresh parsley, for garnish

Place the oil and duck pieces in a large skillet. Sauté over medium-high heat until golden brown, about 3 minutes on each side. Drain off the fat and discard. Add the onion, 1 cup of the stock, vinegar, and salt. Cover and cook over medium-low heat for 45 minutes, turning once. Remove the duck from the pan. Add the remaining ingredients, including the rest of the stock. Place the duck pieces on top of the rice.

Cover, bring to a boil, lower the heat, and cook until the rice and duck are tender, about 30 minutes. Garnish with chopped parsley.

Door County Fish Boil

MAKES 6 SERVINGS

This show-biz method of cooking fish was popular first with the fishermen after a catch, then with Door County church congregations as a fund-raising event. It is quite a production. The fish and vegetables are cooked outdoors in a huge pot over a wood fire. Kerosene is thrown on the flames at the last minute, and then the water boils over with great drama, and everybody claps and has another drink as the food is dished up—it is all great fun and good to eat, too. The fish is usually served with cole slaw and cherry pie.

Though the White Gull Inn does fish boils using enormous amounts of fish and potatoes, they have so many requests for instructions on how to do this at home that they developed this recipe to serve six people. It is done on your kitchen stove without the kerosene. Do not be alarmed by the pound of salt required—it is necessary to elevate the boiling point of the water to keep the fish pieces intact. The food does not absorb the salt—trust me, I've eaten it.

- 3   large pieces of cheesecloth for bags, approximately 24 x 24 inches square
- 12   small red new potatoes, scrubbed
- 1   pound small onions, peeled
- 8   quarts water
- 2   cups salt

1

2

3

4

12 1-inch-thick whitefish steaks (see Note)
1 cup (2 sticks) butter, melted
    Lemon wedges, for garnish

Cut a thin slice from each end of the potatoes and tie them loosely in a cheesecloth square with kitchen twine. Place the onions in another cheesecloth square and tie loosely. In a large kettle, bring the 8 quarts of water to a boil over high heat (if the kettle has a removeable basket, all the better, but it is not necessary).

Add 1 cup of salt slowly so it doesn't lower the boil, then add the potato bag. Partly cover and cook 14 minutes. Add the onion bag and boil 6 minutes longer. Check the potatoes by spearing with a knife; if they are almost done it is time to add the fish.

Wrap the fish in the third piece of cheesecloth and tie the top; there should be enough space that the water can circulate freely about the fish as it cooks. Add the remaining 1 cup of salt and then the fish. Cook for 10 minutes, skimming any fish oils from the cooking water. Drain the fish and vegetables, remove from the cheesecloth, and transfer to a very large platter. Pour the melted butter over all, and serve with lemon wedges.

NOTE: In Door County whitefish steaks are used, but halibut, cod, or haddock would lend themselves equally well.

5

6

7

8

Grilled Bratwurst

MAKES 4 SHEBOYGAN-SIZE SERVINGS

Sheboygan claims to be the sausage capital of the world, and no one quarrels with that. Their specialty is bratwurst, a name that originally meant "lean meat sausage." In comparison to their first cousin, the hot dog, "brats" are pale in color and contain a mixture of veal and pork. The fresh ones are better than the pre-cooked ones, so do look for those at your butcher.

Beer goes well with bratwurst right from the start; marinate them overnight in beer. Be careful not to puncture them or you will lose the good juices during grilling.

- 8 bratwurst
- 1½ cups beer
- 1½ tablespoons vegetable oil
- 2 large onions, coarsely chopped
- 2 tablespoons dark brown sugar
- 2 tablespoons cider vinegar
- 1 tablespoon Worcestershire sauce
- ½ teaspoon salt
- 1 teaspoon paprika
- 1 bay leaf

Place the bratwurst in a shallow glass dish. Pour in the beer, cover, and refrigerate overnight.

Preheat the grill or broiler. In a medium saucepan, heat the oil. Add the onions and cook over medium heat until the onions are lightly browned, about 4 minutes. Add the brown sugar, vinegar, Worcestershire sauce, salt, paprika, and bay leaf. Remove the bratwurst from the beer and add the beer to the onions.

Cook the beer mixture over medium-high heat for 5 minutes. Meanwhile, grill or broil the bratwurst about 7 to 9 inches from the heat for about 20 minutes. Turn with tongs, not a fork, so the bratwurst don't get punctured and the juices escape. Baste with the sauce during the last 5 to 10 minutes. Serve with Sweet Hot Mustard (page 240) and, of course, beer.

Hungarian Cabbage Rolls
(Toltott Kaposzta)

MAKES 6 GENEROUS SERVINGS

Darlene Kronschanabel is a professional food writer from the Midwest, with many cookbooks to her credit. This is her grandmother's recipe, and in their family it is served at their Christmas dinner with turkey, and again at Easter with boiled ham. These cabbage rolls are absolutely first-class eating.

- 1 cabbage, 3 to 4 pounds (see Note)
- 2½ pounds ground beef
- 2 eggs, lightly beaten
- 2 cups cooked white rice
- 1 medium onion, finely chopped
- 1 teaspoon salt
- 1½ tablespoons sweet Hungarian paprika
- 1 garlic clove, finely chopped
- ¼ teaspoon ground pepper
- 3 cups sauerkraut, drained
- 4 cups tomato juice
- 1 cup water
- 2 tablespoons (¼ stick) butter
- 2 tablespoons all-purpose flour

Wash and core the cabbage. Drop the whole head into a large kettle of boiling water and simmer for 5 minutes. Remove, drain, and cool. Carefully peel off the outer leaves; you will need about 15 to 18 cabbage leaves. Chop the remaining inner leaves and set aside.

Mix the beef, eggs, rice, onion, salt, paprika, garlic, and pepper; blend well. Place a portion (about ½ cup) of the meat mixture on the large core end of a cabbage leaf. Fold the sides in over the mixture and roll up carefully, tucking the end in. Repeat with the remaining filling and cabbage leaves.

Spread one-half of the sauerkraut on the bottom of a deep cooking pan. Carefully place the cabbage rolls on top of the kraut, then top with the remaining sauerkraut and the chopped raw cabbage. Pour in the tomato juice and water. Simmer on top of the stove, covered, on low heat for 1 to 2 hours, or until the cabbage leaves are tender—this depends on the age of the cabbage.

Melt the butter over medium-low heat in a small pan and stir in the flour: cook and stir until slightly browned, about 2 to 3 minutes. Whisk in about ½ cup of the cooking liquid from the cabbage rolls, then add 1½ cups more cooking liquid and continue cooking until a thickened sauce forms. Pour over the cabbage rolls; do not stir in; the sauce will cover the cabbage rolls by itself. Simmer for 5 minutes.

NOTE: Sometimes to get the large number of perfect leaves needed, I use 2 cabbages. The bigger the leaves, the easier it is to form the rolls.

Broiled Baby Zucchini with Bacon and Cheese

———— ✱ ————
MAKES 4 SERVINGS

Think you've seen every recipe there is for zucchini? Here's another one and it's worth your attention. For this recipe, use the smallest zucchini you can find. The bacon, a popular country seasoning, forms a crispy topping and bastes the squash with a smoky flavor.

- 4 fresh zucchini, each approximately 4 inches long
  Fresh coarsely ground pepper to taste
- 4 bacon slices, halved
- 1 cup grated Cheddar cheese, approximately
  Chopped fresh parsley, for garnish

Preheat the broiler and place a broiling pan 7 inches from the heat source. Split the unpeeled zucchini lengthwise and sprinkle the cut surfaces generously with pepper. Place the zucchini on the heated pan and broil for 10 minutes. Place a bacon piece on each zucchini half and top generously with cheese. Broil approximately 5 minutes longer, or until the bacon is crisp and the cheese is golden brown and bubbly. Sprinkle with chopped parsley.

Escalloped Tomatoes

———— ✱ ————
MAKES 6 SERVINGS

This can be made only with garden tomatoes, so prepare it during the summer months when the ripened tomatoes are available at farmer's markets or in your own patch. One way to lengthen the season is to gather in all the partially ripe tomatoes just before frost. Wash well and let them dry; discard any with spots or bruises —that's important. Wrap each one individually in a square of newspaper and store in the vegetable drawer of your refrigerator. Remove a tomato or two from the refrigerator as needed and allow them to ripen on the kitchen counter.

This vegetable casserole has just a few ingredients, but they combine to make a savory dish. The bacon adds a very nice flavor—it's quite rich, so serve it with simply prepared broiled fish, chicken, or beef.

- 3 large tomatoes, peeled and cut in ¼-inch slices
- 1 green bell pepper, finely chopped
  Salt and pepper to taste
- ½ pound or more extra sharp Cheddar cheese, thinly sliced
- 2 cups soda cracker crumbs
- ¼ pound bacon, cut in 2-inch pieces

Preheat oven to 350° F. In an oiled, deep 2-quart casserole, layer ⅓ of the tomato slices, ⅓ of the green pepper, salt, pepper, ⅓ of the cheese slices, and a liberal handful of crumbs. Repeat twice more, ending with a layer of crumbs. Arrange the bacon over the top. Cover and bake for 30 minutes, then uncover and bake 35 minutes longer, or until the mixture is bubbling up in the middle.

✳ FRANK LLOYD WRIGHT ✳

Spring Green, sixty miles west of Madison, is where the controversial and colorful architect Frank Lloyd Wright grew up. He built Taliesin East there, which is now the summer campus of the Frank Lloyd Wright Foundation. A personal statement of functioning architecture, it is an example of his organic, or natural, period. Tours are given through the drafting and dining rooms and studio.

During his lifetime, Wright insisted that the other architects and students living there share the responsibility of cooking and gardening and this tradition continues today. At one time there was a dairy herd, and the students made the campus's butter and cottage cheese. They also smoked hams and made kraut. And they played chamber music in the evening.

Wright's legacy lives on and you feel his spirit at Taliesin in a most tangible way.

Butternut Squash with White Beans Taliesin

———— ✱ ————

MAKES 4 SERVINGS

While visiting Taliesin, we were invited to stay for dinner. The students there take turns cooking the meals, which emphasize healthful ingredients and food preparation. Served with a savory meat loaf, this flavorful and colorful squash and white bean vegetable dish filled the bill quite perfectly.

1 pound butternut squash, peeled and cut in 1-inch cubes
1 tablespoon olive oil
1 cup coarsely diced onion
1 large garlic clove, peeled and minced
1 cup diced tomato
1 cup diced green bell pepper
½ teaspoon powdered sage
¼ teaspoon ground allspice
   Liberal pinch of ground red pepper
1 bay leaf
¼ teaspoon salt
⅓ cup Chicken Stock (page 239)
½ cup cooked white beans
   Splash of vinegar
   Fresh sage leaves, for garnish

In a deep saucepan, parboil the squash in water until it is almost tender, but not mushy. The time will vary and can take anywhere from 15 to 30 minutes; keep testing the squash pieces with the tip of a sharp knife. Drain well and set aside.

In a deep sauté pan, heat the oil over medium heat. Add the onion and garlic and sauté for 1 minute. Reduce the heat slightly, cover the pan, and cook for 5 minutes longer, or until the onions are soft. Add the tomato and green pepper and cook another 2 minutes. Add the drained squash, seasonings, and stock, and cook, covered, over medium heat for 15 minutes longer, or until the squash is tender. Add the beans, increase the heat to high, and cook just until any remaining liquid evaporates. Discard the bay leaf. Add the vinegar and toss to combine. Garnish with fresh sage leaves, if desired.

Creamy Cheese Potatoes

———— ✱ ————

MAKES 8 SERVINGS

Wisconsin currently produces more cheese than any other state in the country; early Swiss and German immigrants began the industry, attempting to duplicate the cheeses they had known at home. In 1885, Colby cheese was developed in Wisconsin and named for the county where it originated. Pale orange in color, a bit soft and moist with a milk tang, country-style Colby is good sliced in sandwiches, with fruit, and in sauces.

Prepared in a seasoned cheese sauce and combined with sliced potatoes, this is a good family dish to serve with grilled or roasted meats.

¼ cup (½ stick) butter
3 tablespoons all-purpose flour
2 cups milk
3 tablespoons finely minced onion
2 teaspoons Worcestershire sauce
¾ teaspoon celery salt
¼ teaspoon white pepper
¼ teaspoon dry mustard
1½ cups grated Colby cheese
6 boiled potatoes, peeled, chilled, and cut in ⅜-inch slices
   Paprika
   Minced parsley, for garnish

Preheat the oven to 350° F. In a medium saucepan, melt the butter; add the flour and cook over low heat until the mixture bubbles. Add the milk and the seasonings, increase the heat to medium, and continue whisking until the mixture bubbles up again in the center. Add the cheese gradually and return to a boil, whisking smooth. Butter an 11 x 8 x 2½-inch oval gratin dish and layer the potatoes in it alternately with the cheese sauce. Dust paprika over the top. Bake for 45 minutes, uncovered, or until the top is golden brown and bubbly. Top with the parsley.

Limas and Peas Baked with Herbs

—✳—

MAKES 4 TO 6 SERVINGS

Every once in a while there comes a time when you have to rely on frozen vegetables, which can be better than what passes for "fresh" at the supermarket much of the time. This is an ideal recipe for one of those days when you are preparing an oven meal—try this with meat loaf.

1   10-ounce package frozen lima beans
1   10-ounce package green peas
½ teaspoon salt
½ teaspoon dried basil, or 1 tablespoon fresh
2   scallions, thinly sliced, including part of green tops
2   tablespoons (¼ stick) butter
2   tablespoons water
    Pinch of sugar

Thaw the lima beans and peas for several hours at room temperature. Preheat the oven to 325° F. Place the thawed lima beans and peas in a greased 1½-quart casserole dish and add the remaining ingredients; stir to combine. Cover and bake for 45 minutes.

Vegetable Jam

—✳—

MAKES ABOUT 18 QUARTS

I have pleasant memories of my mother making home-made beef vegetable soup in late September in order to use up all the vegetables before a killing frost spoiled the result of her summer's work. She would cook beef shank, add it to the vegetables, and can it together right then. Sometimes she just canned the produce and called it vegetable jam. During the winter, she would add the vegetables to cooked beef and its stock, and we were able to enjoy the bounty of her summer garden all over again. To can this recipe, you must use a pressure canner, not a hot water bath. Occasionally there might be some shrinkage of vegetables in the jar, leaving a space at the top, but the mixture is perfectly safe to eat. An alternative is to freeze it in quart containers.

1   peck ripe tomatoes, cored, peeled, and chopped (approximately 17 pounds)
2   quarts peeled, coarsely chopped carrots (approximately 2 pounds)
2   small heads cabbage, cored and coarsely shredded
12 ears fresh corn, cob cut off
12 medium onions, coarsely chopped
3   red bell peppers, coarsely chopped
3   green bell peppers, coarsely chopped
1   tablespoon ground pepper
5   bay leaves, crumbled
4   quarts water
9   teaspoons salt, approximately

Combine all the ingredients except the salt in a large stock pot or divide between 2 pots. Cover and bring to a boil. Then lower the heat and simmer, uncovered, for 1 hour, stirring occasionally. Pour the hot mixture into hot jars, leaving 1 inch of head space. Add ¼ teaspoon salt to each pint, or ½ teaspoon salt to each quart. Adjust caps and process pints 1 hour, quarts 1 hour 15 minutes, at 10 pounds pressure.

Welsh Saffron Bread

—✶—

MAKES 1 LOAF

Wisconsin food lore is absolutely fascinating. In the town of Mineral Point is a restored street named "Shake Rag Under the Hill." Originally lined with the stone and log homes built by the Cornish lead miners, the street went down the hill to the mines. The miners' wives would signal mealtime to their husbands by shaking their dishrags out their doors, an action that gave the street its name.

Saffron bread would have been one of the staples those hungry hard-working miners found on their tables. This recipe makes an outstanding savory bread; consider it for tea as well. It is adapted from Recipes from Wisconsin with Love, *by Laurie Gluesing and Debra Gluesing.*

 3 cups boiling water
 1 cup dried currants
 1 cup raisins
 ⅛ teaspoon saffron threads (or ½ teaspoon mace and ½ teaspoon grated lemon rind)
 ½ cup (1 stick) butter, at room temperature
 1 cup sugar
 2 eggs
 1 teaspoon lemon extract
 2 cups unbleached all-purpose flour
 2 teaspoons baking powder
 1 teaspoon salt
 ½ teaspoon grated nutmeg

Preheat the oven to 350° F. Pour 2 cups of the boiling water over the dried currants (not the raisins); soak 15 minutes, then drain. Pour the remaining water over the saffron and allow to steep until cool. Cream the butter and sugar until well blended, about 3 minutes. Then add the eggs one at a time, blending after each. Add the lemon.

Combine the dry ingredients in a bowl with a whisk and add to the sugar-butter mixture alternately with the cooled saffron liquid, beating until just blended. Stir in the raisins and drained currants. Pour into a greased and floured 9 x 5 x 3-inch loaf pan. Bake 40 to 50 minutes, or until the top is golden brown and has shrunk away slightly from the sides of the pan. If the top is getting too brown, cover with a foil tent. (For added assurance the bread is done, a toothpick or skewer inserted into the middle of the loaf should come out clean.) Tip out onto a rack to cool.

BELOW: The hardworking Cornish miners at Mineral Point lived in tiny houses like this, built around 1830. OPPOSITE: The Pendarvis Cornish Restoration looks very similar to the homes families left in Cornwall.

Swedish Limpa Bread

———— ✴ ————
MAKES 2 LOAVES

On a visit to Door County, my husband and I fell in love with Swedish limpa bread. One of the loaves we brought home was labeled with a list of ingredients, and I kept that label for two years, attempting to duplicate the bread. After much research and experimentation, I believe I have achieved a nearly perfect Swedish limpa. The secret I discovered (from an old regional cookbook) is to simmer the herb seeds in hot water first to release their flavor.

The loaves are velvety textured, firm, with a great chewy crust. Though this recipe is for just two loaves, I know why most limpa bread recipes yield six: The bread is absolutely addictive. And do try it toasted, as well.

1	teaspoon anise seed
1	teaspoon caraway seed
1	teaspoon fennel seed
1¾	cups water
⅓	cup dark molasses
¼	cup dark brown sugar
1	tablespoon salt
2	tablespoons vegetable oil
3	tablespoons grated orange rind
2	envelopes active dry yeast
2½	cups medium rye flour
2	cups unbleached all-purpose flour
¼	cup yellow cornmeal

In a small saucepan, combine the anise, caraway, and fennel seed with the water. Simmer, covered, for 5 minutes, then cool to lukewarm. Transfer the mixture to a mixer bowl—there should be 1½ cups of liquid.

Add the molasses, brown sugar, salt, oil, and orange rind and stir together. Whisk the yeast into the cooled seed mixture, then add the rye flour and beat until smooth, using the beater paddle of your mixer or a wooden spoon. Gradually add the all-purpose flour and continue mixing until thoroughly blended. Allow the dough to rest in the bowl for 15 minutes; it will be very stiff. Knead 10 minutes or until smooth (or transfer to the food processor, and using the plastic blade, process the dough for 45 seconds).

Grease your hands with vegetable shortening and form the dough into a smooth ball. Place the dough in a large greased bowl and turn greased-side up. Cover tightly with plastic wrap, and allow the dough to rise for 1 hour or until double in size.

Punch down vigorously and divide the dough into 2 pieces. Cup each piece of dough tightly between your hands to form a round ball. Grease a 12 x 17-inch pan and sprinkle with the cornmeal. Place the loaves in opposite corners of the pan and flatten slightly—you will have a pattie 5 inches in diameter. Allow to rise 45 minutes. (Once in a while a loaf will not remain in a smooth round loaf during the second rising and will open up in a rather addlepated way. If that happens, re-knead it thoroughly and reshape it again tightly into a ball and let it rise a third time.)

Preheat the oven to 375° F. 20 minutes before baking. Lightly slash an *X* across the top of each loaf with a razor blade or very sharp knife. Bake for 30 to 35 minutes. When done, the loaves will be dark and crusty, and the bottom should sound hard and hollow when tapped with your hand (turn it over with a spatula). If not, return the loaves to the oven for 5 or 10 minutes more, covering them with a piece of foil so they don't get too brown. Remove them to a wire rack to cool.

NOTE: If you do not have a warm place for the bread to rise, turn on your oven for 3 minutes at 140° F. Turn it off immediately and put in the bread to rise.

Special flours, like rye and whole wheat, can be kept refrigerated up to 9 months to maintain their flavor and freshness. Rye flour has little gluten, so most recipes combine it with all-purpose flour so the loaves will rise better. Rye batters also are a bit stickier to work with but the end result is worth it.

Cranberry Mousse with Raspberry Sauce

---★---

MAKES 16 SERVINGS

Anything that cranberries can be made into, stuffed into, or spread upon can be found at the Cranberry Festival held every September in Warrens, a small town of 300 people. This is the cranberry bog center of Wisconsin, and the fruit is a very important crop. Recipes for every sort of cranberry dish under the sun are available in locally printed cookbooks; I especially liked this cranberry mousse. Rose-pink in color, with a deep red accompanying sauce, it is elegant, serves a large number of people, and can be made two days in advance of serving. Add all that up, and you have a perfect company dessert.

MOUSSE

- 3 cups fresh or frozen cranberries (12-ounce bag)
- 2 cups sugar
- 4 cups cranberry juice cocktail
- 3 envelopes unflavored gelatin
- ⅓ cup kirsch or light rum
- 2 teaspoons grated orange rind
- 2 cups heavy (whipping) cream
  Pinch of salt

RASPBERRY SAUCE

- 1 10-ounce package frozen raspberries, thawed
- 1 12-ounce jar seedless raspberry preserves
- ¼ cup kirsch or light rum

Rinse the cranberries, discarding any stems and blemished berries. Transfer to a medium saucepan and combine with the sugar and 1 cup of the cranberry juice. Bring to a boil, then reduce the heat and simmer for 5 minutes, uncovered.

In a small bowl, whisk the gelatin into 1 cup of cranberry juice and allow the gelatin to soften, about 5 minutes. Stir the gelatin into the hot cranberry mixture, then add the remaining 2 cups of cranberry juice, kirsch, and orange rind. Transfer to a large bowl and refrigerate until slightly thickened, about 2 or 3 hours.

In a chilled mixer bowl, whip the cream and salt until stiff peaks form. Fold the whipped cream into the slightly thickened gelatin mixture. Pour the mixture into a 2-quart mold that has been sprayed with vegetable spray. Chill until firm, about 4 hours or overnight.

To prepare the sauce, press the raspberries and juice through a sieve and discard the seeds. Stir in the preserves and kirsch; mix well. Cover and refrigerate.

When ready to serve, dip the mold into lukewarm water for a few seconds, tap to loosen, and invert onto a serving platter. Serve with a little raspberry sauce spooned over each serving.

OVERLEAF: The Warrens Cranberry Festival weekend is full of activities, with the town's side streets serpentining into flea markets as enticing as the food. Tours of the marshes give the 40,000 visitors a glimpse of how these tart red berries are raised and harvested. Since cranberries are perennials, an established bed may be in production for a hundred years. CLOCKWISE FROM TOP LEFT: Local residents enjoy a waltz in front of the Warrens Fire station (turned into a temporary beer hall for the event), which will be rebuilt with the proceeds from the festival. Cranberry pizzas are tangy, sweet, and quite irresistible. Nodji Van Wychan (second from left, wearing her daughter Leona's jacket) has been promoting the festival for many years, with lots of assistance from other family members and residents, including the Cranberry Queens. The fruit is water-harvested, with lightweight machines resembling oversized egg beaters on wheels popping the berries off the vines. Wooden frames called booms corral the berries into huge circles, where they are drawn out of the water and into trucks bound for processing plants. Cranberry honey has a distinctive flavor all its own and is a popular seller at the festival.

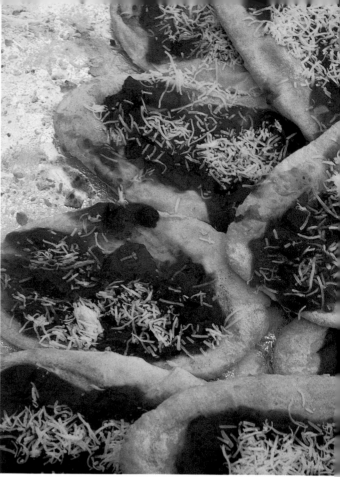

CRANBERRY HONEY

CRANBERRY HONEY

Door County Montmorency Cherry Pie

———— ✳ ————

There is no way you could eat anywhere in Door County and escape the fact that this is cherry country. Every hostess and every restaurant has dozens of cherry desserts to serve, but the favorite is old-fashioned cherry pie. Make this one with a lattice crust—the red juice oozes up and out through the lattice while baking and it makes a pretty pie. Serve slightly warm with a scoop of ice cream.

Pastry for a 2-crust 9-inch pie (½ recipe
    Never-Fail Pie Crust, page 244)
4 cups pitted red sour cherries
1 cup granulated sugar
½ cup brown sugar
3 tablespoons quick-cooking tapioca
½ teaspoon almond extract
¼ teaspoon ground mace
    Red food coloring (optional)
3 tablespoons butter, cut into small pieces

Line a 9-inch pie pan with pastry and set aside. Preheat the oven to 425° F. In a large bowl, combine the cherries, sugars, tapioca, almond extract, mace, and food coloring. Allow to stand for 15 minutes. Pour into the shell and dot with the butter. Top with a lattice crust and bake for 10 minutes. Lower the temperature to 350° F. and continue baking for 30 to 35 minutes longer, or until the juices are bubbling up in the center of the pie. Remove to a rack to cool briefly; this pie is really best when served warm.

Apple Cheese Crisp

———— ✳ ————

Fruit crisps often appear on Midwestern tables as a family dessert, served warm with ice cream or heavy cream. In west-central Wisconsin, where there are great apple orchards in which over a hundred varieties are being raised, apple crisp is a favored dessert. This one has Wisconsin cheddar among its ingredients as well, and all these good things add up to an exceptional and easy-to-prepare treat.

FILLING
5 medium apples, preferably Jonathan or
    Paula Reds
½ cup granulated sugar
½ cup brown sugar
1 teaspoon grated lemon rind
½ teaspoon ground cardamom
½ teaspoon ground cinnamon
2 tablespoons water or cider
1 tablespoon fresh lemon juice

TOPPING
1 cup all-purpose flour
½ cup granulated sugar
1 teaspoon salt
1 cup shredded sharp Wisconsin cheddar
½ cup (1 stick) butter

Preheat the oven to 325° F. Peel, core, and slice the apples into a buttered 8-inch square baking dish. In a small bowl, combine the sugars, rind, cardamom, and cinnamon. Sprinkle over the apples and mix with your hands. Sprinkle the water or cider and lemon juice over the apples.

In a medium bowl, combine all the topping ingredients and mix to a crumbly consistency. Pat over the apples. Bake for 55 to 60 minutes, or until the mixture is golden brown and bubbles up in the center. Serve warm with cream.

Black Forest Torte

from Mader's

———— ✳ ————

MAKES 12 TO 16 SERVINGS

Mader's has been a tradition in Milwaukee since the turn of the century. Serving Bavarian specialties and local beers, Mader's first opened its doors with dinner at 20 cents and beer at 3 cents a glass. This was the era when "bucket boys" made the rounds of office buildings, toting a board dangling with a half-dozen pails of Cream City Beer. This was Milwaukee's interpretation of a coffee break.

Today, Cream City Beer is no more, but at Mader's you can still enjoy this torte, which represents the voluptuousness of Bavarian sweets. It is surprisingly easy to make, and is visually very dramatic. The people at Mader's add, "We substitute a buttercream frosting for the whipped cream frosting, but the whipped cream frosting is more traditional."

CAKE

- ¾ cup all-purpose flour
- ¼ cup sifted unsweetened cocoa powder
- ¼ teaspoon salt
- 6 eggs, separated and at room temperature
- 1¼ cups granulated sugar
- 1 teaspoon vanilla extract

GLAZE

- ¼ cup granulated sugar
- 1 tablespoon water
- ¼ cup brandy
- 2 cups pitted and halved Bing cherries, stewed or canned

FROSTING

- 2 cups heavy (whipping) cream
- ¼ cup confectioners' sugar
- 2 tablespoons brandy

Shaved chocolate, for garnish (see Note)
Maraschino or candied cherries, for garnish

Preheat the oven to 350° F. Sift flour once, measure, add cocoa and salt, and sift again.

In a mixer bowl, beat the egg yolks until thick and lemon colored. Gradually add ¾ cup sugar and continue to beat until the mixture is thick and light. Transfer the mixture to a large mixer bowl.

In a medium bowl, beat the egg whites until frothy, then add the remaining ½ cup sugar gradually, beating constantly. Continue to beat until stiff peaks form. Fold the whites into the egg yolk mixture, blending gently but thoroughly. Sift the flour mixture gradually over the egg mixture, folding gently but thoroughly. Add the vanilla and blend. Turn into 2 deep 9-inch round cake pans, the bottoms of which have been lightly greased and floured. Bake for 25 minutes or until the cake tests done. Remove from the oven and cool in the pans for 10 minutes.

Combine the sugar and water for the glaze in a small saucepan. Stir over low heat until the sugar is dissolved. Remove from the heat and cool slightly, then add the brandy and cherries.

Release the cake layers from the sides of the pans with a knife and remove to wire racks. Brush the brandy glaze over the tops of the warm layers and allow to cool.

Combine the cream and confectioners' sugar for the frosting. Chill thoroughly, then beat until thick and light. Add the brandy and combine.

Spread the frosting on one layer of cake. Top with second layer. Use the remainder of the frosting to coat sides and tops. Sprinkle with shaved chocolate and garnish with well-drained cherries. Keep refrigerated.

N O T E: To make shaved chocolate, shave thin strips of chocolate from a bar, using a swivel-type vegetable peeler.

Prune–Black Walnut Cake

— ✳ —

MAKES 10 TO 12 SERVINGS

Prune cake sounds so odd! Yet during the early 1900s, it was a popular cake, served at special occasions in the Midwest, owing to the availability of prunes. It is a spicy, moist cake that deserves a comeback. Frost it with Lemon Buttercream Frosting (page 245) or the caramel frosting used on the Cider Cake (page 174). This can also be made in a 9 x 13-inch pan.

1 cup moist pitted prunes
1 cup granulated sugar
¼ cup vegetable shortening, softened
2 eggs, at room temperature
1½ cups all-purpose flour
1 tablespoon baking powder
1 teaspoon baking soda
¼ teaspoon salt
½ teaspoon ground cinnamon
¼ teaspoon ground allspice
¼ teaspoon ground cloves
¼ teaspoon grated nutmeg
1 cup buttermilk, at room temperature
1 cup chopped black walnuts

Grease and flour three 8-inch or two 9-inch round cake pans. Cut wax paper to fit the pans and place in the bottom of each pan. Preheat the oven to 350° F. With scissors, cut the prunes into ½-inch pieces; set aside.

In a large mixer bowl, beat together the sugar and shortening for 3 minutes. Drop in the eggs one at a time, beating 1 minute after each addition. Sift together the flour, baking powder, baking soda, salt, and spices. Gradually add to the creamed mixture. Add the buttermilk and prunes alternately to the mixture, then add the nuts. Pour into the prepared pans and bake for 45 to 50 minutes for the 9-inch pans, or 30 minutes for the 8-inch pans. Cool and frost.

Pumpkins and baskets of all sizes are available at the Wisconsin farmer's market.

Rich Custard Peach Ice Cream

—— ✱ ——

MAKES 1 QUART

Ice cream, one of the most beloved American desserts, came as an immigrant to this country, as did most of its citizens. Baltimore was the first city to make it commercially, in 1851, but the Italians had brought this treat to these shores a hundred years earlier.

Cream, eggs, and fresh peaches makes this one of summer's most enjoyable desserts. The custard should be very cold before proceeding with the rest of the recipe and can be made a day in advance.

> 1 cup sugar
> 4 egg yolks
> ⅛ teaspoon salt
> 1 cup milk
> 2½ pounds fresh peaches, peeled, halved, and pitted
> 3 tablespoons almond-flavored liqueur (optional)
> 1 cup heavy (whipping) cream

In a mixer bowl, beat together the sugar and egg yolks on slow speed until the mixture is pale yellow and thick, about 3 minutes. Stir in the salt and the milk with a whisk.

Transfer the mixture to the top of a double boiler with several inches of water in the bottom; the water should be at a low boil. Cover and cook for 12 to 15 minutes, stirring constantly. The custard should be thick enough to coat a spoon and be between 165 and 175° F. Don't let it go above 180° F., or it will curdle.

Remove the top of the double boiler and set in a sink filled with cold water or in an ice-water-filled bowl. Stir the custard for a couple of minutes to cool it down, then transfer it to a bowl, cover, and refrigerate until it is very cold.

Meanwhile, puree the peaches in a food processor. Measure out 2½ cups puree and refrigerate. When the custard is completely chilled, stir in the puree and the liqueur.

Whip the cream until soft peaks form and fold it into the chilled custard-peach mixture. Transfer it to an ice cream machine and freeze according to the manufacturer's directions.

Cranberry Salsa

—— ✱ ——

MAKES 2 CUPS

Cranberries are sometimes called bounce berries because the ripe berries really do bounce when they are dropped. They were also called "crane berries" by early settlers because their slender cone-shaped blossoms reminded them of the beak of a crane.

Cranberries keep well because of their high acidity and can be frozen almost indefinitely. After the holidays they are hard to find, so buy up several bags and freeze them so you can have cranberry dishes all year long. They are too versatile a fruit to be eaten just with Thanksgiving turkey, as this salsa, which is a marvel of flavor, proves. Serve it as an accompaniment to any roast beef or chicken.

> 1 12-ounce bag fresh cranberries
> 2 fresh jalapeño peppers, seeded and minced
> 4 tablespoons chopped cilantro (fresh coriander)
> 2 tablespoons grated onion
> ⅓ cup fresh lime juice
> ½ cup sugar
> ½ teaspoon salt
> ¼ teaspoon freshly ground pepper

Rinse the cranberries, discarding any stems or blemished berries. Transfer them to a medium saucepan, cover with water, bring to a boil, and cook over medium-high heat for 2 minutes. Drain well and transfer to a plastic or glass container. Add the remaining ingredients and combine with a wooden spoon. Cover and refrigerate until needed. This can be stored up to 1 week.

Fruit Chili Sauce

———— ★ ————

MAKES ABOUT 10 PINTS

Thrifty country cooks, faced with baskets of this and that to use up (God forbid they throw anything away or let it go to waste!), would create the most interesting combinations from the rich bounty of their gardens and orchards. This condiment calls for all the glorious fruits of Wisconsin.

Handsomely red, Fruit Chili Sauce is traditionally served as an accompaniment to chicken and red meat dishes.

30 medium tomatoes, peeled and cored
 6 medium onions, peeled and chopped
 6 medium peaches, pitted, peeled and chopped
 6 medium pears, cored, peeled, and chopped
 3 medium firm cooking apples, such as Yellow Delicious or Northern Spy, cored, peeled, and chopped
 4 cups sugar
 2 cups cider vinegar
 2 tablespoons grated lemon rind
 1 tablespoon salt
 1 teaspoon mustard seed
 1 tablespoon celery seed
 2 teaspoons ground cinnamon
 2 teaspoons ground ginger
 2 teaspoons ground allspice
 1 teaspoon black pepper

In a large heavy pan, combine all the ingredients. Bring to a boil, lower the heat, and cook uncovered until the mixture is as thick as regular chili sauce, about 1 to 2 hours. (The amount of time will vary widely, depending on the juiciness of the fruit and the size of the pan.) Stir the sauce frequently to prevent sticking.

Pour the hot mixture into hot pint jars, leaving ⅛-inch headspace. Adjust caps and process in a hot-water bath for 40 minutes.

Apple Cider Marmalade

from the Old Rittenhouse Inn

———— ★ ————

MAKES 10 CUPS

Vacationers going to Lake Superior's Apostle Islands stop off in Bayfield to stay and eat at the Old Rittenhouse Inn. A restored three-story Victorian mansion, the inn has a spacious wraparound front porch, while the interior is filled with period furniture. Owners Jerry and Mary Phillips prepare delectable meals plus jams, jellies, cheesecakes, fudge, and sundae toppings that are available by mail (see Source List).

Apples, always a prolific Wisconsin crop, are preserved for winter in this citrus-laced marmalade. Be sure to always use red-skinned apples.

 6 firm apples, such as Cortland or red Delicious, unpeeled, cored, and cut in sixths
 ¼ cup apple cider
 1 package powdered pectin
 7 cups sugar
 ½ cup grated orange rind
 ½ cup grated lemon rind

Use the fine-slicing blade of a food processor to thinly slice the apples—you will have about 5 cups of apple slices.

Transfer them to a deep saucepan and combine with the cider and pectin. Cover and bring to a rolling boil over high heat. Add the sugar and stir until completely dissolved. Add the rinds and bring to a rolling boil again. Boil 1 minute longer, stirring constantly, then remove the pan from the heat and cool for 3 minutes. Skim off any foam with a slotted spoon and discard. Pour into half-pint jars, seal, and process for 10 minutes in a hot-water bath.

✴ HEARTLAND ✴ BASICS

Where is a recipe for white sauce? How do I make a meringue topping that doesn't weep? Questions like these certainly go through most cooks' minds as they work in their kitchens, usually in a hurry and without time to leaf through a half-dozen cookbooks to find what they need. I get phone calls about these kinds of recipes frequently, especially from beginning cooks. ✴ You'll find all those basic recipes collected here, plus others that are needed to complete many of the recipes in this book, such as the sponge cake called for in the delectable Rhubarb Trifle, or Crème Anglaise, another name for what we call vanilla pouring sauce. And for good measure, I have also added a Midwestern spice blend. ✴

BEEF STOCK ✴ CHICKEN STOCK ✴ SWEET HOT
MUSTARD ✴ TARTAR SAUCE ✴ CLASSIC WHITE SAUCE
✴ PUFFY DUMPLINGS ✴ ROASTED GARLIC ✴ ROASTED
BELL PEPPERS ✴ MIDWESTERN SPICE BLEND ✴
NEVER-FAIL PIE CRUST ✴ EASY COUNTRY SPONGE
CAKE ✴ QUICK CHOCOLATE FROSTING ✴ LEMON
BUTTERCREAM FROSTING ✴ VERY SPECIAL HARD
SAUCE ✴ CIDER SAUCE ✴ BUTTERSCOTCH VELVET
SAUCE ✴ CRÈME ANGLAISE ✴ WHIPPED CREAM
TOPPING ✴ MERINGUE TOPPING

Beef Stock

───── ✦ ─────

MAKES 2½ TO 3 QUARTS

No cookbook worth its salt would omit a recipe for a basic brown stock. This may look like a lot of work, but it's worth it.

- 5 pounds beef soup bones, cut in 6-inch lengths
- 6 medium carrots, scrubbed and halved
- 3 large onions, unpeeled and quartered
- 6 celery stalks, including the leaves
- 1 turnip, scrubbed and quartered
- 3 bay leaves
- 12 whole cloves
- 12 black peppercorns
  Large handful of parsley
- 5 quarts water

Preheat the oven to 400° F. Place the bones in an oiled 12 x 17-inch pan and bake for 30 minutes. Add the carrots and onions and bake another 30 minutes, turning the vegetables and bones at least once during the last cooking period. When the bones are deeply browned (and this may take a few minutes longer), transfer them along with the browned vegetables to a large stockpot. Pour the fat out of the pan, then deglaze with a little water and add this to the stockpot. Add the remaining ingredients, cover, and bring to a boil. Place in a 140° F. oven for 12 hours (I like to do this overnight) or simmer on top of the stove for at least 12 hours.

Remove the bones and vegetables with a slotted spoon, then strain the stock through a fine sieve. (If you want a clearer broth, line the sieve with cheesecloth. I must admit, I generally skip that step.) Refrigerate for several hours, or until the fat rises to the top and forms a hard layer. Discard fat and transfer the stock to 1-quart containers. It can be frozen for up to 3 months.

Chicken Stock

───── ✦ ─────

MAKES 4 TO 4½ QUARTS

This makes an enormous amount, so there will be plenty to freeze.

- 1 large roasting chicken, about 4 to 5 pounds
- 2 medium onions, quartered
- 2 large carrots, halved
- 2 celery stalks, halved
- 1 green bell pepper, halved
- ½ cup parsley sprigs
- 6 whole cloves
- 2 bay leaves
- 1 teaspoon salt
- ½ teaspoon white pepper
- 12 to 14 cups water

Place the chicken, including the neck and giblets (but not the liver), in a large stockpot with the remaining ingredients. The water should cover the chicken completely. Cover, bring to a boil, and simmer for 2 hours, skimming off froth as it forms on top. Remove the chicken to a dish, allow to cool a bit, then remove the meat and skin, reserving the meat for another use. Return the bones and skin to the pot and simmer, covered, for 2 hours more.

Strain the stock through a sieve into a bowl, pressing out the excess juices with a rubber spatula. Chill the stock in refrigerator and skim off the fat. Transfer to 1-quart containers and freeze for up to 3 months if desired.

Sweet Hot Mustard

★

MAKES 1 SCANT QUART

And when I say "hot" I mean hot. Start the mustard the night before—it has a deeper flavor. In the Midwest, it is not uncommon to serve a mustard such as this as a dollop on top of cheese and crackers. It keeps indefinitely in the refrigerator.

- 1½ cups white wine vinegar
- 6 ounces dry mustard (see Note)
- 2 eggs
- 1½ cups sugar
- 2 teaspoons salt

In a glass bowl, combine the vinegar and mustard; allow to stand overnight. The next day, place the eggs in the top of a double boiler and beat slightly. Add the sugar and beat smooth, then beat in the vinegar-mustard mixture. Cook over simmering water until the mustard is thickened and begins to bubble in the middle. Transfer to an electric mixer bowl and beat for 5 minutes; add the salt. Pour into a 1-quart glass jar or four 8-ounce jars and store in the refrigerator.

NOTE: Use a domestic brand of dry mustard or the sauce will be intolerably hot.

Tartar Sauce

★

MAKES 1½ CUPS

Most Midwesterners prefer a tartar sauce that has a touch of sweet pickle. The dill should be fresh; dried dill is not fit for consumption.

- 1 cup mayonnaise
- 2 tablespoons chopped sweet pickle
- 1 tablespoon minced onion
- 2 tablespoons minced fresh dill
- 1 tablespoon minced fresh parsley
- 2 teaspoons cider vinegar
- 1 teaspoon sugar
- ½ teaspoon hot red pepper sauce

In a small bowl, combine all the ingredients and blend well. Cover and refrigerate until ready to serve.

*ABOVE: **A pepper vendor at the Madison Greenmarket has anticipated his customers' questions.** RIGHT: **One of the first steps at Sechler's to create crisp pickles is washing them and getting them into the brine.***

Classic White Sauce
(Sauce Béchamel)

MAKES 1 CUP

Every Midwestern cook should have a foolproof basic white sauce among her or his collection of recipes; it will be used many times. The most reliable white sauce is made from a roux, a cooked mixture of fat and flour. The cooking of the flour in the fat takes away the flour's bitter taste and also swells the starch particles in the flour so it will absorb the liquid and thicken. By varying the proportion of fat and flour, you can vary the sauce's thickness rather easily.

Be sure to cook the roux over even, medium-low heat; high heat will cause the starch granules to shrink and your sauce will be too thin. For a white sauce, do not allow the roux to brown. Butter is by far the best fat to use.

This mixture can be halved or increased (see Note). Be fearless about making this sauce; it is simplicity itself.

- 2 tablespoons (¼ stick) butter (1 tablespoon for a thinner sauce; 3 tablespoons for thicker)
- 2 tablespoons all-purpose flour (1 tablespoon for thinner sauce; 3 tablespoons for thicker)
- 1 cup milk
  Salt and pepper

In a deep saucepan, melt the butter over medium-low heat. Add the flour, mix well, and cook for about 2 minutes. Do not allow the mixture to brown; it will be a bit yellow and should be bubbling on the bottom of the pan.

Add the milk all at once, and continue cooking and whisking until the mixture comes to a boil and thickens. Add salt and pepper to taste. This can be made several days in advance and refrigerated. When the sauce is cooled, a skin will form on top; whisk that back in. It is not necessary to reheat the sauce if you are adding it to another recipe as an ingredient.

NOTE: If you increase amount of the roux ingredients, cook it longer: 3 tablespoons of fat and flour should cook about 5 minutes, 4 tablespoons of fat and flour should cook about 6 minutes and so on.

Puffy Dumplings

✦

MAKES 4 SERVINGS

So many of us have fond memories of dumplings! They were dropped on top of simmering stews, fricassees, and soups (as well as cooked fruits) to extend a simple meal. These dumplings are foolproof with a fine light cakelike texture.

- 1 cup unbleached all-purpose flour
- 1½ teaspoons baking powder
- ½ teaspoon salt
- ⅛ teaspoon grated nutmeg
- ⅛ teaspoon celery seed
- 1 tablespoon cold butter
- 1 egg, lightly beaten
- 6 tablespoons milk
- 1 tablespoon finely minced fresh parsley
- 3 cups stock or other liquid

In a medium bowl, combine the flour, baking powder, salt, nutmeg, and celery seed. Cut in the cold butter with a pastry blender or a fork until the mixture resembles coarse oatmeal. Add the egg, milk, and parsley. Blend lightly, being careful not to overmix. Drop by tablespoonfuls (approximately 6) on top of simmering stock, cover tightly, and simmer over medium-low heat for 20 minutes. Do not lift the cover during the cooking period or the dumplings will fall.

Roasted Garlic

Recipes of the 1980s began requesting roasted garlic among their ingredients. The trend is still with us, and I'm glad, for roasted garlic is a much smoother, sweeter seasoning than raw garlic.

You can increase the number of garlic heads to any number, then serve them as an appetizer, one per person, on individual plates with chewy French bread slices, butter, and goat cheese, too, if you are so inclined. Just pop the roasted garlic cloves out of their skins with your fingers right onto the buttered bread and spread the garlic around with a knife. It's messy but divine.

- 1 large garlic head
- 1 tablespoon olive oil
- ⅛ teaspoon ground pepper
  Pinch of salt
- ⅛ teaspoon dried herbs—any kind but only if using as an appetizer

Preheat the oven to 350° F. With a sharp knife, cut off the top eighth of the garlic head, exposing the cloves. Place in a small foil-lined pan. Drizzle over the oil and sprinkle on the pepper and salt (add the herbs if you are using this as an appetizer). Roast for 30 minutes, then reduce the heat to 250° F and bake 1 hour longer, or until the garlic is very tender when pierced with a knife.

Remove from the oven and cool for at least 30 minutes. Squeeze out the garlic and use as directed. Any extra garlic can be added to salad dressings or other meat and poultry dishes.

Roasted Bell Peppers

I often see very complicated suggestions on how to roast peppers, including holding the peppers over the burner of a stove at the end of the fork. What a time-consuming mess that is! A caterer friend of mine, Nancy Sideris, told me about this method and it is marvelously simple.

- 6 red or green bell peppers
  Olive oil

Preheat the broiler. Cut the peppers in half and core. Place skin side up on a foil-lined baking pan. Flatten the halves firmly with the palm of your hand. Rub the surfaces with olive oil. Broil about 6 inches from the heat for 10 to 12 minutes, or until the skin is black and charred.

With a spatula, transfer the peppers to a brown paper bag, roll shut, and allow the peppers to steam for 15 minutes. Remove from the bag and, with a sharp knife, peel away the charred outer skin and discard. The peppers may be kept covered with olive oil for several days in the refrigerator.

Midwestern Spice Blend

Most serious French cooks create an individual spice mixture they add to dishes that need an extra fillip of flavor. Midwestern cooks do, too, and this savory combination is ideal to rub on roasts and chops. Put a liberal pinch of it in pâtés, meat loaves, and casseroles. Packed in small jars and tied with a ribbon, it also can be given as a little bread-and-butter gift.

- 2 tablespoons ground white pepper
- 2 tablespoons ground black pepper
- 1 tablespoon coarse salt
- 1 tablespoon grated nutmeg
- 1 tablespoon ground cinnamon
- 1 tablespoon dried thyme
- 1½ teaspoons ground ginger
- 1½ teaspoons mace
- 1½ teaspoons ground cloves

In a small bowl, combine all the ingredients and store in a tightly covered jar; it will remain fresh for several months.

Never-Fail Pie Crust

――― ✯ ―――

MAKES ENOUGH PASTRY FOR TWO
9-INCH 2-CRUST PIES

Quickly combined with an electric mixer, this pie crust uses vegetable shortening and freezes well. The baking powder gives it a nice flaky quality.

    4 cups all-purpose flour
    1 teaspoon baking powder
    1 teaspoon salt
    1 teaspoon sugar
 1¾ cups solid vegetable shortening
    1 egg
    1 teaspoon cider vinegar
    ½ cup cold water

In a large mixer bowl, combine the flour, baking powder, salt, and sugar. Add the shortening and beat until the mixture is crumbly, about 2 minutes. In a small bowl, beat the egg well and add the vinegar and water. Pour over the flour-shortening mixture and beat until well combined, about 1 minute. Form the dough into 4 balls, wrap, and refrigerate overnight.

To make pastry shells, roll out one of the balls of dough ⅛-inch thick on a lightly floured board. Rerolling the pastry on your rolling pin, transfer to the pie tin, gently unrolling it in place over the top of the pan. (This pastry is not fragile, but if it does tear, just press it together again with your fingers.)

Ease the dough into the pan without stretching it, and pat it in firmly so there won't be air pockets. If it is an open-faced pie or if it is to be prebaked, form a decorative rim and trim off the excess with a sharp knife or scissors.

If it is to be a filled pie, add the filling and set aside. Incorporating any leftover dough from the bottom crust, roll out another chilled ball of pastry into a circle and, using a larger pie plate or dinner plate as a pattern, cut around it to form a circle. Place it on top of the filling and crimp the top and bottom crust together. Slash the top so steam can escape and, if desired, sprinkle the top with granulated sugar, about 1 tablespoon. Bake according to the recipe's instructions.

To prepare a baked shell, preheat oven to 425° F. Roll out one chilled ball of pastry as directed above. With a fork, prick the shell all over. Bake for 10 to 15 minutes, or until the crust is golden. Check it often and, if necessary, prick again to release any bubbles that may be forming. If the crust begins to slip down the sides of the pan, pat it back up with the back of the fork. Cool before filling.

Easy Country Sponge Cake

――― ✯ ―――

MAKES 1 LARGE CAKE,
12 SERVINGS

Sponge cake is the classic base for trifles and is also used for strawberry shortcake.

    6 eggs, separated, at room temperature
    ¼ teaspoon cream of tartar
    1 cup sugar
    ¼ teaspoon salt
    1 tablespoon fresh lemon juice
    1 tablespoon grated lemon rind
    1 cup sifted cake flour

Preheat the oven to 325° F. In a large mixer bowl, beat the egg whites until foamy. Add the cream of tartar and continue to beat until stiff peaks form when the beater is raised; set aside. In another mixer bowl, beat the egg yolks on high speed for 1 minute. Add the sugar, salt, lemon juice, and rind and beat on high speed for 5 minutes longer. By hand fold the cake flour quickly into the egg yolks, about 15 strokes.

Add about one-third of the whites to the egg-yolk mixture and, with a large rubber spatula, fold until incorporated. Gently fold in the remaining whites in 2 batches. Little patches of white will still be showing. Transfer to an ungreased 10-inch tube pan and bake for just 40 minutes. The top will be golden brown.

Remove cake to a rack to cool for 1 hour. Loosen the sides with a knife and separate the center of the pan from the sides. Then loosen the bottom of the cake from the pan with a knife and tip out onto a rack. Let the cake cool completely before serving or storing.

Quick Chocolate Frosting

MAKES FROSTING FOR ONE 9 X 13-INCH SHEET CAKE

This is such a quick frosting that you will use it often. My mother used to make this and use it as a filling between graham crackers for a kiddie snack when I had other children in to play. Ah, memories.

½ cup (1 stick) butter or margarine, softened
4 cups confectioners' sugar
1 egg white
1 teaspoon vanilla extract
   Pinch of salt
3 packets premelted unsweetened chocolate, or
   3 ounces (3 squares), melted

In a large mixer bowl, combine all the ingredients and beat until thoroughly blended. If the mixture is too thick, add a bit of hot water.

NOTE: For a layer cake, make 1½ times the recipe, using 2 whites and adding a bit more sugar, if necessary.

Lemon Buttercream Frosting

MAKES 4 CUPS

Creamy and tart, this excellent frosting can be used on many kinds of cakes. There's enough for one 9 x 13-inch sheet cake or a 2-layer, 9-inch round cake.

½ cup (1 stick) butter, at room temperature
1 teaspoon grated lemon rind
1 teaspoon vanilla extract
   Pinch of salt
3½ cups confectioners' sugar
¼ cup milk
1 tablespoon fresh lemon juice

In a mixer bowl, cream the butter, lemon rind, vanilla, and salt until light, about 2 minutes. Add the confectioners' sugar alternately with the milk until the mixture is creamy and smooth, beating well after each addition. Beat in the lemon juice.

Very Special Hard Sauce

MAKES 2½ CUPS

This is a hard sauce that uses cream cheese instead of butter. It is a pleasant change. Try it on warm mincemeat pie, as well as steamed pudding.

> 3 ounces cream cheese, at room temperature
> 3 cups confectioners' sugar
> 3 tablespoons sweet sherry
> ¼ teaspoon ground cinnamon
> ¼ teaspoon grated nutmeg
> ¼ teaspoon salt

In a mixer bowl, blend all the ingredients together until smooth. Cover and chill.

Cider Sauce

MAKES A SCANT 2 CUPS

This can enhance any number of dishes—pork chops, pancakes, apple pie, steamed puddings—your imagination is the only limit.

> 1½ cups apple cider, plus 2 tablespoons
> ½ cup brown sugar
> ¼ cup applejack or calvados
> 1 tablespoon butter
> 1 tablespoon fresh lemon juice
> ¼ teaspoon ground cardamom or allspice
> ¼ teaspoon salt
> Pinch of ground black pepper (this adds depth of flavor—don't omit)
> 1 tablespoon cornstarch

In a medium saucepan, combine all but 2 tablespoons of the cider and the cornstarch. Boil over medium heat for 3 minutes. In a small bowl, combine the cornstarch with the remaining cider and pour into the hot liquid. Cook and whisk until the sauce is clear. Serve hot.

Butterscotch Velvet Sauce

MAKES 2½ CUPS

This is a rich sauce that would enhance any ice cream sundae or ice cream pie. It is very thick, a deep rich golden brown. Make a double batch—one for yourself and one for giving. The sauce should be stored in the refrigerator, but bring it to room temperature and warm it in a pan of hot water for about 10 minutes to soften it before serving.

> 1¼ cups brown sugar
> ¼ cup strong hot coffee
> 4 tablespoons (½ stick) butter
> Pinch of salt
> 1 14-ounce can sweetened condensed (not evaporated) milk

In a heavy saucepan, combine the brown sugar, coffee, butter, and salt. Cook over moderate heat until the sugar dissolves, about 5 minutes. Add the condensed milk and cook, stirring constantly, for 5 more minutes. Remove from the heat and allow to cool. Pour into jars and refrigerate.

Crème Anglaise

MAKES 3½ CUPS

This thin English or stirred custard can be used with many desserts. Some cooks complain they have trouble getting it to thicken, so I have provided detailed instructions to assure a perfect sauce. Use a candy thermometer the first couple of times, or until you are comfortable with the technique.

> 3 cups milk
> 9 egg yolks
> 6 tablespoons sugar
> Pinch of salt
> Vanilla extract to taste

In the top of a double boiler, bring the milk almost to a boil over direct heat. In a mixing bowl, beat the egg yolks with the sugar and salt until thick and light. Whisk in half the hot milk, then whisk the mixture back into the remaining milk. Don't whisk excessively. Cook over hot water, stirring constantly with a wooden spoon. When the custard thickens slightly, draw a finger across the back of the spoon. If it leaves a clear trail, it is cooked; it will register 165° F. on a candy thermometer. The sauce will curdle at 180° F., so watch it carefully.

Remove the custard from the heat at once and strain it into a bowl. Cool it quickly by placing the bowl in another large bowl filled with ice to hasten the chilling process. Add just enough extract to scent it. (The strength varies from brand to brand.) Let the sauce cool completely, then cover tightly and chill. (The sauce can be made several days in advance.)

Whipped Cream Topping

MAKES 2 CUPS

The addition of light corn syrup to the cream helps stabilize it so the whipped cream does not go flat and stays nice and perky for a couple of days, though most pies don't last that long. Older cream (check the date on the box) whips better than fresh and the bowl and beater should be well chilled.

    1   cup very cold heavy (whipping) cream
    ¼   cup confectioners' sugar
    1   teaspoon vanilla extract
    1   teaspoon light corn syrup
        Pinch of salt

In a mixer bowl, combine all the ingredients and whip until the cream is stiff and well-defined peaks form. Don't walk away and leave the mixer on though; the mixture can turn into butter in a matter of seconds.

Meringue Topping

MAKES ENOUGH MERINGUE FOR ONE 8- OR 9-INCH PIE

To keep the meringue from weeping, never add more than 2 tablespoons of sugar for each egg white; also the oven temperature for browning it should not be above 325° F. The addition of cream of tartar also gives the whites stability.

    3   egg whites, at room temperature
    ¼   teaspoon salt
    ¼   teaspoon cream of tartar
    6   tablespoons sugar
    1½   teaspoons cornstarch

Preheat the oven to 325° F. In a large mixer bowl, beat the egg whites, salt, and cream of tartar until soft peaks form. Gradually add the sugar a tablespoon at a time and continue beating until stiff peaks form. Just before the beating is completed sprinkle in the cornstarch. The peaks should not topple over when the beater is raised, but the meringue should appear moist, not dry.

Spread the meringue on lukewarm filling in the pie shell (this helps keep it from shrinking away from the filling as it cools), clear over the edge of the crust. Swoop the meringue into attractive peaks. Bake for 15 to 18 minutes, or until the peaks are golden brown. Cool the pie gradually (there should be no warmth left in the meringue at all), and then refrigerate.

APPLES AND APPLE TREES (Antique)

APPLESOURCE
Route 1
Chapin, IL 62628
A selection of antique apples (fruit only) can be sent in sampler boxes or by the bushel. No apples sold on site. Write for informative free catalog.

DOUD ORCHARDS
Route 1
Denver, IN 46926
(317) 275-6100
Many varieties of antique apples can be sent though the mail. Write for brochure. Apples and cider sold on site. Annual apple festival last weekend of September.

SOUTHMEADOW FRUIT GARDENS
Lakeside, MI 49116
(616) 469-2865
This nursery offers a marvelous selection of 250 varieties of antique apple trees. The $8 illustrated catalog has comprehensive descriptions and history. The list of apple varieties and order form is free.

TREE MENDUS FRUIT FARM
Eau Claire, MI 49111
(616) 782-7101
Apples and other fruits from the Southmeadow Fruit Gardens are raised at this fruit farm, which is a U-Pick-It operation.

ASPARAGUS (White)

EARTHLY DELIGHTS
618 Seymour St.
Lansing, MI 48933
(800) 367-4707
Michigan baby white asparagus, winter mushrooms, dried mushrooms, fresh herbs, edible flowers, special salad greens, and chevre are all available by mail order. Write for price list and descriptions.

BLACK WALNUTS

MISSOURI DANDY PANTRY
212 Hammons Dr. East
Stockton, MO 65785
(417) 276-5181
Free catalog and many other nut products available.

BLUE CHEESES

MAYTAG DAIRY FARMS
P.O. Box 806
Newton, IA 50208
(800) 247-2458

NAUVOO CHEESE CO.
Young and Wells Sts.
P.O. Box 188
Nauvoo, IL 62354
(217) 453-2213

BUFFALO MEAT

BUFFALO GAL
Route 1
Houston, MN 55943
(800) 562-2425
Buffalo meat, all cuts, canned meat, pâté, summer sausage, jerky, smoked tongue, bratwurst, party and gift packs. Write or call for price list.

CAVIAR

CAROLYN COLLINS CAVIAR
925 West Jackson Blvd.,
Third Floor
Chicago, IL 60607
(312) 226-0342
Available through mail order nationwide. Fresh salmon and trout caviars, as well as whitefish and American sturgeon. Flavored caviars include golden whitefish roe with a touch of citrus and spicy hot pepper caviar. Write or phone for information.

DRIED CHERRIES, MORELS, SAUCES, PRESERVES

AMERICAN SPOON FOODS
1668 Clarion Ave.
P.O. Box 566
Petoskey, MI 49770-0566
(616) 347-9030
Free catalog.

DUCKS AND DUCK BREASTS

MAPLE LEAF FARMS
Route 1, Box 308
Milford, IN 46542
(219) 658-4121

FLOURS (Specialty)

NEW RINKLE FLOUR
Route 3
Greenfield Mills, IN 46746
Send for price list.

HAM

HoneyBaked Brand Ham
HoneyBaked Foods, Inc.
P.O. Box 7043
Troy, MI 48077-7043
(800) 892-4267
Fully cooked, spiral-sliced, delicately flavored ham, topped with a crunchy honey and spice glaze. Write or call for illustrated catalog.

HONEY

Dave Laney Family Company
25725 New Rd.
New Liberty, IN 25725
(219) 656-8701
Wildflower, Michigan star thistle, blueberry blossom, trefoil, dune country, and autumn wildflower honey available. Write for information.

JAMS, JELLIES, FUDGE SUNDAE SAUCE

Old Rittenhouse Inn
Box 584
Bayfield, WI 54814
(715) 779-5111
Write for information.

KRINGLE

O and H Danish Kringle
1841 Douglas Ave.
Racine, WI 53402
(414) 637-6665
Old World kringles in assorted flavors can be shipped year round. Write for brochure.

MINTS (Frango)

Marshall Field's
111 North State
Chicago, IL 60690
(312) 781-3693
Call or write to the candy department for information.

PERSIMMON PULP

Dymple's Delight
Route 4, Box 53
Mitchell, IN 47446
Canned sweetened persimmon pulp available by mail. Write for price list.

PICKLES

Ralph Sechler and Sons
St. Joe, IN
Sweet pickles, dills, and relishes. Send for mail-order information.

SAUERKRAUT COOKBOOK

One Nation Under Sauerkraut
Dennis Dalton
P.O. Box 419
Waynesville, OH 45068
Cost: $6 prepaid.

SAUSAGES AND BRATWURSTS

Fred Usinger, Inc.
1030 North Old World Third St.
Milwaukee, WI 53203
(800) 558-9998

SCANDINAVIAN FOODS

Wikstrom's Delicatessen and Gourmet Foods
547 North Clark St.
Chicago, IL 60640
(312) 275-6100
Mail-order source of Scandinavian foodstuffs—breads, lefse, brown beans, nonperishable seafood including lutefisk, preserves, and juices, including lingonberries, plus some meats available for shipping. Write for list of items.

SPECIALTY COOKWARE

Maids of Scandinavia
3244 Raleigh Ave.
Minneapolis, MN 55416
(800) 328-6722

VENISON

Buckmaster Fallow Deer
Capoli Ranch
Lansing, IA 52151-9728
(800) 252-IOWA
Venison products, including summer sausages, peppersticks, breakfast sausages, bratwurst, etc. Write for catalog.

WILD RICE

Nature's Best Wild Rice Company
2575 University Ave.
Madison, WI 53705
(800) 369-7423
Wild rice in several grades, dried cranberries and cherries, maple syrup, honey, fruit butter, and gift baskets. Send for free catalog, which includes a few recipes.

WINES

Madron Lake Hills
Winegrow, Inc.
14387 Madron Lake Rd.
Buchanan, MI 49107
(616) 695-5660
Open house every Saturday afternoon, noon to 5:00 P.M., until harvest in October. White Riesling, Gewürztraminer, Chardonnay, and Pinot Noir. Write for information.

* GUIDE TO RESTAURANTS, *
BED-AND-BREAKFASTS,
AND INNS

Listed below is information on the regional restaurants and accommodations mentioned in the text. (R) indicates a restaurant only; (R, A) signifies both food and accommodations are available.

ILLINOIS

ED DEBEVIC'S
840 North Wells St.
Chicago, IL 60611
(312) 664-1707   (R)

PRINTER'S ROW RESTAURANT
550 South Dearborn St.
Chicago, IL 60605
(312) 461-0780   (R)

MARSHALL FIELD'S
The Walnut Room
111 North State
Chicago, IL 60690
(312) 781-3693   (R)

TERCZAK'S
2635 North Halsted St.
Chicago, IL
(312) 404-0171   (R)

INDIANA

CHECKERBERRY INN
62644 County Rd. 37
Goshen, Indiana
(219) 642-4445   (R, A)

CLASSIC KITCHEN
13400 Allisonville Rd.
Noblesville, IN 46060
(317) 773-7385   (R)

COLUMBUS INN
445 Fifth St.
Columbus, IN 47201
(812) 378-4289   (R, A)

OYSTER BAR
1830 South Calhoun
Fort Wayne, IN 46807
(219) 534-3790   (R)

PETER'S
936 Virginia Ave.
Indianapolis, IN 46203
(317) 637-9333   (R)

RED GERANIUM
508 North Street
New Harmony, IN 47631
(812) 682-4431   (R)

IOWA

LA CORSETTE MAISON INN
629 1st Ave. East
Newton, IA 50208
(515) 792-6833   (R, A)

STRAWTOWN INN
1111 Washington St.
Pella, Iowa 50219
(515) 628-4043   (R)

KANSAS

K. C. MASTERPIECE BARBECUE
AND GRILL
10985 Metcalf
Overland Park, KS 66213
(913) 345-1199   (R)

MICHIGAN

RATTLESNAKE CLUB
300 River Pl.
Detroit, MI 48207
(313) 567-4400   (R)

ROWE INN
CO Road C48
Ellsworth, MI 49729
(616) 588-7351   (R)

TAPAWINGO
9502 Lake St.
Ellsworth, MI 49729
(616) 588-7971   (R)

MINNESOTA

THE 510
510 Groveland Ave.
Minneapolis, MN 55540
(612) 874-6440   (R)

MISSOURI

FEDORA CAFÉ
167 St. Louis Union Station
St. Louis, MO 63103
(314) 436-0855   (R)

OHIO

INN AT HONEY RUN
6920 County Rd. 203
Millersburg, OH 44654
(216) 674-0011   (R, A)

PEASANT STOCK
424 East Stroop Rd.
Kettering, OH 45429
(513) 293-3900   (R)

THE PHOENIX
30 Garfield Place
Cincinnati, OH 45200
(513) 721-2255   (R)

WISCONSIN

AL JOHNSON'S SWEDISH
RESTAURANT
702 Bayshore Dr.
Sister Bay, WI 54234
(414) 854-2626   (R)

L'ETOILE
25 North Pinckney St.
Madison, WI 53700
(608) 251-0500   (R)

OLD RITTENHOUSE INN
Box 584
Bayfield, WI 54814
(715) 779-5111   (R, A)

QUIVEY'S GROVE
6261 Nesbitt Rd.
Madison, WI 53719
(608) 273-4900   (R)

WHITE GULL INN
Fish Creek, WI 54212
(414) 868-3517   (R, A)

MADER'S
1037-41 North Third Street
Milwaukee, WI 53203
(414) 271-3377   (R)

✳ MUSEUMS, HISTORIC SITES, ✳ AND OTHER PLACES TO VISIT

ILLINOIS

THE BISHOP HILL STATE
HISTORIC SITE
P.O. Box D
Bishop Hill, IL 61419
(309) 927-3345

NAUVOO RESTORATION AND
VISITOR'S CENTER
Young and North Main Sts.
Nauvoo, IL 62354
(217) 453-2237
*Former 1840s Mormon and
Icarian historical sites and
restoration.*

INDIANA

AUBURN CORD DUESSENBERG
MUSEUM
1600 S. Walnut St.
Auburn, IN 46706
(219) 925-1444
*Vintage cars on display in an Art
Deco museum.*

CONNER PRAIRIE SETTLEMENT
13400 Allisonville Rd.
Noblesville, IN 46060
(317) 776-6000
*Award-winning pioneer living
history museum.*

HISTORIC NEW HARMONY
P.O. Box 579
New Harmony, IN 47631
(812) 682-4482
*Restored site of two former utopian
communities, guided tours.*

JAMES WHITCOMB RILEY
MEMORIAL
528 Lockerbie Square
Indianapolis, IN
(317) 631-5885
*Splendidly restored Victorian
house, guided tours.*

SUMMER HOUSE
Oris Hippensteel
Rural Route #4, Box 134
North Manchester, IN 46962
(219) 982-4707
Herb garden and shop.

MINNESOTA

SINCLAIR LEWIS BOYHOOD HOME
612 Sinclair Lewis Ave.
Sauk Centre, MN 56378
(612) 352-5201

**SINCLAIR LEWIS INTERPRETIVE
CENTER AND MUSEUM**
Box 228
Sauk Centre, MN 56378
(612) 352-5201
*Sinclair Lewis Days is second week
of June.*

OHIO

**THE CIRCLEVILLE PUMPKIN
SHOW**
Post Office Box 188
Circleville, OH 43113
*Held third weekend of October;
write for free bochure.*

GERMAN VILLAGE
624 South Third St.
Columbus, OH 43206
(614) 221-8888
*Old Columbus restored, charming
neighborhood.*

MALABAR FARM STATE PARK
Route 3, Box 469
Lucas, OH 44843
(419) 892-2784
*The restored 32-room country
home of Louis Bromfield, Pulitzer
Prize–winning author and
conservationist; guided tours.*

MEIR'S WINE CELLARS
695 S. Plainfield Pike
Cincinnati, Ohio 45236
(513) 891-2900
*Tours of the winery every hour on
the hour. Call for information.*

OLDENBURG BREWERY
I-75 and Buttermilk Pike
Ft. Mitchell, KY 41011
(606) 341-2804
*Tours of brewery. Just over the
Ohio border. Call for information.*

THE SAUERKRAUT FESTIVAL
Chamber of Commerce
P.O. Box 201
Waynesville, OH 45068
*Held second weekend of October;
write for brochure.*

WISCONSIN

PENDARVIS
114 Shake Rag St.
Mineral Point, WI 53565
(608) 987-2122
*A group of meticulously restored
1840s Cornish miner's furnished
houses. Guided tours. Call or write
for brochure and information.*

TALIESIN FELLOWSHIP BUILDINGS
Taliesin Foundation
Spring Green, WI 53588
(608) 588-2511
*Guided tours of the Frank Lloyd
Wright Foundation campus—a
"must see." May through October.
Call or write for information.*

WARRENS CRANBERRY FESTIVAL
P.O. Box 146
Warrens, WI 54666
*September weekend festival with
foods, antiques, flea market; write
for dates and information.*

WILD GOOSE DAYS FESTIVAL
Chamber of Commerce
Waupun, WI 53963
(414) 324-3491
*Hike or bicycle on the wild goose
trail and observe an estimated 750
thousand migrating geese flying in
to feed. Mid-October. Marsh-area
bus tours during festival, arts
and crafts show, collector-car
show. About 54 miles northeast
of Madison.*

✳ SELECTED BIBLIOGRAPHY ✳

All-American Barbecue Book, The, Rich Davis and Shifra Stein. New York: Vintage Books, 1988.

American Cooking (Foods of the World Series), José Wilson. New York: Time/Life Books, 1971.

American Food, The Gastronomic Story, Evan Jones. New York: Random House, 1981.

American Gothic Cookbook, The, Joan Liffring-Zug Iowa City, IA: Penfield Press, 1986.

American Regional Cookery, Sheila Hibben. New York: Gramercy Publishing Company, 1952.

Aspic and Old Lace, Diane L. Barts. South Bend, IN: Northern Indiana Historical Society, 1987.

Bernard Clayton's New Complete Book of Breads, Bernard Clayton. New York: Simon and Schuster, 1987.

Centennial Cook Book. Ellison Bay, WI: Trinity Lutheran Church.

Cooking of Scandinavia, The, Dale Brown. New York: Time/Life Books, 1968.

Cook's Encyclopedia, The, Tom Stobart. New York: Harper and Row, 1981.

Czech Book, The: Recipes and Traditions, Pat Martin. Iowa City, IA: Penfield Press, 1981.

Down to Earth Vegetable Cookbook, The, Circle Arts. Fish Creek, WI: The Settlement, 1982.

Eating in America, Waverly Root and Richard de Rochemont. New York: William Morrow & Co., 1976.

Flavor of Wisconsin, The, Harva Hachten. Madison, WI: State Historical Society of Wisconsin, 1986.

Food for Thought, Joan and John Digby, eds. New York: William Morrow & Co., 1987.

Food in History, rev. ed., Reay Tannahill, New York: Crown, 1989.

Food of the Frontier: Minnesota Cooking from 1850 to 1900, Marjorie Kreidberg. St. Paul: Minnesota Historical Society Press, 1975.

Jewish Holiday Kitchen, The, Joan Nathan. New York: Schocken Books, 1988.

L. L. Bean Game & Fish Cookbook, The, Angus Cameron and Judith Jones. New York: Random House, 1988.

Louis Bromfield at Malabar: Writings on Farming and Country Life, Charles E. Little, ed. Baltimore: Johns Hopkins University Press, 1988.

Minnesota Ethnic Food Book, The, Anne R. Kaplan, Marjorie A. Hoover, and Willard B. Moore. St. Paul: Minnesota Historical Society Press, 1986.

Minnesota Heritage Cookbook, American Cancer Society, Minnesota Division. Minneapolis: Bolger Publications, Creative Printing, 1979.

Notably Norwegian, Louise Roalson. Iowa City, IA: Penfield Press, 1982.

Pella Collectors' Cookbook. Pella, IA: Central College Auxiliary, 1982.

Putting Food By, 4th ed., Greene, Hertzberg, and Vaugn. Lexington, MA: Stephen Greene Press, 1988.

Recipes from Wisconsin with Love, Laurie Gluesing and Debra Gluesing. Chanhassen, MN: New Boundary Designs, 1984.

Red Flannel Hash and Shoo-fly Pie, Lila Perl. New York: World Publishing Co., 1965.

Scandinavian Cookbook (Adventures in Cooking Series), Culinary Arts Institute. New York: Delair Publishing Co., 1982.

Victorian Kitchen, The, Jennifer Davies. London: BBC Books, 1989.

Wines of America, The, 3rd ed., Leon D. Adams. New York: McGraw-Hill, 1985.

❋ CREDITS ❋

Heartland came into being because so many people were gracious about sharing their time and knowledge. I want to personally acknowledge the following individuals whose experiences and recipes appear on these pages. They helped make this book very special, and I am forever grateful to every one of them.

Marcile Anderson ❋ Colleen Benninghoff ❋ Laura Bixler ❋ John Boch ❋ Connie Brothers ❋ Creighton Brothers ❋ Gail Bryan ❋ June Bryan ❋ Betsy Chapman ❋ Sue Clutter ❋ Larry Coble ❋ Melissa Creassy ❋ Scott Daley ❋ Dennis E. Dalton ❋ Yvonne Diamond ❋ Charlene Dixon ❋ Scott Dody ❋ James Eschner ❋ Elinor Fox ❋ Eric Freeman ❋ Sue Fuson ❋ Camille Glenn ❋ Esther Grabill ❋ Jane Grossnickle ❋ Carmen Hall ❋ Suzanne Hall ❋ Lois Hamilton ❋ Marion Hansen ❋ Kerry Hippensteel ❋ Holley and Max Hobbs ❋ Kay Johnson ❋ Connie Ker ❋ Darlene Kronschnabel ❋ Lannie Lawler ❋ Verna Majewski ❋ Michael Mankin ❋ Maple Lane Bakery, Claypool, Indiana ❋ Tom Maze ❋ Judy Merkle ❋ Jean Muhe ❋ Kori Oberle ❋ Carol Piecuch ❋ Cecelia Piecuch ❋ Michelle Rich ❋ Phyllis Ritenour ❋ Hyacinth Rizzo ❋ Lois and Larsh Rothert ❋ Bonnie Rothgeb ❋ Sue Schieler ❋ Karen Schloss-Saad ❋ Don Schroeder ❋ Martha Schueneman ❋ Elaine Schultz ❋ Nancy Sideris ❋ Eva Slayton ❋ Mathew Staublin ❋ Paul Staublin ❋ Mary Lib Stewart ❋ Mary Sullivan ❋ Sandra Sullivan ❋ Peggy Tagliarino ❋ Becky Thomas of Ike's Daughter's Antiques, Silver Lake, Indiana ❋ Dolores Tomusk ❋ Linda Van Osdol ❋ Nodji Van Wychan ❋ Jane and Wayne Vincent ❋ Dyllis Walley ❋ Teresa Walther ❋ Jo Wolf ❋ Hannah Zacher